JAMES WYATT

Frontispiece: James Wyatt by Sir William Beechey

(*Reproduced by kind permission of the Royal Academy*)

JAMES WYATT

by

ANTONY DALE

BASIL BLACKWELL
OXFORD
1956

By the same Author

FASHIONABLE BRIGHTON 1820-1860
THE HISTORY AND ARCHITECTURE OF BRIGHTON

FIRST PRINTED 1956

PRINTED BY
THE DITCHLING PRESS, DITCHLING, HASSOCKS, SUSSEX

AND BOUND BY THE KEMP HALL BINDERY
IN THE CITY OF OXFORD

To my daughter
MADELINE
in the hope that she
may have a happy life.

ACKNOWLEDGMENTS

The Author and the Publishers wish to express their acknowledgment to the following for their permission to reproduce the illustrations of this book:

The National Buildings Record: Plates 3, 4, 21, 25, 26, 27, 31, 37, 55, 56, 57, and 58; Country Life Ltd.: Plates 6, 7, 8, 9, 10, 11, 13, 14, 15, 16, 17, 18, 20, 23, 32, 33, 34, 35, 38, 39, 40, 45, and 63; the Cobham Hall Estate Company: Plate 12; and Mr W. Carpenter-Jacobs: Plate 19.

CONTENTS

LIST OF ILLUSTRATIONS

PREFACE

IN the demolition-fever which has afflicted England since the war James Wyatt has perhaps been more unfortunate than most classical architects. Badger Hall, Shropshire; the wings of Chiswick House, Middlesex; Fornham Hall, Suffolk; Henham Hall, Suffolk (though altered); Hothfield Park, Kent; Lee Priory, Kent; and (after enemy action) 22 St James's Place, London, have all been demolished. At least two other major works at one time gave rise to considerable anxiety, fortunately since allayed. It is to be hoped that this melancholy process will not be allowed to continue further.

The first version of this book was published in 1936. Since then much new information about James Wyatt has come to light. To incorporate a more detailed consideration of Wyatt's principal works, which the first version of the book did not pretend to provide, the latter has, with the exception of certain chapters, been entirely rewritten.

The disadvantages probably outweigh the advantages in all methods of arranging the biography of an architect. If the treatment is entirely chronological, it is necessary to change the subject as often as in a dictionary and with as little connection between one paragraph and another. If however it is by subject matter, there is bound to be some overlapping and apparent illogicality. It is possible that, if I had been approaching Wyatt's life entirely *de novo*, I might not have followed the framework of my first work. But, on reflection, the disadvantages of its arrangement seem no greater than those of any other. I have therefore adhered to it.

The publication of the 1936 version brought me into touch with several members of the Wyatt family to whom I am indebted for the loan of letters, photographs of portraits and information concerning the genealogy of the family and other points; in particular to the late Brigadier General L. J. Wyatt who was the last descendant of James to bear the name of Wyatt; to Mrs J. S. Budenberg; and to the late Mrs M. Wyatt-Smith.

I have particular reason to be grateful to the Queen's Librarian, Sir Owen Morshead, for information and assistance concerning Frogmore House, supplied with that particular courtesy of which he alone has the secret; to the President of Magdalen College,

Oxford, for most kindly allowing me to see in advance of publication his article on the architectural history of the College at the end of the eighteenth and beginning of the nineteenth centuries; to the Vicomte de Noailles for the loan of an album of Wyatt drawings and photographs thereof; to Mr Ralph Arnold for information concerning Cobham Hall and to the National Buildings Record for generosity concerning photographs.

I have to thank the owners and occupiers of many Wyatt buildings for permission to view, and in some cases photograph, their houses. Amongst these I am specially grateful to the Hon. Andrew Vanneck and to Miss D. Ramsay for help and information concerning Heveningham Hall and the late Lee Priory respectively.

My last debt is to my wife for her invaluable help in the abominable task of making the index of the book.

46 Sussex Square   A.D.
Brighton   *October, 1956.*

Chapter I

EARLY LIFE

In an article contributed to *Country Life* of 26th April 1919, dealing with Trinity House, Tower Hill, London, Mr H. Avray Tipping, speaking of the architect of that building, namely Samuel Wyatt, wrote: 'When we consider the enormous architectural output of this family from the year 1770, when James Wyatt designed the Pantheon, to the year 1851, when Lewis Wyatt died',—Lewis Wyatt actually died in 1853—'it is strange that there is no biographical and critical account of all or any of its members, nor, it seems, material for its production.' Mr Tipping need not really have limited himself to 1851 as the termination of the activities of the Wyatt family, as James Wyatt's second son, Matthew Cotes, though he was an historical painter and sculptor and not an architect, outlived this date by eleven years; and the two brothers Thomas Henry and Sir Matthew Digby Wyatt, members of a collateral branch of the family, did not die until 1880 and 1877 respectively. Between these dates of 1770 and 1880 no less than thirteen members of the family practised the profession of architecture; whence has arisen much confusion and incorrect attribution of their works.

Mr Tipping continued his remarks thus: 'Such slight and fragmentary information as was obtainable was laboriously collected by Mr Papworth when Curator of the Soane Museum and put together by him as an article for the Dictionary of the Architectural Publications' Society.' Mr Papworth's Christian name was Wyatt, and, as there was some relationship between him and the family of that name, some of his information may have come to him from private sources. His article was published in 1891 and in the absence of any more comprehensive material still remains the central authority on the subject. The list of works attributed to the Wyatts is incomplete and must be supplemented, but a student of any member of the family or of their work is bound to be more in the debt of Mr Papworth than of any other authority.

I

Far more is known of James Wyatt than of any other of the early members of his family. When Horace Walpole enquired from him in 1772 whether he was descended from the poet Sir Thomas Wyatt of Henry VIII's time, whose life Walpole was then engaged in writing, James Wyatt replied that his knowledge of his family, derived as it was from oral tradition only, went no further back than his great-grandfather, who was a farmer in Staffordshire. The Wyatt family had very extensive connections with this county. Branches of the family lived at Tamworth and at Burton-on-Trent. But Weeford near Lichfield was its real home. The fifth entry in the parish register of that village for the year 1562—the first year in which a register was kept—was that of a Wyatt; and as late as the middle of the last century there were still members of the family living in the parish. Probably the Wyatts had been yeoman farmers there for the whole period of 150 years that separated the commencement of the parish registers and the beginning of the eighteenth century.

The home of the family at Weeford was a house called Thickbroom which is still standing. It is an L-shaped timber-framed farmhouse of moderate size with a tiled roof. The house has lost much of its character in modern times by having been refaced with roughcast and refenes-trated. Here lived James's grandparents, John Wyatt (1675-1742) and Jane Jackson (1677-1739), who are both buried in Weeford church-yard.

John and Jane Wyatt had nine children, of whom eight were sons. The sixth of these was Benjamin Wyatt who was baptized in Weeford church on 17th September 1709. He became a farmer and timber merchant but also practised as a builder and architect. James Elmes, in an article which is full of inaccurate statements,[1] called him an opulent and eminent builder of London who was much concerned with government and other large contracts. But there seems no evidence for this statement. All that is really known of this Benjamin Wyatt is that between 1769 and 1772 he erected the Stafford General Infirmary. There is in the William Salt Library, Stafford, a print of this signed 'Benj. Wyatt and Sons, Archit.' The original plans are still in the possession of the Infirmary.

On 27th May 1731 Benjamin Wyatt married Mary, daughter of William and Anna Wright of Coton, near Tamworth. They occupied a farmhouse in the parish of Weeford named Blackbrook which is also still standing. This is one of those delightful large mid-eighteenth-

[1] *Civil Engineer and Architect's Journal*, Vol. 10, 1847.

century red brick houses which are such a special feature of the English landscape. It was no doubt built by Benjamin Wyatt for himself on his marriage. He died there in July 1772 and his wife in March 1793. Both are buried in Weeford churchyard.

Benjamin Wyatt was the founder of the architectural traditions of his family. Seven of his ten children were sons. Of these, no less than five adopted their father's profession. The exceptions were John, the second son (1735-1797), who became a surgeon, and Charles, the youngest, who died at the age of four. The sons who were comprised in the firm's name 'Benj. Wyatt and Sons' were probably William, the eldest (1734-1780), Joseph (1739-1785) and Benjamin (1744-1818). In 1803, after the death of the two eldest brothers, Benjamin Wyatt the second, who was then living at Sutton Coldfield, rebuilt Weeford church, though it seems that the plans were provided by James.

The third son, Samuel (1737-1807), in due course achieved celebrity as an architect. But the most famous was James Wyatt, the sixth son, who was born at Blackbrook Farm, Weeford, on the 3rd August 1746. He was baptized in Weeford church on 30th August of the same year. There is a curiously persistent legend, about which the authorities are in almost unanimous accord, that he was born at 'Burton Constable in Staffordshire'; but there is apparently no such place.

James Wyatt is said to have attended the 'village' school, by which Lichfield was probably meant. We are then told that he became the pupil of W. Atkinson. Who this gentleman was, and whether he taught drawing or ordinary studies, has not been explained, but he may have been a relation of the architect Thomas Atkinson of York. Presumably he was a drawing master, as the boy James Wyatt is said by *The Gentleman's Magazine* to have shown sufficient talent in drawing and taste for the same to attract the notice of 'Lord Bagot then about to depart for Rome as the Ambassador of Great Britain at the Ecclesiastical States'.[1]

This last statement, however, is more than a little difficult to interpret. Most authorities agree that Wyatt left England at the age of fourteen. This would be in the year 1760; but at that date there existed no such person as 'Lord Bagot'. Sir William Bagot, the sixth baronet of Bagots Bromley and Blithfield, Staffordshire, was not created a peer until 1780. Secondly, throughout the whole of the eighteenth century England sent no diplomatic representative to the Papal Court.

[1]*Gentleman's Magazine*, Sept. 1813, Vol. 83, Pt. II, p. 296.

The Monthly Magazine, in its obituary of Wyatt, has quite a different account to give. It makes out that it was in the company of the seventh Earl of Northampton, who had been ruined in the destructive contest for the parliamentary seats of Northamptonshire, that Wyatt visited Italy.

Both these statements can to some extent be brought into harmony with each other. In 1762, not 1760, Lord Northampton was appointed Ambassador Extraordinary and Plenipotentiary to the Republic of Venice; and with him travelled as Secretary to the Embassy, his friend Richard Bagot, brother of the Sir William Bagot who was later elevated to the peerage.

There does not appear to have been any motive behind this embassy other than to return the compliments paid to George III on his accession by the Venetian Republic, which had sent a special embassy to congratulate His Majesty. Northampton's stay was very short. He arrived in Venice on 17th October 1762 and left immediately after making his state entry and presenting his credentials, a ceremony which was delayed until six months after his arrival only on account of his own illness and the death of the Doge.

Northampton's wife, who had also been ill, left Venice before the ambassador and travelled to Naples. When asking to be recalled, Northampton requested permission to follow his wife thither for the benefit of his own health before returning to England. As he obtained his recall, presumably he obtained this permission also. But when he left Venice on 8th June 1763 he proceeded first to Verona, and apparently thence to Geneva, to consult a special doctor. Later he continued his journey to Naples, only to die there before the year was out.

These movements of Northampton's are a little difficult to fit in with the facts related of Wyatt's visit to Italy. The latter is said to have first spent four years at Rome studying architecture with a thoroughness which is well attested. He is reported to have drawn crowds both in the Pantheon and in St Peter's on account of the precarious process by which, lying flat on his back, he was slung horizontally upon a ladder without cradle or siderail into the void of the dome in order that he could draw and measure every portion of the latter. These youthful exploits did not however inspire him with special respect for Bramante and Michelangelo's great masterpiece, as in after years Wyatt told Farington that he thought 'St Peter's at Rome bad architecture—it is divided into little parts. It is the size which makes it striking.—There is

4

1. Unidentified drawing dated 1771

(Reproduced by kind permission of the Royal Institute of British Architects)

2. Interior of the Pantheon. By William Hodges and Zoffany

(Reproduced by kind permission of Temple Newsam House, Leeds)

3.
Cobham Hall.
The ceiling in the
vestibule

4.
Cobham Hall.
The chimney piece
in the vestibule

5.
Stoke Poges Park.
Detail of the
staircase handrail

no good modern architecture in Rome—the best specimens are by Raphael.—That of Michael Angelo is very bad.'[1]

At the end of these four years, so *The Gentleman's Magazine* tells us, he passed on to Venice, where a further two were spent in working under Antonio Viscentini. (There appear to be at least four different ways of spelling this gentleman's name.) There is an extraordinary entry in the unpublished portion of Farington's Diary about Viscentini, or 'Visantini' as Farington called him. On one occasion in 1798 when Farington visited Wyatt's house, Wyatt showed Farington a portrait of Wyatt's old drawing master and said that he 'was a hundred years old when Wyatt first saw him at Venice'.[2]

Here he made unusual progress, especially in architectural painting, his few works in this line being held by flattering admirers to rival those of Panini. It is said that his talents in architecture, painting and music were so equally developed that it was only his preference for the first which decided his career.

But if Wyatt accompanied Lord Northampton and Richard Bagot to Italy, the order of these visits to Rome and Venice must evidently have been reversed. This is quite possible, as the only evidence supporting the order given is provided by *The Gentleman's Magazine*, and the statement may well be as inaccurate as that which accounts for Wyatt's arrival in Italy.

In 1768 Wyatt returned to England and for two years remained wrapped in a silence which is so complete that we know nothing of his doings until he emerged into fame as the successful architect of the Pantheon. These two years of apparent inactivity are the most mystifying and intriguing period of his life. Knowledge of his whereabouts and occupation then might prove very valuable. Presumably he returned to Staffordshire and worked in co-operation with his father and brothers. But it is only a supposition. Everything is dark until 1770, when he emerges suddenly into the limelight and remains a noticeable figure until his death.

[1]*Farington Diary*, 7 Nov. 1797.
[2]*Farington Diary*, 28 July 1798.

CHAPTER II

THE PANTHEON

How did this sudden transformation from insignificance to celebrity come about? When the old opera house in the Haymarket was burned down the proprietors of the Pantheon in Oxford Street determined to take this opportunity of converting their own building for the holding of masquerades and dramatic representations. There are two theories of how James Wyatt came successfully to compete for the appointment as architect.

The Monthly Magazine relates that he owed the commission to the influence of his brother John, who was the only surviving member of his generation that had not adopted architecture as a career. John Wyatt was a surgeon and fairly successful in his profession. He became in due course a Fellow of the Royal Society and Master of the Corporation of Surgeons of the City of London. There is a portrait of him in the board-room of the Middlesex Hospital. Amongst other things he was concerned with the construction of canals from Hull to Liverpool and from Burton-on-Trent to Lichfield. On James's return from Italy he found John Wyatt practising in Newport Street. The latter was a zealous promoter of the scheme of conversion of the Pantheon and one of the committee of proprietors supervising its execution. He it was who induced his brother to submit a design to the committee and added a recommendation of James as the architect. The committee approved the designs and acquiesced in the appointment. In 1770 James Wyatt was living in Great Newport Street, probably with John Wyatt and his wife. An advertisement of the Pantheon in a contemporary newspaper gives the name of the Treasurer of the building as 'W. Wyatt'. There was another brother named William who was a builder-architect. But possibly this entry was a mistake for John Wyatt. However, whether there were two brothers concerned in the scheme or only one, the suggestion was that their or his influence prevailed to obtain the commission for James.

The second account of Wyatt's appointment comes from T. F.

6

Hunt's *Archittetura Campestre*. He tells us that, while at Venice, Wyatt became acquainted with Joseph Smith who for nearly twenty years held the position of English Consul in that city. No doubt he was introduced to Smith by Viscentini, who had designed two houses for the Consul, one at Venice and one at Mojano sul Terraglio. The villa at Venice, Terra Firma, which Smith had filled with artistic objects and curiosities, became a meeting-place of the numerous connoisseurs who visited Italy. Here Wyatt met Richard Dalton, with whom he contracted a lifelong friendship. Dalton had been sent to Italy by George III for the purpose of collecting pictures; and when he returned, Wyatt travelled in his company. It was therefore through Dalton's influence that Wyatt was successful in the competition for the Pantheon appointment.

This second explanation is confirmed by the mention in Wyatt's obituary in *The Gentleman's Magazine* of the fact that someone, whose name is not given but who was influential in the Pantheon concern, exercised his good offices in his favour, having met and formed an esteem for him in Italy. There is, however, no extant contradiction of the former theory, and there is nothing to prevent their both being true. Influence was probably necessary to enforce consideration of the claims of such an unknown artist. But whether this came from John or William Wyatt, or from Richard Dalton, or from both, the deciding factor must have been the designs themselves. It is most unlikely that the drawings of a building which so overwhelmed contemporaries when it was constructed, should not themselves have been proportionately striking. So James Wyatt was quite as essential a factor in his own appointment in 1770 as his sponsor.

The building took two years to complete. There are various accounts of its cost. In April 1771 Horace Walpole wrote that this was to amount to £50,000. The *Dictionary of Architecture* gives £60,000 as the price. Yet Wyatt himself told Farington in 1797 that it had cost £25,000, of which £1,500 was spent upon the composition pillars. These were formed of scagliola, which was thus for the first time used in England.

The expense was defrayed by subscribers who held shares of £500 each. Wyatt himself owned two, which at the end of two or three years he sold for £900 apiece. When the building was finished, he offered the shareholders £500 for the privilege of showing it during the first year. They demanded £600, and he, being piqued, refused to give so much. As a result, if his own statement may be believed, at least £3,000 was actually gained by the exhibition of the building. As half

7

a guinea per person was at first charged for admission, though later five shillings or half a crown, and as the whole of fashionable and curious London flocked at once to inspect the premises, this may well be believed.

The building consisted of a large central apartment with apsidal ends and arcaded sides of two storeys, the upper storey forming galleries. Behind the columns on each floor were statues standing in niches lit by green and purple lights. Above was a painted frieze and a coffered dome, from which hung lights in the form of gilded vases. (Plate 2.) Behind was an L-wing containing smaller rooms of interesting shapes, one oval and one circular, with four semi-circular recesses at the corners. Beneath was an underground storey comprising a tea-room of equal area to the cupola room and intended as a foil to it; also a few more small apartments as above. There were entrances in Oxford Street and Poland Street. The outside was not particularly prepossessing and when mentioned at all by those who visited the Pantheon, is generally condemned. The portico in Oxford Street was added by Sydney Smirke in 1834.

The opening took place on 27th January 1772. *The Gentleman's Magazine* wrote: 'Was opened for the first time the much talked of Pantheon to a crowded company of between fifteen hundred and two thousand people. Imagination cannot well surpass the elegance and magnificence of the apartments, the boldness of the paintings, or the disposition of the lights, which last are reflected from gilt bases, suspended by gilt chains. Beside the splendid ornaments which decorate the rotundo or great room, there are a number of statues, in niches, below the dome, representing most of the heathen gods and goddesses, supposed to be in the Pantheon at Rome. To these are added three more of white porphyry, the two first representing the present King and Queen, the last Britannia. The whole building is composed of a suite of fourteen rooms, all of which are adapted to particular uses, and each affording a striking instance of the splendour and profusion of modern times.'[1]

This is very high praise and is only to be expected from a fashionable periodical. But the writer's opinion was shared by a large band of his contemporaries. It is of interest to note a few of these.

Horace Walpole visited the building for the first time in April 1771 before it was completed. Its luxury amazed him. He wrote: 'Imagine Balbec in all its glory! The pillars are of artificial "giallo antico". The

[1]*Gentleman's Magazine*, 1772, Vol. 42, p. 44.

ceilings, even of the passages, are of the most beautiful stuccos in the best taste of grotesque. The ceilings of the ball-room and the panels painted like Raphael's "loggias" in the Vatican. A dome like the Pantheon' (at Rome) 'glazed. It is to cost fifty thousand pounds.'[1] The French Ambassador, the duc de Guisnes, who accompanied him on the visit, commented: 'Ce n'est qu'à Londres qu'on peut faire tout cela.'[1] Two years later Walpole thought the Pantheon 'still the most beautiful edifice in England',[2] compared with which the Adelphi buildings were 'warehouses laced down the seams, like a soldier's trull in a regimental old coat'.[2]

Gibbon in a more aloof manner agreed with him. 'The Pantheon, in point of ennui and magnificence, is the wonder of the eighteenth century, and the British Empire',[3] he wrote. Dr Burney was equally sweeping. 'This most excellent building so far surpasses in beauty any other place appropriated to public amusements throughout Europe, that it is infinitely more the wonder of foreigners than of natives; and yet these, however often they may have seen it, still regard it with admiration.'[4] Even Henry Angelo, whose *Reminiscences* were published as late as 1824, called it 'certainly the most elegant and beautiful structure that had been erected in the metropolis'.[5] Ralph, in his *Review of the Buildings of London*, wrote with a more distinct guide-book flavour: 'Much taste and invention is displayed in the building called the Pantheon. Its exterior has nothing to demand our attention: on the contrary, the entrance from Oxford Street may justly be deemed a deformity in itself, and an encumbrance to the street. But the interior is adorned with all the embellishment that modern luxury can wish for. The principal room is truly magnificent.'

But there were a few who were not quite so enthusiastic. Fanny Burney's heroine, Evelina, was probably expressing the opinion of the authoress herself when she remarked: 'I was extremely struck with the beauty of the building, which greatly surpassed whatever I could have expected or imagined. Yet it has more the appearance of a chapel than a place of diversion, and though I was charmed with the magnificence of the room, I felt I could not be gay and thoughtless there as at Ranelagh; for there is something in it which rather inspires awe and

[1]Walpole to Sir Horace Mann, 26 April 1771.
[2]Walpole to Rev. William Mason, 29 July 1773.
[3]Edward Gibbon, Letter to J. B. Holroyd, 3 Feb. 1772.
[4]Charles Burney, Account of the Handel Festival.
[5]Henry Angelo, *Reminiscences*.

solemnity than mirth and pleasure. However, perhaps it may only have this effect upon such a novice as myself.'[1]

Dr Johnson and Boswell both preferred Ranelagh. Mrs Powys also noted in her diary: 'As a fine room, I think it grand beyond conception, yet I am not certain Ranelagh struck me not equally at first sight, and as a diversion, 'tis a place I think infinitely inferior, as there being so many rooms, no communication with the galleries, the staircase inconvenient, all contributed to lose the company than to show them to advantage.'[2]

Wyatt himself has said that the object of the rebuilding of the Pantheon was to make it a town Ranelagh, or as Walpole wrote, a winter Ranelagh. For a time this was achieved. All the fashionable world rushed to see and admire the magnificence of the building. The early seventies were probably the gayest and most care-free period of the eighteenth century in England, and the fêtes and masquerades, for which the Pantheon had been reconstructed, at first took the town by storm. The King and Queen attended, and admission was regulated by persons of distinguished rank and reputation. One would gather from a satirical poem called 'The Pantheon Rupture' written on this subject in 1772 that more emphasis was placed upon the rank than on the reputation, and a title was a better recommendation for admission than a spotless character. But in any case, the company was selected, if not select, the suppers hot and sumptuous and the wines choice and abundant. 'People of the first fashion of both sexes went in character and many eminent wits also, in appropriate costume, sustained their assumed parts with that spirit and vigour which may vainly be sought in a modern masquerade.'[3]

But the novelty of these Venetian masquerades soon began to pall, and as the real leaders of fashion became bored, they ceased attendance. In 1774 Gibbon wrote: 'Last night was the triumph of Boodles. Our masquerade cost two thousand guineas. A sum which might have fertilised a province, (I speak in your own style), vanished in a few hours, but not without leaving behind it the fame of the most splendid and elegant fête that was perhaps ever given in a seat of art and opulence. It would be as difficult to describe the magnificence of the scene as it would be easy to record the humour of the night. The one was above, the other below, all relation.'[4]

[1] Fanny Burney, *Evelina.*
[2] Passages from the Diary of Mrs Philip Lybbe Powys.
[3] Angelo, *Reminiscences.*
[4] Gibbon, Letter to J. B. Holroyd, 4 May 1774.

But the best demonstration of how the lapse of time altered the opinion entertained of these fêtes comes from Horace Walpole. In 1772 he was in raptures. 'There has been a masquerade at the Pantheon, which was so glorious a vision that I thought I was in the old Pantheon, or in the Temples of Delphi or Ephesus, amidst a crowd of various nations, and that formerly

Panthoides Euphorbus eram,

and did but recollect what I had seen. All the friezes and niches were edged with alternate lamps of green and purple glass that shed a most heathen light, and the dome was illuminated by a heaven of oiled paper well painted with gods and goddesses. Mr Wyatt, the architect, has so much taste that I think he must be descended from Sir Thomas.' (Walpole was then engaged in editing Sir Thomas Wyatt's letters and speeches.) 'Even Henry VIII had so much taste that, were he alive, he would visit the Pantheon.'[1]

Seven years later it was quite a different tale. 'The town has wound up the season perfectly in character with a fête at the Pantheon by subscription. Le Texier managed it, but it turned out sadly. The company was first shut in the galleries to look at the supper, then let descend to it. Afterwards they were led into a subterraneous apartment that was laid with mould and planted with trees, and crammed with nosegays: but the fresh earth, the dead leaves, and the effluvia of breaths made such a stench and moisture that they were suffocated: and when they remounted, the legs and wings of chicken and remnants of ham (for supper was not removed) poisoned them more. A Druid in an arbour distributed verses to the ladies: and the Bacelli and the Dancers of the Opera danced: and then danced the company: and then it being morning, and the candles burnt out, the windows were opened, and the stew-danced assembly were such shocking figures that they fled as the ghosts they looked.'[2]

At first both building and pleasure were new and attractive. As acquaintance with them increased the pleasure waned, and even the most fervent admiration for the building was inadequate to supply its place. The result was well exemplified in Gibbon's rather cynical utterances and Walpole's boredom. The proprietors of the Pantheon, naturally alarmed for their revenue, relaxed the regulations governing admission, as the usual tendency is, and the assembly rooms thus gradually lost caste until, in 1783, at the fortnightly balls

[1]Walpole to Rev. William Mason, 6 May 1772.
[2]Walpole to General Henry Conway, 16 June 1779.

which were held, anyone was admitted who had previously purchased a ticket. In addition to this, there was a certain limitation of festivities owing to the war; and also, the rival and confessedly more licentious establishment of Madame Corneilly's in Soho Square drew off many who still sought amusement.

So it was as a concert hall that the Pantheon came to be known, in opposition to the Opera House in the Haymarket. Even at the beginning of its existence the Italian singers who had performed there for the sum of fifty guineas a song had proved a great attraction; and it was probably their success which suggested the idea of the transformation into a concert hall.

In May 1784 the performance on the second day of the Handel Festival was held there, and the result was a fresh outburst of enthusiasm for the building and its architect. Wyatt was called in to design the temporary fittings, as he had done in Westminster Abbey for the previous day's concert. Over the entrance and opposite the orchestra was erected a large box for the Royal Family and their attendants. Critics agreed that though beforehand they had thought that the splendour of the Pantheon could not be increased, yet Wyatt's new decorations had actually improved its appearance.

Besides concerts, other attractions were employed to draw people to the building. In 1777, lightning conductors were exhibited in the cupola room of the Pantheon, and demonstrations given of their efficacy. Likewise in 1784 Vicenzo Lunardi's famous balloon was displayed there. Prints of both these two exhibits laid out in the interior of the Pantheon still exist.

Its final stage of existence was as an actual theatre. In 1789 the opera house in the Haymarket was again destroyed by fire, and the proprietors of the Pantheon transferred to their own establishment the Italian ballet and opera formerly playing at the Haymarket theatre. The grand saloon was converted into a permanent auditorium. The building was leased to a Mr O'Reilly for £3,000 a year; and the opening as the King's Theatre took place in 1791.

Opinions evidently differed as to its effect in its new capacity. Walpole wrote to Mary Berry: 'The Pantheon has opened, and is small, they say, but pretty and simple; all the rest ill-conducted, and from the singers to the scene-shifters imperfect; the dances long and bad, and the whole performance so dilatory and tedious that it lasted from eight to half an hour past twelve.'[1] Angelo, however, found the

[1]Walpole to Mary Berry, 18 Feb. 1791.

pit, boxes and gallery spacious and well adapted to receive an audience, the stage of vast extent, and the scenery and costumes most effective. Everything was proceeding satisfactorily when the end came.

This took place in the early hours of the morning of 14th January 1792. A fire broke out in the region behind the stage; and as the persons who lived on the premises did not awake until stones were thrown up at their windows by a neighbour who had himself been roused by the intense heat coming in at his window, the whole building was consumed, leaving only the walls standing. The dome had been built of timber, owing to the niggardliness of the proprietors, and similarly much lath and plaster was used throughout. In addition to these materials, the scagliola work proved very inflammable. When efforts were made to quench the fire, it was too far advanced, and the coldness of the night made the procuring of water more difficult, as it was everywhere frozen.

It is interesting to note that Angelo records that Wyatt himself saw the glare of the fire in the sky from his post-chaise as he was crossing Salisbury Plain, on his way back to London from the west. He observed to Dixon, his clerk: 'That vast light is in the direction of London; surely, Dixon, the whole city is on fire', 'little dreaming that this awful spectacle was blazing away so fatally for himself'.[1] This story is so picturesque that one hesitates to question whether the greatest conflagration imaginable in London could be seen as far away as Salisbury Plain.

After 1792 the Pantheon was rebuilt in a simpler fashion but perished again nearly twenty years later. A reference to this occurs in one of Wyatt's few surviving letters. On November 21st 1811 he wrote to his son Matthew Cotes: 'Your mother and Charles' (another son) 'both had informed me about the Pantheon. I wize it had all been consumed except the fronts and I believe they [are] all that remain of the Original Building.' It would be difficult to be more matter-of-fact on such an occasion.

The building was reconstructed by Cundy as a theatre in 1812, remodelled as a bazaar and picture gallery in 1834 by Sydney Smirke, when the portico in Oxford Street was added, converted into Messrs Gilbey's offices and wine warehouse in 1867 and finally demolished in 1937 to make way for the new premises of Marks and Spencers.

As Wyatt's Pantheon has vanished, it is fortunate that there exist sufficient reproductions of it to enable us to see what manner of

[1] Angelo, *Reminiscences*.

13

building it was. The original drawings, which were exhibited in the Royal Academy of 1770, no longer exist, but before their disappearance, Sir John Soane caused copies to be made of them for his lectures as Professor of Architecture at the Royal Academy. These consist of a sectional drawing of the interior, a plan of both floors, and an elevation of the Oxford Street entrance, and are to be found in Sir John Soane's Museum. Messrs Gilbey, who occupied the premises of the Pantheon from 1867-1937, possess a very wide range of prints of the building at various stages in its history, and the series is so numerous and varied that the history of its architectural development is fairly complete.

CHAPTER III

THE ADVENT OF FAME

THE celebrity to which Wyatt attained at one fell swoop with a single work, and that his first, was almost unparalleled. It was certainly unique for a man of his age. It might naturally be asked how it came about that his advancement was so much more spectacular than that of the Adam brothers. The only reason seems to have been that the Pantheon was a public place of amusement, whereas the Adams never had the good fortune to design such a building in England. Instead therefore of the architecture being admired only by a small circle of friends who were invited to stay in the country or who visited in town, the Pantheon was inspected by the whole of London. The novelty and attractiveness of the fêtes held there and the suitability of the lightness of this style of decoration ensured the appreciation of the building by those who frequented it. Thus was the reputation of its architect made.

In 1770, on the strength of three drawings of the Pantheon on view in that year's exhibition, Wyatt was elected an Associate of the Royal Academy. He became an Academician in 1785. At the period of his election as an Associate, he was living in Great Newport Street, probably at his brother John's establishment. In 1774 he moved to Newman Street. This may have been his first separate establishment, and his move to it may have coincided with his marriage. Of his wife, Rachel Lunn, the only information that we have is that *The Monthly Magazine* called her 'the niece of a medical gentleman',[1] and that she was the cousin of a certain Matthew Yatman of Chelsea who bequeathed to her an annuity of £100 when she was a widow. Their first child, Benjamin Dean Wyatt, was born, presumably in Newman Street, in 1775, their second son, Matthew Cotes, in 1777. Two more sons, Charles Burton and Philip William, and one daughter, Jane, followed.

In the very year in which Wyatt moved to Newman Street he

[1]*Monthly Magazine*, Oct. 1813, Vol. 36, p. 266.

obtained from Lord Foley the lease of a long narrow plot of land over-looking the grounds of Foley House, Portland Place. On this site he built a house for his own occupation which was finished by 1783. He resided there from that year until his death in 1813. It was at first called No. 69 Queen Anne Street East. In 1810 this was changed to No. 1 Foley Place, in 1822 to No. 8 Langham Place and subsequently to No. 8 Portland Place. The house was one of the most delightful small buildings ever designed by Wyatt, and it is immensely to be regretted that it was demolished about 1928.

The principal front, which looked into Langham Street and Foley Place, was faced with stucco and was somewhat of a forerunner of the style more associated with Nash and the Regency thirty years later. It comprised a main block of three storeys and two single-storeyed pavilions. The principal feature of the ground floor consisted of two tripartite windows and a central doorway flanked by slit windows, all three of which were surmounted by segmental tympana containing bas-reliefs of two gryphons with an urn between them. The first floor windows were flanked by twin Corinthian pilasters standing on an enriched stringcourse. Over each window was a Coadeware plaque of one or two figures. Above the main entablature stood plain twin pilasters. The whole was topped by a parapet of imitation balustrading.

Inside, the main doorway was flanked by Ionic columns and surmounted by a half-dome with enriched plasterwork in ribs. On the right of the hall was the dining-room. The west end was screened off by two Ionic scagliola columns. The cornice of the whole room had small heads in the place of modillions. Four heads of approximately similar size, but this time of goats, topped the jambs of the chimney-piece, above two shields containing figures in low relief. The chimney-piece in the library on the opposite side of the hall had a centre panel of Callimachus sketching the first Corinthian capital and in the angles medallions possibly of Inigo Jones and Palladio. The drawing-room above the dining-room was segmental-ended east and west with a single window flanked by recesses. The mantelpiece had three vignettes of Cupids and reeded jambs. The chief feature was the elaborately enriched plaster ceiling. Probably the most charming portion of the whole house was the landing and staircase approaching the first floor. This had an elaborate cross vault and a finely panelled barrel ceiling, in the spandrels of which were radiating fans of plaster-work. Below these were panels of arabesques in stucco containing a

16

figure standing on a pedestal at an altar. The whole was finished by a beautiful wrought iron handrail to the staircase. (Plate 16.)

When James Wyatt died in 1813 he was succeeded in occupation of the house by his nephew, Captain Charles Wyatt, who had been Chief Engineer in Bengal. The latter resided there until his death in 1819. The astonishing architectural genius of this family is never better displayed than in Government House, Calcutta, which Charles Wyatt, though an engineer and not an architect, had designed in 1798 during his career in India. How beautiful would be our towns and villages today if the engineers to whom so much of their construction and ornamentation is, alas! entrusted could produce or inspire buildings like this!

At some time after his success Wyatt acquired, in addition to his town house, a country seat. This is generally called Hanworth Park, Middlesex, but Farington, who dined there on several occasions, called it Hanworth Farm, 'an estate of about 90 acres'.[1] When James's sons, Benjamin and Charles, were in India between 1798 and 1802 their letters home were filled with nostalgic references to the delights of their childhood at Hanworth. There is considerable doubt as to the identity of this house. A building named Hanworth Park exists today which is a hotel attached to Hanworth air-port. This has been so much altered and enlarged that it is difficult to unravel the various stages of its growth. The interior contains nothing that one can associate with Wyatt. Of the exterior, the only portion that might be his work is the two-storeyed portico in the centre of the main front, which is not unlike those built by Wyatt at Goodwood and elsewhere. But the double veranda of Regency pattern, though it could have been designed in the last years of his life, was more probably added soon after his death together with the central pediment above it and the two flanking hips. It seems however that this house was not called Hanworth Park until 1870.

About a quarter to half a mile to the north-west of the latter was another house which apparently bore this name before 1870. This was a moated Tudor building which was used as a hunting lodge by Henry VIII. After his death it passed to his widow, Katherine Parr, who lived there with her fourth husband, Sir Thomas Seymour. It was in this house that took place the famous familiarities between Seymour and Princess Elizabeth which led to his impeachment after Katherine Parr's death. This building is said to have been in the hands of the

[1]*Farington Diary*, 28 Aug. 1797.

Duke of St Albans in 1786 and to have been burned down in 1797. Its stables however survive and are unquestionably by Wyatt. They are now converted into flats known as Tudor Court. They form a vast L-shaped castellated rudimentary Gothic edifice of harsh brown brick. This has no less than nine window-bays on each front with square battlemented towers in the centre and at each end and a castellated parapet over the portions of lower elevation between the towers. All the window openings have pointed tympana, though modern casement windows have been inserted in them. The central tower on each front contains a carriage archway with double doors, the principal one having a pointed head. The building is singularly ugly and presumably was one of Wyatt's very early experiments in Gothic, when he was not at all at ease with the medium.

There is another house in the neighbourhood which, from the character of some of its interior work, may be associated with Wyatt. This is just within the parish of Feltham but near enough to the boundary between the two parishes to have been thought of as being in Hanworth, before the area was built up. It is now the officers' mess in a large Royal Army Service Corps depot but was previously called Feltham House. The very plain exterior of stock brick is relieved by a projecting bay in the centre of the south front and wings with Venetian windows breaking forward on the north side. The principal apartments are on the first floor and are approached by a flight of fourteen steps with an iron handrail leading up to the bay on one side and a pair of curved steps of sedan pattern on the other side. The house has not been improved by the addition of a tile-hung third storey in modern times.

The southern bay contains the staircase, of which the south wall within is curved and contains a niche. At first floor level is a band with a design of vases, lyres and rams' heads in plaster work. The uprights of the handrails are joined by small ovals set between pairs of scrolls above and below. The central room behind the staircase, now the officers' dining-room, is almost certainly older than Wyatt's time. But the two Corinthian columns which divide it nearly in half may have been inserted by him. The room in the south-west corner of the house, now called the ante-room, retains only a contemporary door-case with a frieze of anthemia and corn-stooks alternately. The billiard-room behind has a ceiling frieze of female figures linked by festoons of husks with paterae above. The chimney-piece is of composition imitating marble with anthemium capitals to the jambs and a

18

central plaque of a lyre and a beribboned pineapple-headed rod in a festoon. Above it is a round bas-relief of four classical figures, one holding a lyre and another a serpent twisted round a column which is topped by a vase. The whole panel is encircled by a festoon of small ovals made of corn heads. This room has a strong suggestion of Wyatt, and the house may very well be that which he occupied. But there is no certainty, and it is equally possible that his house may have been demolished.

He also rebuilt the parish church of Hanworth between 1808 and 1813. But the version of Gothic which he used pleased the succeeding generation so little that it in its turn was demolished and rebuilt in 1865.

We are told that after the opening of the Pantheon Wyatt's house was surrounded by the carriages of the nobility and of the foreign ambassadors, and that his rooms were crowded with their owners who had come to lavish their praises upon this prodigy. As Peter Pindar picturesquely puts it:

'I know the foolish kingdom all runs riot,
Calling aloud for Wyat, Wyat, Wyat,
Who on their good opinion hourly gains.
But where lies Wyat's merit? . . . Where his praise?
Abroad this roving man spent half his days,
Contemplating of Rome the great remains.'[1]

But it was not mere laudatory phrases without any practical import that these distinguished personages came to utter. They were also armed with offers of employment. Amongst this vague assembly of people, only three have been actually named. Of these, two were English noblemen, the Dukes of Richmond and Northumberland. Their particular mention by name is rather remarkable, as there is no record that Wyatt began work for the Duke of Richmond at Goodwood until at least fifteen years later, or that he ever worked at all for the Duke of Northumberland, who indeed was one of Adam's most important patrons.

The third specified was the Russian Ambassador, who was empowered by the Tsarina Catherine to offer Wyatt any salary that he chose to demand if he would settle in St Petersburg as her architect. Hunt[2] records that he was dissuaded from acceptance of this offer by a certain Mr Wright, who had acquired a large fortune in Russia by coach-building. He told Wyatt that Catherine would keep all her promises with regard to reward—did she offer him a million of money

[1]Peter Pindar, *Works*, Ode 22.
[2]T. F. Hunt, *Archittetura Campestre*.

she would give it—but she would never allow him to leave the country.

Probably more effective than this factor in keeping Wyatt at home was the employment offered him in England. To prevent his acceptance of the proposal of the Russian, or of any other, ambassador, several English noblemen combined together, contributing various sums of money, to pay him a retaining fee of £1,200 a year to act as the architectural supervisor of their houses.

The result of all these attentions was that Wyatt became acknowledged as the most fashionable architect of his day. He began to travel constantly up and down the country and had his coach fitted up so that he could work in it, though how this was possible in a jolting vehicle along the bad roads of the eighteenth century it is difficult to imagine. In 1796 he told Farington that he reckoned he travelled 7,000 miles a year. His fees were a commission of 5 per cent on the cost of the work carried out, plus 2s. 6d. a mile and five guineas a day for personal attendance on the spot; or when he was merely called upon to give advice without any agreement being entered into, ten guineas a day.

Even the King, followed by the Queen, noticed Wyatt with favour. The stars of the Adams were somewhat dimmed by his appearance, and besides them there was hardly another who could afford serious competition. Sir William Chambers must perhaps be mentioned, but he was growing old, and his period of supremacy was well on the decline. Strangely enough, though he had always been antagonistic to the Adam brothers and had been influential enough to exclude them from the Royal Academy, yet he appears to have welcomed Wyatt and to have encouraged his advancement. He may even have recommended him as his successor as Surveyor General to the Board of Works. This post George III conferred on Wyatt on Chambers' death in 1796. He was in fact the last architect to be the holder of the position, as after his death the title was given to a civil servant and the technical duties assigned to three 'attached architects' (Nash, Soane and Smirke). This was Wyatt's second official appointment. In 1776 he had succeeded Henry Keene as Fabric Surveyor and College Surveyor of Westminster Abbey and the remains of the Palace of Westminster attached to it, including the Houses of Parliament. On his death this post passed to his eldest son, Benjamin Dean. He was also 'Surveyor of Somerset Place' (Somerset House) at a salary of £200 a year, the appointment having been made, according to Farington, against the King's wishes. In 1806 Wyatt acquired one further appointment, namely that of Architect to the Board of Ordnance.

6 and 7. Brocklesby Park. The Mausoleum
(*Country Life Photographs*)

8. Heaton Hall
(*Country Life Photograph*)

9. Castle Coole
(*Country Life Photograph*)

10. Heaton Hall. The Cupola Room
(*Country Life Photograph*)

11. Castle Coole. The Saloon
(*Country Life Photograph*)

12. Cobham Hall. The Mausoleum

13. Heaton Hall. The Temple
(*Country Life Photograph*)

14. Heveningham Hall. The Orangery
(*Country Life Photograph*)

Chapter IV

GENERAL CLASSICAL WORK

(1.) 1770-1775

THE earliest surviving drawing of Wyatt's is dated 1771 and is in the Library of the Royal Institute of British Architects. The building concerned has not been identified. It has some affinities with Bowden House, Wiltshire, which Wyatt built for B. Dickenson in 1796, though it is considerably larger and more elaborate. The main feature of the house is the centre-piece made up of four pilasters and six engaged columns all of the Corinthian order. Between them are statues in niches on the ground floor with an enriched stringcourse above, Coadeware stone plaques of various shapes at first floor level and, over this, a frieze enriched with swags and paterae. Above the entablature is a parapet decorated with a design of gryphons and arabesques and surmounted at the ends by recumbent figures which flank a stepped saucer-dome. If this design was never executed, it is much to be regretted. (Plate 1.)

At least two commissions were however carried out by Wyatt in this same year, though neither was very important. One was for a ceiling at Hagley in Staffordshire, shown in the Royal Academy of 1771, and the other for the ceilings and chimney-pieces in the library and the small drawing-room at Fawley Court, Oxfordshire, which had been built by Sir Christopher Wren in 1684-8.

Wyatt probably began work as early as 1771 at a house with which he was connected on and off for the whole of his working career, namely Cobham Hall, Kent. The *Dictionary of Architecture* dates his work there at 1783, no doubt because that was the year in which the mausoleum in the grounds was built. But Mr Ralph Arnold, who has fully examined the surviving accounts for work done at Cobham Hall, has ascertained that the third Earl of Darnley's operations there began in 1768, when he added a parapet to the south front. Sir William Chambers was paid £20 for making a journey to Cobham in 1770 and for preparing some plans. In that year an extra storey was added to the

C

west front, but whether it was for designing this that Chambers was paid, it is not possible to say.

At that time the house consisted of a half-H plan: parallel north and south wings erected between 1584 and 1602 and a connecting block built between 1662 and 1672 and probably designed by John Webb. The first alteration which can safely be attributed to Wyatt is the addition of a wide service corridor along the east face of the centre block with the portrait gallery above it. This was executed between 1771 and 1773. At the same time he probably began the extension eastward of the two parallel wings to form a complete H and eventually become the kitchen court. These additions were carried out in a style matching the Elizabethan character of the old work.

Following this, in 1773-4, Wyatt redecorated several of the rooms in the house in the Chinese manner. The room in the south wing known as Lady Darnley's drawing-room and the ante-room adjoining it which was called the Fruit room were hung with very fine blue Chinese wall-papers which are referred to in the accounts as 'India' papers. Wyatt similarly decorated two rooms on the first floor of the centre block known as the Blue Damask room and the Blue Damask dressing-room. The bedroom, which was then the third Countess's sitting-room, has a white marble chimney-piece with a frieze of putti in relief and in the centre an odd kind of vase with half a fabulous bird springing from each side of it. This and the handsome doorcases and shutters in both rooms of eight reeded panels with rosettes in the angles were carved by Thomas Varley. The furniture was upholstered with thirteen pieces of blue damask of eighteen yards each, purchased in 1774 at the cost of £109 4s. This furniture may possibly have been designed by Wyatt, but the bed had been bought in 1768. Both rooms have elaborate plaster ceilings, the design of that in the dressing-room being octagonal, though the room is not quite of this shape.

Contemporary with the decoration of these rooms was the creation of the vestibule in the centre of the west front of the main block. This formed the principal entrance until the porte cochère and entrance hall on the west side were added by Wyatt some years later. The vestibule is the most complete of Wyatt's alterations or additions surviving at Cobham. It is a charming little room. The walls are pale green, painted with panels of grey, pink and pale blue. The side walls each contain a doorway in the centre surmounted by a rectangular trempe l'oeil painted panel between round-headed niches surmounted

22

by similar oval panels. Opposite to the main entrance is a screen separating from the main hall an apse that is slightly more than a semicircle. This screen consists of a round-headed archway with pink scagliola borders decorated with white scroll plasterwork, with oval openings above. The ceiling has a central circular panel with a green background and a pink border linked by a pattern of arabesques to four lunettes of two white sphinxes flanking an urn on a pink ground. (Plate 3.) The fireplace is in the centre of the apse and is an exceptionally delightful one. (Plate 4.) It is in three portions, all of white marble, and was probably carved by Thomas Varley. The centre projects slightly and has a fine continuous frieze of amorini more boldly carved than those on the fireplace in the Blue Damask room. Its jambs are fluted half-columns. The outer portions have only a frieze of triglyphs but the uprights are whole columns. Between these and the half columns of the centre portions stand enchanting pairs of embracing figures on pedestals. No house in England contains a more beautiful example of a chimney-piece designed by Wyatt than this. The ceiling of the apse has a scrolled frieze of similar design to the borders framing the openings in the screen, and this appears again in the ceiling itself round the central rosette. The room contains four fine gilt settees with inward-curving scroll ends which have been attributed to Wyatt but have more affinity with the Regency.

Adjoining the vestibule is the magnificent Gilt Hall or music-room. This was built in 1672, but the only portion of its internal decoration which is indisputably of that date is the gilded ceiling. It was originally a banqueting-room but was converted into a music-room at the time of Wyatt's alterations in the eighteenth century. At each end of the room he erected a gallery supported on yellow scagliola columns. The organ in the north gallery dates from 1779. About twelve years later he added the yellow scagliola pilasters round the walls with the white marbling of the wall surface between. The very fine mahogany doors of the same design as those in the Blue Damask room upstairs are certainly Wyatt's. So probably is the chandelier consisting of two circular tiers of lights decorated with gryphons and hanging from a palm branch. The elder Westmacott and not Wyatt was responsible for the chimney-piece, more typical of that monumental exuberance which one has come to associate with the long reign of a female sovereign. There remain the plaster panels above the level of the galleries and of the pilasters. They are the chief glory of the room. They were gilded in 1791-3, but when were they inserted and by whom designed? The panels comprise most beautiful clusters of musical trophies and wreathed cameo heads alternately. As the room was converted into a music-room in 1779, it would seem reasonable to assign the musical trophies to that date and it is therefore tempting to attribute them to Wyatt. But it is difficult to point to other work of similar character from his hand. Most of the few other cases in which he employed groups of musical trophies occur in houses built towards the end of his life. The quality of the work is so excellent that one thinks at once of Joseph Rose as the craftsman who would have carried it out. But the scagliola pilasters were made by Dominick Bartoli, and so it is likely that the trophies may have been executed by him also. On the north wall are two fixed stone side-tables decorated with figures engaged in pressing grapes and with gryphons in the angles. These again may be Wyatt's work. Tradition at Cobham Hall maintains that George IV is said to have considered the Gilt Hall the finest room in England. It is certainly surpassed by few.

The third Earl of Darnley died in 1781, and his successor was a minor. There was therefore a pause in building operations at Cobham Hall at this date, though under the terms of the third Earl's will Wyatt built a mausoleum in the grounds in 1783 to receive his body. From 1789 onwards the fourth Earl continued his father's work. The old stables opposite the south front were demolished and a new block erected beyond the kitchen court. The latter was probably completed at this date. The finishing touches were added to the Gilt Hall, as has already been mentioned. Humphrey Repton was also commissioned to landscape the park.

There was then another pause until about 1801. In that year Wyatt began the addition of the entrance hall or cloister which is a wing projecting at right angles to the north front with an archway in the centre forming a porte cochère. The roof makes a bridge connecting the first floor of the house with the long terraced garden. The exterior of the wing is of red brick in harmony with the Tudor north wing, which it adjoins, and the archway of Roman cement. There is the date 1801 over this, but the work was not finished until 1809. Inside there is a complete transformation from Wyatt's earlier work at Cobham. The style is Gothic. The outer hall or corridor has ribbed plaster vaulting, the inner hall a screen of three four-centred arches at the foot of the staircase. One wonders whether this change of style was because the new Earl, being a young man, was an enthusiast for the new ideas then just becoming fashionable, or whether it was solely due to the fact that his architect was, by the turn of the century, well launched on his Gothic career. Between 1806 and 1809 Wyatt reconstructed the picture gallery in the north wing and the large dining-room beneath it. But the Elizabethan character of the former was not altered. The latter was redecorated about 1840. Wyatt's last work at Cobham, in 1812-13, was the reconstruction of the chapel, now the small library, in the same wing. He inserted in this two Gothic screens similar to that in the hall. These have since been glazed.

Wyatt's work at Cobham Hall is not amongst the most important or significant that he executed but is chiefly interesting as having covered the whole period of his working career, and as showing the evolution of his taste or styles during forty-two years.

The mausoleum stands at the top of the slight rise in the Park known as William's Hill. A design of it was exhibited in the Royal Academy of 1783. Wyatt was paid fifty guineas for his plans. The building is sometimes said to have cost £30,000, but if the fee was the usual commission of five per cent, the cost would have been only £1,000, which seems more probable. (Plate 12.)

The mausoleum is built of Portland stone and is set in a circular ditch with a vallum surrounding it. The plan is an irregular octagon consisting of four main sides and four small projections at the angles. It is of two storeys, the entrance being at first floor level by a bridge across the ditch. Each of the main sides has two engaged fluted Doric columns standing on the rusticated base of the ground floor, and each of the small sides two free-standing similar columns. A triglyph frieze runs round the whole. Above this is a segmental arch on each of the main sides and a small sarcophagus on each of the projections. Over these again are a cornice and parapet, on which stands a large solid pyramid topping the whole building. Within, the tombhouse was on the ground floor containing sixteen recesses round the outside, beside the places intended for the third Earl and Countess of Darnley in the centre. The first floor room formed a chapel finished in Brocotello marble and stained glass. The building was never actually used as a mausoleum and is now out of repair. It cannot be called a successful composition, as the pyramid is too heavy for the structure below it and looks somewhat out of place hoisted aloft.

Wyatt built another mausoleum in the grounds of Brocklesby Park, Lincolnshire, for Charles Anderson Pelham, later first Earl of Yarborough, for whom he also worked at Apuldurcombe in the Isle of Wight. The building was in memory of Pelham's wife, Sophia Aufrere.

25

It belongs to the period between 1787 and 1794, and Wyatt's design for it was not shown in the Royal Academy until 1795. But it may be convenient to consider it at this point. It is a very different construction from the mausoleum at Cobham Hall and must be one of the most exquisite small buildings in the whole of the British Isles. In scale, delicacy of craftsmanship and position it somewhat resembles James Paine's chapel at Gibside, Durham, and Sir William Chambers's Casino at Marino, Clontarf, Dublin, though the exterior is more delightful than either. It did not however find favour with all contemporaries. John Byng, later fifth Viscount Torrington, visited it during 1794 when it was still in course of construction. After calling it 'a little Ratcliffe library',[1] which is not inappropriate, he went on to say that it was 'a lumbring Grecian building . . . I never saw a heavier clump',[1] than which there could be few more untrue comments.

The design is based on the temples of Vesta at Rome and Tivoli. It stands on a slight mound set in trees and is surrounded by an iron railing interspersed with stone piers decorated with swags and topped by pediments. Like the mausoleum at Cobham, it is of two storeys with the land round the ground floor slightly scooped away. The building is circular. The ground floor again is rusticated, and on this base stands a colonnade of sixteen fluted Roman Doric columns. The first floor is inset within this and behind the columns are four round-headed niches containing sarcophagi standing on high plinths. Above the columns is a very beautiful frieze enriched with swags, a modillion cornice and a most delicately-proportioned balustraded parapet. Behind the gallery formed by this balustrade rises a copper dome surmounted by a small circular feature. (Plate 7.)

The main room is on the first floor approached by broad converging flights of gradual steps. Eight porphyritic columns support the coffered dome which is lit from a skylight in the centre. Between the columns are four recesses containing sculptured groups executed in Italy commemorating various members of the Pelham family. In the centre is a circle of dove-coloured marbles set in bronze. On this stands a drum supporting a beautiful white marble figure of Sophia Pelham by Nollekens. Nowhere is the elegance of the eighteenth century, even in death, better demonstrated than in this building. (Plate 6.)

Wyatt also designed several small garden ornaments at Brocklesby such as urns. The house itself had been built about 1730. It is not possible to say whether he did any work to the interior as this was

[1] *The Torrington Diaries*, 12 July 1794.

26

gutted by fire in 1898. But it is likely that he may have designed for the house some furniture which survived the fire, particularly the organ-case in the chapel.

The year 1772, in which the Pantheon was opened, brought a more important commission in Heaton Hall, Manchester. An elevation of the house was shown in the Royal Academy Exhibition of that year. About 1750 Sir Thomas Egerton, the sixth baronet, had built a house there of brick which was the size of the present central block. His son Sir Thomas, the seventh baronet, who was later created Earl Grey de Wilton, employed Wyatt to enlarge this building. Wyatt added a new south front in sandstone ashlar, consisting of a two-storeyed centre and single-storeyed octagonal pavilions linked to this by colonnaded corridors. (Plate 8.)

The principal feature of the central block is a curved bay of three windows, the centre window flanked by engaged Ionic columns rising the whole height of the building, and the outer windows by part-pilasters which die into the walls on each side. Below the stringcourse of guilloche moulding at the sill level of the first floor windows are three Coadeware plaques showing classical groups. Above the entablature is a flat saucer dome. The outer window bays of the central block are flanked by similar Ionic pilasters and have Venetian windows on the ground floor. Flanking the central segmental steps are the figures of a lion and lioness. The colonnaded corridors are surmounted by massive square blocks of chimneys, each shaft linked to the others by the entablature and the base. The three sides of the octagonal pavilions facing south have pilasters which support a fluted frieze, continued over the corridors, with an ox-skull above the capital of each pilaster or column. Venetian windows in the centre of each pavilion balance those in the main block, and the outer windows are surmounted by rectangular panels of Coadeware swags.

The stone of this façade is now partly blackened by the smoke from the city of Manchester, whose expansion has overtaken the house, but, when new, the sandstone must have gleamed brightly in the sunlight. Heaton Hall was the first house of several in which Wyatt used the plan very popular with eighteenth-century architects of a central block and flanking wings. One of the octagonal pavilions contains the library, and the other the kitchen with two monumental ranges facing each other in the centre of its east and west walls. There was no basement. This had the convenience all too uncommon in eighteenth-century mansions that the kitchen was only separated from the

27

dining-room by the intervention of two small service rooms in the western colonnade. With many clients of the period this would not have found favour, as it was generally held that the kitchen should be neither seen nor smelt.

On the north or entrance front the pre-existing block of the house was encased between long flat wings of seven window-bays, of which the three centre windows are emphasized by pilaster treatment. The main block has a slight central break forward with a pediment over and a tetrastyle portico. The whole front was stuccoed to match the stone of the new garden front but is unfortunately now even more blackened by smoke than the latter.

Heaton Hall was purchased by Manchester Corporation in 1901 but, to the lasting detriment of the house, the opportunity was not taken of buying all the original fittings or contents which the taste of that date little valued. The house is now suitably used as a Georgian museum, but some of the rooms are rather empty and consequently not seen to the fullest advantage.

The hall, entered from the portico on the north side, is a plain room with apsidal ends each containing a doorway and two niches for statues. Opposite the entrance is a fireplace set between two other beautiful mahogany doors. The doorcases, chimney-piece and ceiling all have a frieze of flutings and large paterae containing three intersecting arrows.

The hall opens into the staircase, and beyond it is the saloon which contains the central bow of the south front. At the opposite end of the room is a screen or passage with a coved ceiling separated from the rest of the room by two black and white scagliola columns having capitals formed of draped masks imitating the Corinthian order. On each side of the fireplaces, which face each other in the side walls, are niches for statuary, and over the chimney-pieces are oval plaques in bas-relief of female figures holding a lyre. These are surrounded by delicate festoons of plasterwork. The ceiling and mantelpieces have a frieze picked out in gold of alternate lyres and paterae containing tiny cherubs' faces.

The chief features of the dining-room are the Venetian window with an enriched soffit and an anthemium frieze matching the pattern of the ceiling frieze, the doorcases and the mantelpiece, and the semicircular side-board recess at the opposite end of the room, of which the head is decorated with plaster arabesques and three painted ovals of female figures. Fitted in the recess is a painted table made in three sections.

The room balancing the dining-room on the other side of the saloon is the billiard-room. The walls are panelled with pictures of Classic scenes which have fortunately been retained as fixtures. They are set in imitation gilt frames of anthemium design almost flush with the wall surface. Tall vases take the place of the honeysuckle motif in the ceiling frieze, the overdoors and the chimney-piece. The ceiling has a design of ornamental plasterwork with an oval in the centre framed by rectangular panels which repeat the urn motif of the frieze linked by arabesques.

The billiard-room leads into the music-room. The chief feature of this room is probably the ingenious manner in which an ogee-shaped recess was contrived in the east wall between the apse of the ante-room and one side of the octagonal library in order to contain the organ. This organ is dated 1790 and was built by Samuel Green of London, but the case was evidently designed by Wyatt as the frieze of the room with a pattern of gilded balls is carried round the top of it. The panels below the pipes are painted with scenes in grisaille and a miniature portrait of a musician, probably Handel. These are the work of Biagio Rebecca. The ceiling has a plain cove. The white marble chimney-piece is less delicate than those in the other rooms. The jambs frame female figures in relief. The wide frieze above has figures of eagles in the angles with wreaths dangling from their beaks and a sleeping cherub in the centre swathed in festoons.

The last room in the suite of reception rooms is the library, which occupies the octagonal pavilion at the east end balancing the kitchen. With its bookcases removed, it is a plain room retaining only its laurel frieze, octagonal ribbed dome and white marble chimney-piece. This last has an architrave of fret pattern supported by composite columns and a fine original grate with brass-fronted hobs. At the north end of the room is an oval ante-room entered through an archway formed by two sienna-coloured scagliola Ionic columns which support the entablature of the ante-room's lower ceiling.

The staircase is the forerunner of many designed by Wyatt. It is situated in the centre of the house, where he always liked to place it if space permitted, and is lit from above. The stair is of that invariably impressive pattern which begins as a single flight and divides into two at the half-landing. The wrought-iron balusters are lyre-shaped, framing an anthemium motif, and topped by a figure eight. The bottom step is flanked by gilded tripods supporting single candlestick shafts. On the first floor a small gallery is formed on each side of the stairs by two pairs of brown scagliola Corinthian columns which hold up the entablature of the staircase-well. The principal bedrooms open off these galleries. Between the pairs of columns and at the head of the stair are three more tripods, as at the foot. The ceiling has a frieze of anthemia and tall vases alternately, a cove with fan radiations in the corners and a small circular dome in the centre. The centre doors in the south gallery and the landing have very elaborate heads enriched with scrolls of plaster-work. In the north gallery is a similar arrangement of arabesques flanking an urn placed over a small circular convex mirror which reflects the staircase. The doors on each side are surmounted by rectangular panels painted in grisaille with imitation drapery in plaster below them.

The finest room at Heaton is not actually one of the reception rooms on the ground floor, but the Cupola-room above. (Plate 10.) This is circular and occupies the central bow above the saloon. It is entered through double doors very slightly curved to the shape of the room. The walls and ceiling were painted in the Etruscan manner which Wyatt also used at Heveningham Hall. But this is much the finest specimen existing of his work in this style. The artist to whom the execution of the design was entrusted was Biagio Rebecca. This was the first instance of the co-operation between Rebecca and Wyatt which was to re-occur on many occasions in their joint careers. The colour scheme is of two shades of green and biscuit-colour. Both walls and ceiling are divided into eight wide and eight narrow sections. The narrow sections of the walls are flanked by pale green pilasters painted all over, the spaces between being of darker green and containing tall rectangular mirrors with roundels above them. The wide sections contain two doorways, three windows, two recesses and the fireplace. All have fan-ornamentation in their semi-circular heads. The doors have six green panels painted with birds and sphinxes and set in surrounds of biscuit-colour. The chimney-piece consists only of a band of white marble, above which gilt sphinxes in relief support a circular panel containing a portrait. The ceiling panels narrow as they rise towards the central circular panel containing a large rosette, from which the chandelier hung, surrounded by eight small diamonds, each painted with a female figure. Probably the most beautiful portion of the whole room consists of the wide ceiling panels. These have a cream ground painted with arabesques and in the centre a cream-coloured figure set in a chocolate-coloured oval. The whole scheme of decoration in this room is as beautiful as anything Wyatt ever designed during his career.

The stables are contemporary but uninteresting. The farm buildings adjoining include some rather unusual two-storeyed hay-lofts, enclosed on the ground floor but open above on one face with circular brick columns supporting the eaves of the roof.

Wyatt also designed a small cottage in the park now known as Dower House Cottage, the Smithy Lodge which is octagonal with the chimneys in the centre and a colonnade round it, and the Grand Lodge or main entrance, consisting of a triumphal arch set between one-storeyed dwellings. But the only building of interest in the park is the temple which is magnificently situated at the crown of the estate commanding a fine view over Manchester. This is a small circular stuccoed building surrounded by a balustrade. It is raised on two steps and consists of a single room set in a colonnade of eight Doric columns supporting a dentil cornice and a leaden dome. Above the latter is a miniature reproduction of the temple, itself forming a cupola containing a large bell. The building badly needs repainting but is a charming little piece of work, worthy to rank with Wyatt's other masterpieces in miniature, the mausoleum at Brocklesby, and the orangery at Heveningham Hall. (Plate 13.)

The grounds were laid out in the style associated with the name of Capability Brown, but it is not known whether they were actually the beginning of an artistic association which, like that between Wyatt and Rebecca, was to re-occur on many occasions in the following years. When Manchester Corporation purchased the estate in 1901, they re-erected on the other side of the lake the Ionic screen from the old Manchester Town Hall designed by Francis Goodwin which had recently been demolished. In its present position it makes an excellent 'eye-catcher', as the eighteenth century would have called it, viewed from the house across the water.

In 1926 Mr H. Avray Tipping, writing in *English Homes, Period VI*, first attributed some of the interior work at Crichel House, Dorset, to James Wyatt. Since that date no documentary evidence has come to light confirming the attribution, but it has been generally assumed by other writers to be correct and probably is so. The house was first rebuilt by Sir William Napier in 1744 after a fire but was greatly enlarged by Humphrey Sturt soon after 1765. Most of the interior work, despite its date, is Palladian in character. The only portions which are in later style and could be from Wyatt's hand are the dining-room, the great drawing-room, the corridor on the first floor and the former boudoir. They were probably executed about 1773.

The dining-room walls are straw-coloured and are decorated with round or oval painted panels in trempe l'oeil style of white figures on a pale blue ground, surmounted by ornamental scrolls of plasterwork. Over the doors are similar lunettes. The chimney-piece has grey marble coupled Ionic columns as uprights with white marble capitals and cornice and a panel in the centre said to have been painted by Sir Joshua Reynolds. The frieze of the ceiling and the doorcase has a pattern of white urns on a blue ground. The chief glory of the room is the magnificent ceiling. This has a wide cove painted pale green and decorated alternately with tall vases on pedestals of white plaster in relief and painted medallions imitating sculpture containing white figures on a purple ground now faded to look almost grey. In the angles are segmental sections of radiating fanwork which Wyatt was very fond of placing in the corners of his coved ceilings. The central flat of the ceiling has a rosette set in a diamond within a scrolled circle of leaves on a green ground and is framed by raised bands of white plasterwork on a purple ground matching the medallions of the cove.

The walls of the great drawing-room are divided into sections by enriched Corinthian pilasters. The frieze has a pattern of octagons and circles alternately. The spectacular barrel ceiling is composed of a series of round, lunette, oblong and rhomboidal panels, probably painted by Biagio Rebecca, with whom Wyatt worked so much, with two parallel bands of raised plasterwork running the whole length of the room.

The ceiling of the staircase may be by Wyatt. Leading off the landing is a corridor of which the walls have oval or diamond-shaped panels painted light green and containing white plaster shells in relief with replicas of cream jugs delicately poised on the side points of the diamonds.

At the end of this passage is a room originally called the boudoir, and now a girls' dormitory as the house is a school. The ceiling has a cove painted with grey and green circular trempe l'oeil panels on a buff ground. The centre portion has a pattern of grey scroll work on a green ground and in the centre a shallow ribbed saucer dome.

Alterations which were carried out at Charlton Park, Wiltshire, for the 12th Earl of Suffolk and Berkshire in 1774 have been attributed to Wyatt, with a reasonable degree of certainty. The house had been built in 1607. Wyatt carefully reconstructed the centre of the south and east fronts in Jacobean style to match the remainder of the house but inserted large sash windows. Inside he converted the internal courtyard, round which the house was built, into a large hall or saloon occupying two storeys, though this was not finished till modern times. It is lit from a central dome decorated with arabesques. On each side is a gallery supported on fluted Ionic columns with similar Corinthian columns above. In the centre of the other two sides is an apse flanked by niches containing three-sided candelabra very similar to those which later Wyatt designed at Heveningham Hall. Above these niches are circular plaques of Coadeware stone. There are similar smaller ones above the door in the galleries. The principal apartment in the east front designed by Wyatt and entered through the doorway in one of the apses of the hall is the dining-room. The walls are decorated with panels of arabesques in stucco with oval plaques containing figures in the centre. He also redecorated the drawing-room, the small dining-room and the billiard-room or library and rebuilt the main staircase. The billiard-room has an unusual ceiling with a cove of pendentives and squinch arches. In the grounds Wyatt erected two gardeners' cottages with a glass-house between them.

Another Wiltshire house of Wyatt's which has not been dated is New Park, built for James Sutton. The print of it in Neale's *Seats* shows it to be one of Wyatt's most attractive smaller houses. It consists of a centre and two wings. The central block of two storeys and attic is fronted by four engaged Ionic columns with a balustraded parapet above, in the centre of which is a raised panel containing a lunette window. The wings are of only one storey and have four round-headed windows, each flanked by pilasters, the end window-bays forming projections.

Another undated house of Wyatt's and one of the few which he built in Yorkshire is Thirkleby Park for Sir T. Frankland. The chief feature of the house is its projecting centre of three window-bays surmounted by a panel of balustrading. A recessed porch is formed by two Corinthian columns rising the whole height of the building. The ground floor window on each side of these is placed in a deep semi-domed recess.

(2.) 1776-1778

Undoubtedly Wyatt's greatest masterpiece was Heveningham Hall, Suffolk. There is considerable confusion concerning the date at which he began operations there. The *Dictionary of Architecture* for some unknown reason mentions 1797-8. This is obviously wrong. The estate had been purchased in 1752 by Sir Joshua Vanneck, who died in 1776. He found there a small rectangular house built by John Bence

33

about 1707. It has not hitherto been thought that Sir Joshua made any alterations to this building, but that it was his son, Sir Gerard Vanneck, who rebuilt and enlarged it. The exterior of the new house is the work of Sir Robert Taylor, and it has generally been held that Taylor was commissioned by Sir Gerard Vanneck soon after the latter's succession in 1776 and worked there until Taylor's death in 1788, when Wyatt succeeded him. But an interesting account exists of a visit paid to the house in 1784 by François de la Rochefoucauld, later duc de la Rochefoucauld, who was then making a long stay in England and wrote notes of his experiences for the benefit of his father, then duc de Liancourt. This makes it quite clear that the various state-rooms which he was shown by Sir Gerard Vanneck were finished at the time and were in the condition in which they are to be seen today. He also refers to Sir Gerard having begun the work 'ten or twelve years ago'.[1] From this it is evident that Wyatt appeared upon the scene at Heveningham long before Sir Robert Taylor's death, and that the latter must have been dismissed by Sir Gerard Vanneck. The eight years between 1776 and 1784 would seem a very short period to include the making of plans by one architect, their part execution, the entire revision of the scheme by another architect, and the completion of the whole work. One wonders therefore whether it was not possible that Taylor was employed to rebuild the house by the first baronet, Sir Joshua Vanneck, at some time between 1752 and 1776 and, the work being unfinished at Sir Joshua's death, his son Sir Gerard preferred to change his architect and entrust the completion of the interior to a younger man whose construction of the Pantheon had so recently made him the most fashionable architect of the day. There is however no evidence to say.

As completed, the house consists of a central block of seven window-bays and slightly recessed wings of five windows each terminating in flanking pavilions of three windows each. The whole of the ground floor is arcaded, the centre and end pavilions being rusticated. On the podium formed by the ground floor stand Corinthian columns which rise through the two floors above fronting the centre and end pavilions. These are free-standing along the centre block and engaged along the pavilions. The latter support pediments, the former a tall parapet which is enriched with Coadeware figures, panels of swags and profile plaques and is surmounted by vases and figures of lions and two reclining females who support an escutcheon. The wings have no second floor windows but in their place rectangular Coadeware

[1] *A Frenchman in England*, 1784.

plaques. Above them are balustraded parapets concealing the galleries which connect the second floor rooms of the centre block and the end pavilions.

The south front facing the formal garden laid out in the nineteenth century is rather a Mary-Anne back, to which neither architect devoted much attention. The wings on this side project nearly flush with the end pavilions instead of being recessed, and the façade of the centre block is probably that of the early eighteenth-century house merely plastered over.

The plans of the interior made by Taylor and Wyatt vary very little in the actual subdivision of the floor space into rooms, though different names and functions are assigned to each individual room. Both architects gave up the whole of the centre block, which formed the old house, to a hall rising to the height of two storeys. Taylor's would have had a gallery at first floor level, but this was omitted by Wyatt. The room is probably the most magnificent that Wyatt ever designed and rivals Adam's hall at Syon House. The walls and ceiling are of pale green with white enrichments. The end window-bays are divided from the main portion of the hall by sienna-coloured scagliola Corinthian columns with white capitals. The long walls are divided into sections by similar pilasters, between which are recesses containing statues or busts with panels of scroll-work above them. The fluted frieze has oval paterae above the pilasters. The barrel ceiling is divided transversally into sections by ribs of double guilloche moulding which rise from above the pilasters. Lengthways the ceiling is divided by strips of imitation drapery, with lions' masks in the intersections, into five centre panels containing oval rosettes and five semi-circular panels on each side. The latter are supported by squinch arches of radiating fan ornamentation, between which are semi-circular wall-spaces containing oval panels of trophies. The same segments but of larger dimensions surmount the end columns. The portions screened by these columns have coffered ceilings lower than that of the centre sections and semi-circular tables painted green and white to match the walls with brown tops painted in imitation of marble. These and the green and white chairs were no doubt designed by Wyatt. The floor, made of white stone and red and black marble, reflects the pattern of the ceiling with stars in the place of the central rosettes. (Plate 16.) De la Rochefoucauld's comment on the hall was: 'It is extremely dignified and magnificent.'[1] Indeed it is so.

[1] *A Frenchman in England,* 1784.

Behind the hall is the staircase. The walls are pale blue with white mouldings. Owing to its position, the stair is not of the usual dividing pattern, but winds around the three internal walls. The balusters take the form of a central oval with a scroll of wrought iron above and below leading to a spray of leaves standing one upon another, which are of lead. Every third oval contains a Wedgwood medallion of a white figure on a pale blue background, the other two having a rosette within a diamond. The staircase and hall between them bisect the house, and owing to the fact that the hall rises to the height of two storeys, there is no communication on the first floor between one end of the house and the other except along the one narrow landing of the staircase on the south side.

On the ground floor the right or west wing contains the private or family rooms. The staircase leads into the study, and beyond this on the south front are the offices as there is no basement. On the north front are the morning-room, the print room and the servants' hall. The morning-room is also called the Waggon room from the shape of its panelled barrel ceiling. The walls are pale green, but were originally blue, and the chimney-piece is of white marble. This leads into the print room which has always been used as the private dining-room. The east wall is flat and the west wall curved so that the windows might be evenly spaced. This was common to both Taylor's and Wyatt's plans of the house. The curve of the west wall is ingeniously contrived in both the chimney-piece and the doors of the cupboards on each side which fill the part of the rectangle cut off by the curve. There are not many of these print rooms in existence in England. That at Woodall Park, designed by Thomas Leverton, is on a much bigger scale. The room at Heveningham more resembles that at Strathfieldsaye. The colour scheme is green, red and cream. The walls are pale green, with a darker dado. The prints have been pasted onto the walls direct, surrounded by a border of dark red edged with cream and then varnished. The doorcases are of cream picked out in red, and the green doors have six panels of darker green matching the dado. The chimney-piece is a simple wooden surround painted cream and surmounted by a frieze of red with cream swags and cornice above. In summer a panel, designed with the room, is fitted into the fireplace opening, onto which more prints have been pasted to match the walls. The ceiling is cream picked out in red with a deep cove.

The left or east wing contains the state-rooms. The first of these on the north front is the dining-room. About two years ago this room was

15. No. 1 Foley Place, London. The head of the staircase
(*Country Life Photograph*)

16. Heveningham Hall. The Hall
(*Country Life Photograph*)

17. The Library

18. The Etruscan Room

(*Country Life Photographs*)

19. Bryanston

20. Blagdon

(Country Life Photograph)

21. Dodington Park

22. Norris Castle

23. Blagdon. The Study
(*Country Life Photograph*)

24. Sandleford Priory. The Octagonal Room

seriously damaged by a fire which started in one of the bedrooms above. It is however being carefully restored by the owner of the house, the Hon. Andrew Vanneck, and is an exact replica of its original condition. The walls are pale blue with white enrichments and the painted panels are of white figures on a dark red background. The long wall contains a curved recess on either side of the fireplace with a half-dome divided into upright panels of arabesques. In the centre of the west wall is a flatter coved recess with narrow pilasters flanking the side of the cove, fan radiation in the head of it and a lunette within this of chiaroscuro painting by Biagio Rebecca imitating bas-relief. All three of these niches contain a fitted sideboard of painted deal with carved and tapered legs, a frieze painted white and red to continue the line of the dado and a red scagliola top. The south and west walls contain doorways on the outer sides of the recesses with friezes of stylised trees alternating with urns or putti, as in the ceiling frieze. In the east wall the doorway is central, inset and framed to match the sideboard recess opposite. The magnificent double doors are veneered with the most choice figured mahogany and have enriched mouldings to the edges of the styles and of the six inset panels. On each side of this door is a plain niche containing a tripod candelabrum. The uprights of these have hoofed feet and female heads with ormolu candle brackets branching from the heads. Between them is a bowl of anthemium design, from which rises a column entwined by serpents with a pineapple finial. This is one of Wyatt's most delicate designs. (Plate 45.)

Above these niches and above the doorways of the other walls are square panels enclosing roundels also painted by Rebecca. Over the fireplace is a long thin panel of white cherubs on a red ground and above this the largest panel in this room painted by Rebecca which is an oval showing two female figures being garlanded by amorini. Above the three main recesses and the doorway of the east wall are rows of festoons, from the ends of which depend tiny white cameos on a red ground. These cameos also occur in the wall lights which are fixed between the windows and in the west recess. From them hang ribboned garlands attached to an imitation lamp in plaster with rams-head corners to support candle brackets. Above the cameos are elaborate scrolls and festoons of plasterwork. In the white marble chimney-piece are two panels of jasper or onyx streaked with red to match that of Rebecca's backgrounds.

The dining-room at Heveningham must certainly be one of the most beautiful rooms in England. François de la Rochefoucauld's comment on seeing it was: 'I have never seen anything to compare with the perfect proportions of this room or with the elegance of its decoration.'[1] The library leads out of the dining-room, and he continued: 'I should continue to think it impossible to see a more beautiful room if we had not immediately afterwards entered the library, which at once blotted it out of my vision. This room is a masterpiece of good taste.'[1]

The library is one of the two rooms in the house which have never been repainted. The colour-scheme is of pale green, white and red, but the red has more of purple in it than that of the dining-room. Of this colour are the scagliola Corinthian columns which screen the west end of the room, forming a lobby that lies outside the confines of the end pavilion of the house. Recessed bookcases line the walls above the dado in both the main room and the lobby. Between the bookcases are narrow panels flanked by thin pilasters of red scagliola with capitals of white lions' masks surmounted by urns with a frieze between of white scrolls on a red ground. These panels are really cupboards which open, and the keyholes are concealed by the swags which link them to a bracket supporting a female figure in plaster. The chimney-piece is of red and white marble to match these pilasters. Above this and above each bookcase and window are recessed semi-circles with plaster enrichment and between them large oval profile heads of English poets painted by Rebecca. These are white on a red ground and, like the painted panels in the dining-room, are intended to give the effect of bas-reliefs. The plaster panels also occur between the windows on the north wall and so left no room for curtains. The reveals contain shutters and above are looped silk blinds which are let down at night. The east wall contains one of those large square-headed tripartite windows invented by Wyatt as a variation on a Venetian window which came to be called after him. It is set in Corinthian pilasters of red scagliola which balance the columns of the opposite end. The doorway leading into the dining-room is treated in the same way as the bookcases and windows. (Plate 17.)

But probably the most beautiful feature of the room is the great coved ceiling. The flat portion is divided into three sections, each containing a roundel painted by Rebecca of white figures on a red ground. The centre one is set in an octagon framing eight similarly painted panels of lions or lionesses which form the dominant motif of this room. The outer ones are set in an oval of sixteen tongue-shaped

[1] *A Frenchman in England, 1784.*

38

scallops containing white anthemia. The border of the ceiling is of scrolls and swags with the figure of a ram in each corner beneath a still more elaborate flourish. Wyatt never designed a more beautiful room than this library.

The dining-room and the library occupy the whole north front of the east wing. They are slightly higher than the space which, in the elevation, appears to be allotted to them. Their ceilings actually come a little above the bottom panes of the first floor windows, of which only the remaining three panes light the upper rooms, and this from the level of the skirting to half-way up the walls—a piece of typical eighteenth-century botching which is partially masked by the construction of the ceilings on the first floors with great coves.

The rooms facing south in the east wing are entered through a small ante-room known as the Etruscan room. As in the case of the print room, there are not many rooms of this character in existence in England. Wyatt had already designed one at Heaton Hall which was far grander and more elaborate in scale than that at Heveningham, but the latter is much purer in style and nearer to the Wedgwood effect that it was desired to give. (Plate 18.)

The walls and ceiling are pale green, the enrichments white and the classical figures painted by Rebecca the reddish-brown that is found on Etruscan vases. The side walls each have a pair of double doors containing four narrow rectangular panels painted with one figure each and two round panels of a vase between these. Over each door is a roundel of several figures. There is no fireplace. Between the doors are shallow recesses containing tripod candelabra with rectangular painted panels above. The candelabra have a flat triangular base, on which stand rams' feet supporting a three-sided pier painted with one figure on each side. At the top is an anthemium frieze with rams' heads in the corners, from which spring ormolu scroll candle brackets similar to those in the dining-room. Above each pier is a two-handled urn painted with figures. The colouring of these is the same green and brown as the rest of the room.

In the centre of the north wall is a fifth doorway of similar design but framed in pilasters and an architrave with a pediment. Above it is another long thin painted panel. The ceiling is composed of a number of sunk panels of various shapes with an oval in the centre, all painted with figures, birds and sphinxes.

The room retains the original green and brown painted furniture which Wyatt designed for it. Between the windows is a semi-circular

39

table. In the centre of the side walls are settees of double-ended scroll type. Finally there is a series of oval-backed chairs with splats shaped like a palm-tree. The whole room is a charmingly complete essay in an unusual medium, though it has a chill chastity about it which seems to call for the warmth of company and a summer afternoon for the fullest appreciation of its beauty.

The Etruscan room leads into the saloon or ball-room. It is in this room that Rebecca was given the fullest scope. Nearly the whole surface of walls and ceiling is painted, the colour-scheme being entirely green on a biscuit ground. The saloon is apsidal-ended with painted pilasters in the angles. Between them on the long wall opposite the windows are upright rectangular panels painted with arabesques and figures. The chimney-piece is only a narrow surround of painted wood. The doors at each end of the wall, of which one is a dummy, are also painted, and over them are rectangular panels of gryphons flanking an urn. These also appear over the curved doors in the end walls. On each side of the latter are semi-circular recesses divided into sections by thin pilasters, with ribbed semi-domes over having fan ornamentation at the base of each rib and a frieze below this which is carried round the soffit. The shutters are painted in panels rather like the doors in miniature.

The frieze of the room is a very beautiful one consisting of octagonal medallions of two putti and a vase alternately with a rosette between them. Above this, the flat cove of the shallow barrel ceiling is painted with a continuous frieze of playing amorini. At the ends, the segments above the apses are ribbed somewhat like the recesses below. The main section of the ceiling has three rosettes from which hang crystal chandeliers between narrow segments of arabesques lengthwise and wedge-shaped panels painted with figures breadthwise. This is the only one of the main rooms which has hanging chandeliers.

The saloon retains its original furniture. Between the windows are semi-circular painted green and white tables with tops also painted brown to imitate marble. Opposite to them are sofas somewhat similar to those in the Etruscan room but with lower ends. There is a series of cane chairs with oval backs, the woodwork being painted green and brown.

Like the library, the saloon has never been repainted. Its colour-scheme, being wholly green, gives it a more restrained note than either the library or the dining-room and on that account it is perhaps slightly less beautiful when empty. But it has an elegance and style

40

which would be unsurpassed when filled with the brightly-dressed figures of dancers.

The last room in this suite is the drawing-room, called the Pink drawing-room from the colour of its chair upholstery. This is unfinished. Only the ceiling has been decorated. This fact has not been explained though François de la Rochefoucauld commented on it. The most natural explanation would be that Wyatt in his dilatory fashion never delivered the plans before Sir Gerard Vanneck's death in 1791. But this is negatived by the fact that there is preserved at Heveningham a painting, apparently by Rebecca, of the ceiling as planned. This comprises a series of painted entaglios set in gilt mouldings. Only the mouldings were carried out, but not in gilt. A design for a chandelier for the room has also been preserved. Mr Avray Tipping in his article in *English Homes, Period VI*, suggested that Sir Gerard Vanneck grew tired of paying the bills for Wyatt's elaborate interior work. But this seems a little difficult to believe when there wanted only one room to the completion of his house.

As is often the case, no designs survive for furniture at Heveningham that was actually carried out. But several of Wyatt's sketches have been preserved for chimney-pieces, mirrors and chandeliers which were never executed. The most interesting of these is for a sofa or day-bed surmounted by a circular tent-shaped canopy of drapery, in the style of Josephine's bed-room at Malmaison, looped up in feathered bows at the sides. The effect when closed would have been rather like a mosquito net to keep off the flies during an afternoon siesta. It would have been more curious than beautiful. (Plate 46.)

Heveningham Hall is still occupied by the Vanneck family, and its great beauty is its completeness. Adam in many instances designed houses in which all the detail of the internal fittings and the furniture was from his hand. But there is no other recorded example of a house in which similar work by Wyatt remains complete and intact. In view of the fact that some of his designs for furniture have survived, it is almost certain that at other houses, like Heaton Hall for instance, he must have given the whole effect the same detailed treatment as at Heveningham, and the furniture was subsequently dispersed when the house ceased to be occupied by the original family for whom it was built. It is a thousand pities that such furniture has been, as so much else, the victim of change and decay.

The park at Heveningham was laid out by Capability Brown in 1781. Miss Dorothy Stroud has attributed the stables to Brown on the strength of the fact that they appear in Brown's plan of that year. But in this they are shown as forming a bisected oval. As built, they are actually the shape of a horseshoe. Amongst the papers preserved at Heveningham is a rough plan of the stables marked 'Executed 1785'. This was two years after Brown's death, and so it looks as if it was more likely that Wyatt was the architect. They are of red brick with a pantile roof and have a series of round-headed arches with lunette windows, two pediments and a little cupola. They are a good example of the charm which eighteenth-century architects never failed to achieve in their stable design.

To Wyatt can also be assigned the orangery facing the kitchen-garden. This has seven tall round-headed windows and at each end a niche containing a statue with a Coadeware plaque above it. In front of the three centre window-bays is a semi-circular tetrastyle portico. The whole is surmounted by an elegant balustraded parapet which now has just the right proportions since Mr Vanneck has removed the domed glass roof added in the late nineteenth century in imitation of the transept of the Crystal Palace. This orangery is another of Wyatt's exquisite little masterpieces, ranking with the mausoleum at Brocklesby and the temple at Heaton Hall. (Plate 14.)

It is likely that Wyatt also rebuilt the Rectory at Heveningham. This is one of those pleasant late eighteenth-century houses affording every opportunity to the younger son of a noble family for that leisured elegant life which the clergy of the period so freely enjoyed. It is of white brick with grooved pilasters flanking the front and the central window-bay, with a pediment over the latter. The central first floor window has a panel of balustrading below it, and in the centre of the ground floor is a stuccoed Doric porch.

Two farms are also contemporary. Valley Farm is a good standard production of the period that may or may not be by Wyatt, but Huntingfield Hall in the neighbouring parish, from which Sir Gerard Vanneck's younger brother, Sir Joshua, took his title when raised to the peerage in 1796, certainly is. This is a rudimentary essay in Gothic. It is built of red brick with projecting end window-bays and is surmounted by a tall castellated parapet with five quatrefoil-shaped recessed panels between stringcourses. The portion of the parapet above the end window bays is carried up higher to give the effect of turrets. The two-light casement windows are pointed on the ground floor and ogee-headed above with dripstones and finials over. The most elaborate feature is the central doorway with 'Gothick' pilasters, an enriched

42

frieze, a parapet pierced with quatrefoils and a cusped ogee-headed fanlight with enriched spandrels framing it. This is a small example of Wyatt's Lee Priory Gothic manner and, like the interior of that house, is charming in its complete unreality.

A house with which Wyatt's connection has been overlooked is Hothfield Place, near Ashford in Kent. This was rebuilt by him in 1776-1780 for the 8th Earl of Thanet. Mr Howard Colvin in his *Dictionary of Architecture* assigns this house to Sir William Chambers (1773) on the strength of correspondence between Chambers and Lord Thanet. But a design by Wyatt for the ceiling in Lord Thanet's dressing-room has been preserved in the Victoria and Albert Museum. From this and from the general character of the building, I have no doubt that Lord Thanet changed his mind and actually gave the commission to Wyatt. His work comprised the central portion only. The wings were added about a hundred years later. But the whole house was demolished in 1954. The elevations were plain but had some affinity with the central block of Wyatt's later Castle Coole, Fermanagh. The house stands on a rusticated podium containing a semi-basement and was built of Portland stone which weathered to a most attractive pinkish hue. The main front faced east. Out of the seven window-bays in all, the three centre ones were flanked by engaged Ionic columns supporting a dentilled cornice. The principal storey, which was above ground level, was approached by two flights of steps joining at a half-landing and continued up to the house in a single flight. The only feature of the west front was a large Venetian window in the centre of the principal storey with a lunette window below it. All the other windows on the main floor had Venetian shutters with false tops perforated like shutters, but they were far too small for the size of the house.

The entrance was unusually placed at the end of the building in the south wall. The hall had a screen of two fluted Doric columns at the north and south ends which served little purpose as the entablature that spanned it was surmounted by nothing but a segmental space. A frieze of large round paterae and flutings alternately ran round the whole room including this entablature. The same motifs figure in the doorcases. The walls had niches for statues.

The hall led into the staircase which had a large semi-domed recess opposite the main doorway. The stair wound round the four walls of the apartment with a mezzanine floor leading off the half-landing and a gallery at the level of the main floor above consisting of

43

two pairs of Ionic columns with a handrail between, which also closed the third side of the well. The balusters were shaped like two archery bows set in an oval with a scroll above and below. The stair was lit from a small oval skylight in a coved ceiling.

The principal reception rooms lay on either side of the hall and staircase, but they had little to show of contemporary decoration except one white marble chimney-piece with bas-relief carving at the head of the jambs. No decoration of any upstairs room prior to demolition corresponded with the design for the ceiling in Lord Thanet's dressing-room, and the ceilings of the ground floor rooms which survive were among the least interesting Wyatt designed.

According to Hutchin's History of Dorset, Bryanston, near Blandford, dates from 1778. Wyatt's house replaced a gabled Tudor building and is said to have been built of stone from Vanbrugh's short-lived Eastbury in the same county. It was illustrated in Watts's *Views of the Seats of the Nobility and Gentry* during 1786. The print shows it to have been a nearly square mansion of freestone with a rusticated ground floor and a central pediment supported by pilasters on one front and, on another, similar projecting wings containing pedimented first floor windows set in round-headed arcading. The 'octangular'[1] staircase was in the centre of the plan with a gallery round it at first floor level formed by eight scagliola columns and eight pilasters. The offices were at some distance to the west, linked to the house by an underground passage. Wyatt did not often employ this inconvenient arrangement, and one suspects that his client must have given him specific instructions to do so in this case.

The house was rebuilt by Norman Shaw in his most lavish Queen Anne manner in 1890. The kitchen block however remains, though now in rather a neglected state. It has a projecting centre portion with a pediment and a series of round-headed arches containing tall windows in the wings and lunette windows in the centre portion above the doorway and its flanking windows. The handsome main lodge is also Wyatt's and can be identified with a rough pencil sketch of his that has been preserved.[2] It consists of a tall round-headed carriage archway flanked by Doric columns with a pediment over and on each side a small square single-storeyed dwelling which is linked by a curved wall to a stone gate pier supporting a heraldic beast. (Plate 19.) The stables date from about thirty years before Wyatt's time, when a

[1]Watts's *Views*.
[2]Now in the possession of the Vicomte de Noailles.

44

small church was also built in the grounds. This still exists but is disused, a new church having been built with the stone from Wyatt's house.

A house in which Wyatt worked at this period was Blagdon, Northumberland, for Sir Matthew White Ridley. This had been built about 1740, and his only contribution to the exterior was the removal of pilasters and a heavy cornice. He also built the lodges and entrance gate. (Plate 20.) But these were not erected until later. The design for them is dated 1787. They are charming little octagonal single-storeyed buildings with a frieze of bows and festoons. They are linked by a Doric colonnade to the wide piers of the carriage drive which contain empty niches and are surmounted by fine recumbent figures of bulls from the arms of the Ridley family. The stables followed in 1789-91. These form a courtyard entered through a round-headed carriage archway with small circular windows in the spandrels and a pediment and cupola over.

Wyatt had previously been working inside the house as his design for the dining-room, now the study, is dated September 1778. One end of the room is screened by two columns with foliated capitals. The two long walls, painted pale green and white, each have a pair of balancing doorways with painted overdoors. Between these are two tall thin panels of arabesques in plasterwork. The space within them contains the chimney-piece on one side with a rather unusual frieze of shields containing a motif somewhat resembling stylized trees. This also appears in the frieze of the ceiling and in the doorcases. Wyatt's design for the room showed a round plaster panel of figures above the chimney-piece encircled by a wreath, but this was not carried out. Instead there is a pedimented overmantel framing a picture of the previous house at Blagdon. In the centre of the opposite wall is a panel in which another picture is inset surmounted by an urn from which depend most delicate festoons of roses. This is one of Wyatt's most delightful pieces of plasterwork. (Plate 23.) The ceiling has fan-radiations in the corners and again the tree motif in the wreath of ovals that surrounds the central rosette. The remainder of Wyatt's work at Blagdon consisted mostly of fittings such as chimney-pieces. But the frieze in the present dining-room is certainly his. This again is unusual and consists of urns alternating with a double-ended scroll like the prow of a ship, with a shell between the two. These are now white against a deep maroon background above dark green walls, but this colour scheme does not date from Wyatt's time.

(3.) 1779-1789

One of Wyatt's plainer works was Badger Hall, Shropshire, which he rebuilt for Isaac Hawkins Brown between 1779 and 1783. This was unfortunately demolished in 1952. It was of red brick with rusticated quoins at each end of the main fronts and in the case of the west front also flanking the three centre bays of the façade. At the south end of the latter one window-bay was added later; so were the two flanking wings, though these probably were by Wyatt. There is a series of signed drawings of the house in the Library of the Royal Institute of British Architects. The east front of six bays can be identified with one of these, but amongst them is a sketch of the north elevation that either was not carried out as depicted or has since been masked by subsequent additions. It shows a stuccoed surface. In the centre is a semi-circular portico with a balcony over it, and in the centre of the first floor a tripartite Wyatt window. Above it on the second floor is a triple lunette window.

The staircase was in the centre of the house and was lit from an oval dome above. The balusters of the handrail formed an arch on each step, between which was a wrought iron scroll twisted to form a heart enclosing a honeysuckle motif with two ovals above it. The design of these balusters was very similar to those which Wyatt inserted at his own house in Foley Place. The landing on the first floor overlooking the staircase was framed in two massive columns with recesses in the wall on each side. (Plate 25.)

The dining-room had a barrel-vaulted coffered ceiling of rosettes and a frieze of scroll-pattern. The walls were divided into panels by enriched mouldings enclosing painted grisaille roundels or ovals of the trempe l'oeil variety. The chimney-piece was of pink and white marble and retained its original grate with a medallion at the back showing a badger in relief. The south end of the room formed an apse separated from the rest of the room by a pair of pink and cream-coloured marble Corinthian columns and containing a fitted table painted white and gold with delicate rich ornamentation. The curtain rods in this room were ornamented with rams' heads and foxes, as if to keep the badger company.

The drawing-room or saloon had a rich coved and panelled ceiling composed of octagons and rectangles. The octagons contained central medallions of classical groups and were connected with the rectangles by half-medallions. The colour scheme was grey and pink. Beneath the cove were small circular green medallions. The north doorway

46

was shaped like a Wyatt window with a semi-circular tympanum over that was painted with figures on a green ground.

This doorway led into the library. The original library was on the first floor above the dining-room. The ground floor room was added but had every appearance of being by Wyatt. It had built-in bookcases of mahogany and, as in the dining-room, the end of the room was screened by two Corinthian columns, this time of grey fonsil marble which framed a Palladian window in the north wall having pilasters and columns of pink marble and gilt Corinthian capitals. Grisaille trempe l'oeil decoration appeared again in a wide frieze of a continuous classical scene running right round the room. The ceiling had a high cove, in the corners of which were large gilt shells in relief—perhaps the most unusual feature of the room. The central flat panel of the ceiling had an intricate pattern of arabesques in plasterwork. The white marble chimney-piece was particularly elegant with female caryatid figures and a wide frieze in high relief. (Plate 26.)

Wyatt built an octagonal pigeon-house in the grounds, of which signed working drawings dated 1779-1781 have also been preserved in the Library of the Royal Institute of British Architects. This somewhat resembled a temple with a frieze of flutings and paterae.

The year 1779 brought a London commission from a Mr Viner. This was for No. 9 Conduit Street which, appropriately enough, was for many years the headquarters of the Royal Institute of British Architects before this body moved to its present premises in Portland Place. Like Wyatt's own house in Foley Place which was completed four years later, the stuccoed façade of No. 9 Conduit Street anticipates Nash and the Regency. It was in fact one of the earliest buildings in London to be faced with the mastic for which several patents appear to have been issued at this period. One was called Wyatt's cement. This was much the same thing as Roman cement or Parker's cement, which latter was patented in 1796. Wyatt's cement was manufactured by a firm called J. and C. Wyatt and Co. in 1837 and Wyatt and Parker and Co. in 1841. If this firm existed as early as James Wyatt's lifetime, it would seem to justify Lyson's private accusation that Wyatt used 'a composition not much cheaper than stone'[1] in the repairs at Westminster because he had an interest in the patent.

The ground floor of No. 9 Conduit Street is rusticated. Four Ionic pilasters, standing on this base, rise through the first and second floors to support an entablature enriched with oval paterae above the

[1] *Farington Diary*, 1 Dec. 1806.

47

capitals and panels of swags between these, which have now been painted black on the cream ground of the stucco—with very considerable effect. The third floor above the cornice has plain pilasters and is only surmounted by a blocking course. The ground floor windows are round-headed and slightly recessed, and those on the first floor emphasized by pediments above them. The hall of the house, with its coffered barrel ceiling, is particularly dignified. The arrangement of the staircase behind this, with a short flight descending as well as ascending, is unusual.

In the seventies Wyatt designed five houses at the north-east corner of Portman Square. Of these, one (No. 15) has been demolished. The adjoining house (No. 14) with a brown brick front is very undistinguished. The next two houses (Nos. 12 and 13) have elevations not dissimilar to that of No. 9 Conduit Street with friezes of paterae and festoons and masks set in swags of drapery, though No. 12 has been spoiled by having been rendered in cement. Most of the original interior of this house, now the Portman Estate Office, has been removed, including the staircase. But the drawing-room retains its original modillion cornice and frieze of vases and scrolls and rather heavy chimney-pieces with console-jambs. These are in fact more typical of the period immediately preceding Wyatt's day or of the style associated with Sir William Chambers and have nothing of his lightness of touch except the central medallions. No. 13, which is now most suitably occupied by the British Colour Council, contains a very fine staircase. The balusters make a design of intersecting arcs of circles with diamond shapes above and below. Opposite the back drawing-room door on the landing is a most unusual bowed recess in the hand-rail, obviously intended to form a vantage-point where the host and hostess should stand to receive guests as they came upstairs. The rear portion of the landing is separated from the stair by a solid balustrade on which stand two columns forming two round-headed arches with a third archway to the left over the actual passage leading to the back rooms of the house. The staircase is lit by a barrel-shaped skylight with a wide frieze of drapery in festoons. The drawing-room retains most of its original decoration. The walls are divided into panels by moulding, and above is a wide frieze of roundels and urns linked by festoons. The arch between the front and back rooms is framed by enriched pilasters and surmounted by a similar entablature with a small curved pediment in the centre. The chimney-piece is of white marble with a frieze of honeysuckle design. The original curtain pelmets remain and repeat the same motif. The very fine mahogany doors are fitted with charming brass finger-plates of an oval rosette surrounded by festoons.

The end house with a plain brown brick façade, originally No. 11 Portman Square, is now known as No. 1 Baker Street. Its staircase is rather similar to that in No. 13 Portman Square but, being a corner house, has a square instead of narrow rectangular well. It is lit by a small oval dome, the ceiling below which has a frieze of flutings interspersed with skeleton ox-heads. Over the first floor doorways are round plaques of bas-reliefs. The design of the balusters is slightly more elaborate than that in the other house. It comprises a rose set in a diamond within a circle with a leaf-shaped ornament above and a scroll beneath it. There is the same bowed recess in the hand-rail opposite the back drawing-room door, but of greater width. The original pelmets have been preserved in the front ground floor rooms. These have a small tablet in the centre showing a vase with fluting and oval paterae on either side. The house is not in as good condition as No. 13 Portman Square and so does not show to as great advantage but must have been a very fine residence in its day.

Wyatt has not really been fortunate in London. Both the Pantheon and his own house having disappeared, this group in Portman Square and No. 9 Conduit Street are almost all his work that survives there. No. 22 St James's Place, which he built for Samuel Rogers in 1806, was badly damaged by enemy action in 1940 and has been since demolished. Devonshire House, Piccadilly, was delivered to the housebreakers in 1924. Here Wyatt added to the house by William Kent a bowed projection on the garden front which contained the magnificent staircase, Kent's approach to the piano nobile having been by means of an outside staircase on the entrance front leading straight into the great saloon. This masterpiece, which was one of Wyatt's last works, executed for the 6th Duke of Devonshire on his succession in 1811, was until its destruction probably the finest staircase in England. It was circular with steps so shallow that they allowed the stair to make the complete circle in rising only one floor. The balusters were alternately a plain upright with a scroll above and below and a more elaborate pattern with a large circle in the centre. The great feature of the staircase was the banister which was made of glass, from which the whole was called the Crystal staircase. (Plate 27.) The destruction of Devonshire House was one of the major architectural calamities of this century.

Wyatt is credited with two houses in Grosvenor Square—one for a Mr Delvine on the south side and one for William Drake—which have not been identified. White's Club, if it was his, was greatly altered in 1850. Of interior work there remain the drawing-room at No. 15 St James's Square, redecorated in 1794 in a house by James Stuart, and the drawing-room at No. 18 New Cavendish Street, which Wyatt similarly redesigned in a house of Adam's.

Neither in London nor in any other town did Wyatt manage to design any architectural estates such as the Adelphi or even any complete squares, terraces or other formal groups of houses. He did however make a plan for a crescent at Bristol which never materialised. In 1791 T. G. Vaughan, John Weekes and James Weeks obtained a lease of the Royal Fort, Bristol, from Thomas Tyndall and certain other land from the Dean and Chapter of Bristol and planned to erect upon this a crescent, a square, a circus and several other streets—in fact another Bath. Each house was to have a frontage of no less than twenty-eight feet. An advertisement in *Felix Farley's Bristol Journal* offering thirty-eight building plots for sale on the 29th August 1792 mentions that 'Royal Fort Crescent, Park Place, Bristol', as this crescent was to be called, was designed by James Wyatt, the surveyor being Charles Melsome. The work seems to have proceeded a little further as an advertisement was subsequently inserted for masons and carpenters. But by 1798 the scheme was abandoned. The foundations of the crescent were levelled. The land was returned to the Tyndall family and soon afterwards landscaped by Repton. This seems to be the nearest Wyatt ever came to designing such an architectural unit, or at least the only record of it that survives. A drawing was preserved in the Bristol City Library that might have been the elevation of Wyatt's Royal Fort Crescent, but this was unfortunately destroyed in the raids on Bristol during the war.

In an album of Wyatt drawings in the Victoria and Albert Museum is a design for the ceiling of the dining-room 'for the house of Charles Kent Esqr. of Fornham' St Genevieve, Suffolk. It is undated but other sketches in the same album bear dates between 1776 and 1783. In a second album are two more drawings of a classical portico. These are of slightly later date as they are headed 'Sir Charles Kent's house at Fornham'. In 1781 Capability Brown was commissioned to produce a design for laying out the grounds at Fornham Hall, though this was apparently never executed. Wyatt's work was no doubt contemporary.

Fornham Hall was unfortunately demolished in 1951, after being unoccupied (except by the Army) for about thirty-five years. But photographs of it exist. From these it is safe to say that the whole house, apart from later internal alterations, was Wyatt's. The dining-room ceiling was almost identical with the design preserved. The two porticos which the house possessed, however, were not. If the one drawn was ever built, it was subsequently altered.

The exterior was not exciting. The entrance front of yellow brick had a central feature of three windows, each flanked by pilasters, with a panelled parapet above surmounted by miniature trees instead of vases over each pilaster. The garden front, which was faced with Roman cement, had a rusticated ground floor, two projecting wings with arcading over the ground floor windows, and in the centre a double-decker semi-circular portico with a tent-shaped canopy over it.

The hall and staircase had been much altered at a later date. But the very beautiful doorways leading out of the hall survived. These were set in coved round-headed recesses, the sides panelled with rams' heads above and fluting in the heads. In each tympanum was a delightful little oval cameo of amorini in a goat carriage set in a wreath flanked by scrolls. The doors had six sunk panels of guilloche moulding. The dining-room doorcases had a frieze of wreaths encircling cherubs' heads and vases alternately. Each room had a fine plaster ceiling and a white marble chimney-piece. Probably the library was the best preserved room. The ceiling there had a cove divided into triangular sections of floral design. The recessed bookcases were framed in guilloche moulding. The chimney-piece had exquisite tiny white marble cameos in low relief on a coloured marble background. Above the overmantel was a cartouche effect of carved and gilded putti acting as the supporters of a clock face, with a coronet above. Though not one of Wyatt's finest works, the whole interior was a good one, and it is infinitely to be regretted that it has been another of the numerous casualties of changing times.

In 1782-1784 Wyatt rebuilt Pishiobury Park, Sawbridgeworth, a late sixteenth-century or early seventeenth-century house which had been destroyed by fire. A mild attempt was made to Gothicise the exterior, but as this was limited to the superimposal of an embattled parapet and the insertion of windows with four-centred heads on the ground floor, Pishiobury can hardly be called a real Gothic house and remains fundamentally classical in conception. It is a moderate-sized house built of red brick. The plan is square with a pediment in the centre of the east front which is embattled like the remainder of the

51

parapet, and a porch in the centre of the west front. The outer ground floor windows on the latter side are recessed in coved reveals with rubbed brick soffits and dripstones over. The equivalent windows on the north and east fronts are of tripartite design with blank tympana in the four-centred heads. All three façades exposed are rather severe, though lightened by the frivolousness of these Gothic details.

The interior is wholly classical. The staircase, as in most of Wyatt's houses, is in the centre and is lit from a small round skylight set in a coved ceiling. Below the cornice on each wall are three delicate plaster panels of figures, two being oval and one rectangular, set in wreaths and linked by festoons surmounted by bows. At first floor level is a wide frieze of medallions and scrolls linked with festoons to flanking urns surmounted by honeysuckle motifs. The stair winds round the four sides of the square hall in which it stands. The balusters are alternately a plain upright and a double 'S' curve containing a honey-suckle motif on its side in the centre volute which is common to both 'S' formations. The chimney-piece is a rather heavy one of white marble. The jambs are formed by female figures standing on pedestals and looking outward. One holds a mask and the other a lyre in a hand extended backwards towards the centre panel which depicts a sleeping cherub in relief. The frieze is a series of inverted shields.

The house is now occupied as a school. The rooms have little decoration beyond the chimney-pieces, of which that in the recreation-room is of imitation stone, probably Coadeware, with a frieze of cornucopiae, scrolls and sphinxes. The dining-room retains some Jacobean panelling from the old house.

From 1783 to 1786 Wyatt assisted his brother Samuel at the Albion Mills, Blackfriars, a carpentry and building speculation, but the premises were burnt by incendiaries in 1791.

The seventeen-eighties brought Wyatt several commissions in West Sussex. The first was the Assembly Rooms at Chichester, built in 1783. These were added to Roger Morris's Town Hall in North Street. They consist of a single very plain room—quite one of Wyatt's dullest works. It is clear that the municipality had very little money available for the usual Wyatt touches. Professor Sir Albert Richardson in his *Introduction to Georgian Architecture* has attributed to Wyatt the hall or corridor in the Bishop's Palace at Chichester. I do not know on what evidence this attribution is based. If on style only, it is certainly quite possible.

Two years later, acting in an honorary capacity, Wyatt provided designs for a new County Prison at Petworth. John Howard had visited

25. The Staircase

26. The Library

27. Devonshire House, London

28. Stoke Poges Park

29. The Kennels

30. The House

31. Goodwood House. The Library

32. Liverpool Town Hall. The Ball Room
(*Country Life Photograph*)

the old prison at Petworth in 1774 and 1776 and had made very unfavourable reports upon it. In 1782 therefore the magistrates decided to rebuild it. The work was carried out between 1785 and 1788. The plan and elevation of Wyatt's building were illustrated in Dallaway's *History of West Sussex*. The elevation has that quiet dignity which the eighteenth century never failed to exhibit even in its most materialistic and, as far as use was concerned, least attractive, buildings. Out of the total of twelve window-bays, the four central ones project slightly and are topped by a pediment. All the windows are of the lunette-shape which is a pleasant feature of so many warehouses of the period. The arches of the ground floor are round-headed to haromonise with these.

The building stood on an open arcade, except for the centre portion which contained two store-rooms. Above were two storeys each comprising sixteen cells, two infirmaries which alone had chimneys, and in the centre a chapel. This contained thirty-two pews with sides so lofty that the prisoners could not see each other, though they were all in view of the chaplain! In 1816 the ground floor was enclosed by Moneypenny to provide work-rooms when it was decided to give employment to the prisoners. At this period, and possibly from 1785, each cell contained a water-closet, which must have been a very unusual provision at the time. Despite this and the alterations, by 1835 it was found that the prison was quite unsuitable to contemporary conditions, though ideas on penology were hardly advanced at that period. It was pulled down and replaced by another building which has since suffered the same fate, except for the Chief Warder's house, now the Police Station.

After Petworth Prison came Stansted Park, Rowlands' Castle. The existing house here had been designed by William Talman and was said to have been very similar in character to Uppark, Harting, which is not very far to the north of it in the same county. Contemporaneously with it three mighty avenues had been cut through Stansted Forest which were said to have been designed by Le Nôtre. They are on a scale only rivalled by those laid out by Lord Bathurst at Cirencester. At the end of 1781 Capability Brown was summoned to Stansted by the then owner, Richard Barwell, and prepared a set of drawings for the alteration of both the house and grounds. Brown's death in February 1783 prevented their execution or completion. Barwell then entrusted the work to Wyatt and Bonomi. Between 1786 and 1791 they removed the existing wings of the house, encased the remainder in white

E   53

brick and added an extra storey and two-tiered porticos facing east and west, each comprising eight columns of the Doric order on the ground floor and the Ionic order above. They then constructed two new wings or pavilions to contain the offices and the stables respectively at some distance from the house on the north side. These they connected with the house by curved colonnades of two rows of Doric columns twelve feet apart which supported lead cisterns concealed in the balustrades. These were supplied with water by a hydraulic machine nine furlongs away and 199 feet below them which pumped up seven hogsheads of water per hour.

The main portion of this house was burned down in 1900 and rebuilt by Sir Reginald Blomfield in his best Wren manner, but the north pavilion containing the stables survives with a service wing behind. There is no written evidence as to the nature of the collaboration between Wyatt and Bonomi and their respective shares in the work. But the similarity of the rather complicated turrets surmounting the stables and service wing at Stansted to the towers which Wyatt designed for his unrealized buildings at Downing College, Cambridge, suggests that the elevation was of his composition. The two buildings form a thin rectangular courtyard, of which the main façade facing west has a small central pediment, a carriage archway at each end flanked by twin columns and a slight projection to each end window-bay. The north and south lodges in the park also date from this period and are no doubt by Wyatt. Between them stretches the great avenue in the forest which was replanted in 1820.

Amongst those who had been active in the rebuilding of the Petworth Prison was the third Duke of Richmond who is said to have been one of the first noblemen to offer Wyatt his patronage after the opening of the Pantheon. But it was apparently not until 1782 that any actual commission materialised, when he executed some alterations at Richmond House, London. In 1787 Wyatt designed the kennels in Goodwood Park. These are built of squared knapped flints, the three centre window-bays and the arcading above the ground floor windows being of yellow brick. The combination of these two materials in a building of this scale is quite successful. (Plate 29.)

Following the erection of the Kennels, Wyatt embarked upon the reconstruction of Goodwood House. The dates assigned to this are usually between 1800 and 1806. This is probably because the work was unfinished at the third Duke's death, which occurred in 1806. But for several reasons it is very unlikely that the house was built as late as

54

this. The original house, an Elizabethan building, had been purchased by the first Duke about 1720. His son added a small simple rectangular wing at right angles soon after he succeeded in 1723. The third Duke inherited in 1750. His first act was to erect from the designs of Sir William Chambers the magnificent stable quadrangle which stands to the south of the house. When this was completed in 1763, it would have been no exaggeration to say that his horses were more handsomely housed than His Grace himself. If his hounds in their turn were spaciously provided for in 1787, it is difficult to imagine that the Duke would have waited until 1800 before commissioning his preferred architect to rebuild the mansion. Moreover the character of the interior work at Goodwood which can be associated with Wyatt is much more in his early manner than that which he would have been likely to use in 1800, when he was well launched in his Gothic period.

The old Elizabethan house was pulled down, and at right angles to the early eighteenth-century wing the Duke planned to build a complete hollow octagon. Only three sides of it were however realized. At the Duke's special insistence the materials used were again obtained locally. But instead of being set with their shining knapped inner surfaces outwards in neat squares, as in the stables and kennels, the flints were placed with their irregular dull exteriors exposed but set in flint chips. This gives a flat, dull effect, quite inappropriate to so large a building as Goodwood House. It is consequently to the general advantage of the house that today it is largely covered by magnolia and other climbing plants. At the ends or junctions of the three sides of the house are round towers of three storeys surmounted by small copper saucer domes. In the middle of the centre side is a two-storeyed portico of six Doric or Ionic columns, as at Stansted, with a balustrade above. (Plate 30.)

On penetrating this colonnade the eye is confronted by a further series of magnificent columns screening from the entrance hall a passage behind it. These are this time of the Corinthian order with shafts of grey scagliola imitating granite and capitals of bronze.[1] The principal room for the decoration of which Wyatt was responsible is the library. (Plate 31.) The walls are lined with bookshelves, the centre of each end wall being surmounted by a small broken pediment containing a bust. Below the book-cases are low cupboards of which the panels were painted by Biagio Rebecca with grisaille figures

[1]Mr Rupert Gunnis tells me that the account for these columns is dated 1815, which was two years after Wyatt's death. In that case they almost certainly replace other columns in the same position erected in Wyatt's time.

on a terra-cotta ground. Above the chimney-piece is a large roundel of the death of Cleopatra, also painted by Rebecca, enclosed in a scrolled wreath flanked by twin pilasters standing on brackets and surmounted by a pediment. The overdoors show reclining figures of Bacchus and Ariadne. A wide frieze runs round the room below the ceiling containing a pattern of festoons encircling oval paterae. The ceiling, also painted by Rebecca, is made up of a series of polygonal sunk panels and is of much the same pattern as that designed by Adam for the red drawing-room at Syon House, which Sir William Chambers likened to a set of skied dessert dishes. The Tapestry drawing-room at Goodwood has a frieze and doorcase of anthemium pattern and a scroll plaster ceiling of Wyatt's design. The chimney-piece is by John Bacon. The Yellow drawing-room has a gilded frieze of stylised trees and a border of scroll-work round the ceiling very similar to designs executed for Liverpool Town Hall and Belvoir Castle. The doorcases are decorated with anthemia and tulips alternately. In the north wall is a semi-domed recess. Most of the other rooms were never finished by Wyatt or in the third Duke's lifetime.

Of the lodges of Goodwood Park, the Kennels Lodge was built in 1789 and Pilleygreen Lodges in 1794. Waterbeach Lodge and Valdoe Lodge are not dated. Probably all were designed by Wyatt. No doubt he was also responsible for the dower house in the park known as Molecombe which was probably built about 1800. This has a simple elevation of a centre portion and two wings. Like the lodges, it is built of flints but is relieved by dressings of red brick on one side and white brick on the other.

There is just one other building which Wyatt may have designed for the Duke of Richmond near but not at Goodwood. This was the stables at West Itchenor on an arm of Chichester Harbour where the Duke kept his race-horses. These stables were built in 1783 and so, if Wyatt was responsible for them, were his first commission from the Duke, antedating the kennels by four years. They are of red brick and grey headers and form a hexagonal courtyard not quite enclosed. A modillion cornice is carried round the five sides which are continuous with a pediment in the centre of each. The sixth side stands free with no pediment over it. Adjoining the stables is a moderate sized house, now known as Itchenor House, which the Duke used as a pied-à-terre when yachting in Chichester Harbour and to accommodate the staff of his racing stable. This is dated 1787. Like Molecombe, it consists of a centre portion and flanking pavilions and is not unlike a sketch of Wyatt's which survives labelled 'Mr Helyor' and consisting of a modest house flanked by stables and a brewhouse.

A house at which Wyatt worked round about 1785 was Sunningdale Park, Berkshire. The plan is L-shaped with three fronts exposed. Each is flanked by Doric pilasters and has a slightly projecting centre portion emphasised by similar pilasters or engaged Ionic columns. These support a heavy double entablature with a pediment above the central portion of the west and south fronts which are the most impressive. The east front has a projecting terrace before it containing basement rooms with round-headed windows and a flight of steps leading down to the garden dividing into two at the half-landing.

The interior has been largely gutted in the present century to make way for a central hall of vast proportions in Hollywood-baronial style. But a few of the original chimney-pieces remain. Those in the dining-room and the adjoining room, now used by the Civil Defence College which occupies the house as a bar, are almost a pair in yellow and white, and green and white marble respectively. The jambs take the form of Ionic columns in coloured marble with white capitals. The frieze is fluted alternately in white and colour, and in the centre is a tablet, that in the dining-room depicting a hunting scene of a dog catching a rabbit, both in white marble on a yellow marble ground, and that in the bar being wholly of white marble and only ornamented with a mask. The room now used as a lecture-room has a pair of exceptionally fine identical fireplaces. These are supported on white marble console brackets. The frieze is of yellow marble bearing a high relief of grapes and vases in white with, in the centre, a tablet of a cherub's head set in sun's rays. The frieze suggests that this room was originally the dining-room. One of the original doorcases also survives.

Wyatt also worked at the adjoining Sunninghill Park, Berkshire, which has since been demolished. The *Dictionary of Architecture* only attributes to him 'alterations and a new disposition of apartments'. But the house, as seen in Neale's *Seats*, has every look of being completely his work. The end window-bays of the main front projected, with Wyatt windows on the ground floor. The side elevation had a central bow.

John Betjeman and John Piper in their Berkshire Guide have attributed to Wyatt a third house in the same district, namely Sillwood Park, which was rebuilt at the height of the nineteenth century. But this was actually designed by Robert Mitchell in 1796.

Another commission of about 1785 was Wynnstay, Ruabon, for

57

Sir Watkin Williams Wynn. In 1782 Sir Watkin had obtained plans from Capability Brown for altering both the house and grounds, but only the latter were carried out. Wyatt exhibited a drawing of a new south front for Wynnstay in the Royal Academy of 1785 and another in 1788. In 1786 he also showed a design for a Doric temple intended to be built on a spot in the park called Nant y Belean. At another place in the grounds he erected a fluted column in memory of Sir Watkin's predecessor at Wynnstay. The house itself was rebuilt towards the end of the nineteenth century. But Neale's *Seats* shows it to have been a large L-shaped classical building, of which one wing terminated in a curved bay surmounted by a small saucer dome rather similar to the centre of Sundridge Park, Bromley, erected ten years later. The side face of the other wing had a projecting centre and Wyatt windows on the ground floor on each side of this. The *Dictionary of Architecture* also attributes the stables to Wyatt. These survived the nineteenth-century rebuilding but almost certainly date from earlier in the eighteenth century than his time.

It was probably at some time in the eighties that Wyatt worked at Ragley Hall, Warwickshire, for Lord Hertford, no doubt at the recommendation of Horace Walpole. He designed sundry ceilings and chimney-pieces, added the fine pedimented east portico with curved sedan steps leading up to it and possibly also the rectangular pediment breaking the balustrade of the west front with its three small circular windows set in swags. At the same time it is likely that he rebuilt the stable yard and laundry court. These form a complete courtyard having round-headed rusticated carriage archways in the centre of the opposite sides with, above, pediments and curious dumpy octagonal superstructures. These and the first floor above the archways have small round windows which are a change from the usual lunettes of stables. The other doorways are recessed in arcading containing semi-circular fanlights suggestive of the centre compartment of Venetian windows. The wing forming the laundry court is colonnaded on the inside. The whole building is a charming piece of simple composition.

Wyatt also worked for Lord Hertford at Sudbourne Hall, Suffolk, in 1784, but this house has since been enlarged and greatly altered.

In the following year he was employed by Lord Suffield at Gunton Hall in the adjoining county of Norfolk. Here Wyatt added to an existing Palladian house (since burned out) a three-storeyed wing of elegant proportions with six pilasters supporting a balustraded parapet, also a lower service block beyond. The offices which this contained were said by Neale's *Seats* to be 'superior to any in the Kingdom'.

Another undated Norfolk house is Worsted Hall, built for Sir Berney Brograve. It has a very plain elevation of red brick with a central bow containing the main entrance. Over the hall is a circular library.

A house for which Wyatt provided the plans and elevations only and did not undertake further responsibility was Ammerdown House, Somerset. He received the commission for this from Thomas Samuel Jolliffe in 1788. Very few of his receipted bills survive, but one has been preserved at Ammerdown and is worth quoting in full:

'1788. Due to James Wyatt. Jan. 14.

Set off from London, time and expenses travelling to Charlton and back	...	...	28	15	0
To 3 days time at Charlton	...	...	15	15	0
To clean drawings of ground. Plans and three elevations	...	...	15	15	0
1789. Ap. 13. By Lee. Basement and principal storey plans	...	...	2	2	0
May 14. Plan of principal and chamber storey. Elevation of the Front, Do of one end	...	...	6	6	0
			68	13	0
Capital for pilasters, entablature for Do; Do for Portico, Ballaster for Do; Base and surbase for do	...	...	1	7	0

Nov. 1789. Recd. of T. S. Jolliffe Seventy Pounds of wch I promise to give a discharge on stamp if required. Witness W. Jolliffe.

(Signed) JAMES WYATT.'

The house has been enlarged on three occasions in the nineteenth century but was originally of very modest proportions. In shape a square, it had two window-bays facing south and three facing east and west and comprised only three reception rooms and a small office on the ground floor, with a tail portion to the north containing the servants' quarters. The material used was Bath stone. The rusticated ground floor has recessed Venetian windows, alternating on the south front with small narrow round-headed recesses. Above, Doric pilasters rise through the two upper storeys to support the entablature. The elevations are very simple and foreshadow Regency taste, which Wyatt did not greatly employ, though he lived long enough to have done so if he had not been so occupied with Gothic enterprises at the end of his life.

The south front originally contained two parlours which have been later thrown into one drawing-room. The ceiling is decorated with simple mouldings in geometric patterns. The chimney-pieces are said to have come from Egremont House, Piccadilly. The dining-room, facing east, though also very simple in decoration, is the most elegant room in the house. The ceiling has an oval rosette in the centre encircled by a festoon of further ellipses. Below it is a frieze of paterae and swags with a fluted cornice. The east wall contains an apsed recess for the sideboard flanked by Ionic pilasters, with a further niche on each side of it containing a bust resting on a cupboard.

The staircase is lit by an elliptical dome supported on Ionic columns which have since been glazed in. At first floor level the landing is screened from the staircase by Doric columns with a balustrade between. The side wall facing the head of the stair contains a blind elliptical arch with squinch brackets on each side of it lined to suggest fan-vaulting. The whole arrangement is very similar to the plan of the more imposing staircases which Wyatt designed for his larger houses.

Between 1787 and 1789 Wyatt first came to be associated with a building on which he worked off and on till the end of his life. This was the Exchange or Mansion House, Liverpool, also called the Town Hall. The building had been originally designed by John Wood the Elder of Bath and erected between 1749 and 1754, the year of Wood's death. Wyatt's first task was the construction of the north addition containing the ball-room on the first floor, below which the Council Chamber was installed at a later date. In 1792 he provided the west front of the building with a new façade when this side of the Mansion House was freed from adjacent structures and Exchange Passage created. But Wyatt's design for this new front was more or less a reproduction of Wood's design for the opposite side. In the same year the whole of the ground floor, which had up till then been an open arcade, was converted into offices.

This would possibly have been the limit of Wyatt's work on the Mansion House if a bad fire had not occurred in 1795 which gutted the whole of the interior. He was consequently given the commission of replanning and redecorating the whole building. This occupied him until at least 1811. The dome was built in 1802 and the south portico added in 1811. Some of the rooms were ready for occupation by 1807, as in a letter of the 9th November in that year to James's son, Matthew, the latter's cousin, Lewis Wyatt, wrote: 'I will therefore be much obliged if you will [?produce] the drawings which Joseph [Dixon] sent you relating to Liverpool, that they may be forwarded, as Mr Foster is desired to get the staircase and a few Rooms in the Exchange furnished for the reception of the new Lord Mayor, and for which my Uncle's designs are wanting.'[1]

The entrance is through a vestibule divided by Corinthian columns. (Plate 33.) Between the two centre columns rises the staircase of the single-divide pattern which is invariably impressive for state rooms and reception purposes. The balusters are of cast iron, which was unusual in Wyatt's buildings, and the handrail of brass. It is lit from the dome above. The staircase leads to a set of reception rooms on the first floor which Edward VII is said to have pronounced the finest in England. The centre-room, into which the landing opens, has a flat dome carried on fluted pendentives with a wreath of Roman Corinthian ornament round its base. On each wall is a segmental arch springing from a cornice enriched with urns and inverted pyramids of fluting. This room is flanked by a pair of reception rooms with a barrel-vaulted coffered ceiling and a simple frieze.

At right angles then come the dining-room and the small ball-room. The former is divided into sections by very handsome scagliola pilasters, between which are niches containing stoves and on one side of the room round-headed window recesses with deep reveals and draped brocaded curtains. The frieze is one of the most beautiful and elaborate that Wyatt designed: in the centre of each panel, a pair of lions flanking an urn, with a scroll on each side of them and beyond again a larger urn above each pilaster. A letter from Matthew Wyatt to John Foster dated the 15th April 1811 refers to designs for the ceiling of the dining-room and says that he was 'particularly happy to be employed in decorating any Room that is designed by my Father'.[1] This is odd as the coved ceiling of the dining-room is not painted but divided into sunk panels of different shapes edged with rich mouldings. But between every alternate pair of pilasters above the recesses on the walls are painted roundels which are no doubt Matthew Wyatt's work.

[1]Letter in the British Museum.

61

The small ball-room has a vaulted ceiling and curved ends. One of these apses contains two semi-domed recesses for the musicians, edged with brass handrails. Round the whole room below the cornice are a series of thin rectangular panels containing scroll ornamentation similar to that edging the base of the dome in the centre room. The window recesses retain their original brocade curtains.

The grandest and possibly the finest room in the series is the great ball-room in Wyatt's annexe of 1789. (Plate 32.) This room, like the dining-room, is pilastered in scagliola of sienna colour. The frieze is an elaborate one of arabesques and large-scale anthemia. The ceiling is a magnificent barrel-vault returned at the ends and decorated with enriched bands and sunk panels. Above the main windows are smaller round windows of which the reveals are framed in rich mouldings. In the centre of the opposite wall is another recessed musicians' gallery but at higher level than those in the small ball-room. This has a richly coffered semi-dome and another delicate brass balustrade.

The chimney-pieces throughout the building are of simple design. But one of the principal and most unusual features of the Exchange consists of the cast-iron stoves of different patterns which Wyatt designed for each room. The dining-room contains two varieties, one topped by great jasper vases and the other by more elaborate vases decorated in brass with a glass bowl at the top and flanked by candelabra. Those in the centre-room are oval and are surmounted by winged sphinxes holding up a lamp-bowl. But possibly the most ingenious and elegant of the whole series are those in the staircase hall which take the form of a Greek Doric column on a plinth decorated with a design of wings and bearing aloft a three-pronged finial or cap. The reception rooms also contain a notable collection of fine furniture, but this was not designed by Wyatt and dates from slightly after his day. Altogether the Mansion House at Liverpool is a magnificent composition and is certainly Wyatt's finest surviving town work which would at least have rivalled the Pantheon if this was still standing.

(4.) 1790-1813

In 1790 Wyatt had been practising for twenty years. Robert Adam had only two years to live. New ideas of Greek or what came to be Regency simplicity were beginning to dawn. Most of Wyatt's work after this date was Gothic in style. But in his classical buildings he also began to move away from elaboration of detail in interior decoration and in the direction of the Greek revival in exteriors. This is well exemplified in Castle Coole, Fermanagh, his most important Irish house, which was begun in 1790. This is built of Portland stone shipped direct from Portland to Ballyshannon at immense expense. The total cost of the house is said to have been £54,000. Lord Belmore in fact ruined himself over it. The plan of the house is the same as that of Heaton Hall and many contemporary mansions: a centre block with a portico on one side and a semi-circular projection on the other, and flanking pavilions of one storey linked to the centre by corridors which are colonnaded on the entrance front. The central feature on each side has four engaged and fluted Ionic columns of which the capital volutes are set at an angle of almost forty-five degrees. The entrance portico also has a pediment which interrupts the balustraded parapet of the centre block. The pavilions have a similar parapet and two niches to each front flanking a Venetian window on the garden side and a loggia with two fluted Doric columns on the entrance front. The ends of the wings have solid raised panels in the centre of the parapet and four fluted Doric columns supporting the entablature below this. The whole arrangement is a singularly fine composition, but its effect is greatly mitigated by the emphasis falling on the black voids of the windows through the sash bars being painted a dark colour instead of white. (Plate 9.)

The hall has a simple triglyph frieze with paterae in the metopes and a border to the ceiling of chequered and diamond pattern. The end opposite the door has a screen of porphyry scagliola columns. The door in the centre leads into the oval saloon which is the principal apartment. This is divided into twelve compartments by grey, black and white mottled Corinthian pilasters which, like the columns in the hall, were the work of Dominick Bartoli. The frieze has a pattern of swags enclosing oval paterae, and the ceiling a series of concentric mouldings of festoons and anthemia encircling a central oval rosette. (Plate 11.) All the stucco work in the house was executed under the direction of Joseph Rose who worked so much for Adam. His greatness in his own craft is well illuminated by the fact that he was long remembered at Castle Coole after his visits as 'Sir Joseph Rose'. The doorcases repeat the design of the ceiling and frieze, and the doors are inset with six panels painted in grisaille.

The saloon leads on one side into the dining-room and on the other into the library. The dining-room gives a foretaste of Regency elegance and chastity and shows considerable influence of Henry Holland. The walls are divided into panels to contain pictures edged with simple mouldings. The frieze is composed of a series of enlaced garlands, which are again echoed by the doorcases and by the ceiling, of one large and two small rosettes enclosed in a border patterned with a motif of octagons. Most of the furniture in the house was acquired by the second Earl of Belmore at a later date. But the sideboard with a sarcophagus wine-cooler beneath it and urns on pedestals on each side of it, also the dining-table of six separate sections which can be bolted together, and the semi-circular side-tables were all made in the house in 1797 and 1798 and so possibly were designed by Wyatt.

The bookcases in the library have reeded frames and architraves and a guilloche moulding to the dado above the cupboards beneath them. The chimney-piece, executed by Richard Westmacott at the cost of £126, is of white marble imitating drapery. It is by no known standard beautiful. It can only be considered as a joke but is rather a too permanent one to be amusing. It would have been more in place in the Great Exhibition of 1851. The ceiling has a central rosette set in a cusped octagon and is edged with a border of small rosettes in rectangles.

Between the library and the drawing-room is the staircase. This is of the usual pattern branching into two flights at the half-landing. But owing to its position in the house it is rather narrow in proportions, like the very similar staircase at Frogmore which Wyatt built at about the same period. The wrought iron balusters, too, of the design of two lyres, the lower one inverted, with a rosette between, are rather similar to those of Frogmore and are almost identical with a sketch of Wyatt's which has survived in an album marked 'Mr D. Smith'.[1]

Probably the most unusual feature of Castle Coole is the plan of the upper floors. In the centre of the first floor is a lobby approached by four doors symmetrically placed with a gallery running round this at second floor level. The gallery has the same wrought iron balustrade as the staircase, and the ceiling is supported by coupled Doric columns painted yellow. The lobby is lit by an oval skylight set in an enriched ceiling, and at each end the gallery expands into a landing which is lit by a similar smaller oval skylight on the opposite axis to the centre one. Wyatt's design for this lobby and gallery has been preserved at Castle Coole. The whole detail of the house shows another aspect of Wyatt's many-sided genius in full flower in the nineties.

Wyatt's other work in Ireland consisted of Ardbraccan House near Navan for the Bishop of Meath, and the decoration of the picture gallery over the supper-room at Leinster House, Dublin, executed

[1]In the possession of the Vicomte de Noailles.

about 1785. But it is not known whether he visited Ireland in connection with any of these commissions.

Another work of the seventeen-nineties which shows Wyatt's leanings towards simplicity at this time was Frogmore, built for Queen Charlotte. This is described in Chapter XII.

Sundridge Park, Bromley, Kent, dates from between 1792 and 1795 and was designed for Edward George Lind. Its architectural history is complicated. An earlier house on the site was demolished and the new one erected in a higher position chosen by Humphrey Repton who designed the landscape setting. In 1796 the estate was sold to Claude Scott, later knighted, who carried out further work on the house. In 1799 Nash exhibited two designs in the Royal Academy for work at Sundridge Park. But these may not have been executed. Angus's *Seats* (1804) however attributes the interior decoration to Samuel Wyatt. The natural interpretation would be that Nash added the flanking L-wings which Samuel Wyatt decorated, but the accompanying print in Angus's *Seats* shows the house without the wings. The responsibility for them therefore remains uncertain. But the bulk of the house, including its fine internal decoration, was almost certainly James Wyatt's.

The house is a very unusual shape, originally hexagonal, with three porticoes. In the centre facing south six free-standing Corinthian columns form a curve of what is, inside, a round room. They are surmounted by a small dome inset within a balustrade above the attic storey. On each side is a splayed portion and then a wing at right angles, in the centre of which is another Corinthian portico, surmounted by a pediment, the west one containing a recessed porch, the east one forming only a balancing projection. From the outside the building has considerable affinities with Goodwood and appears to be slightly more than half a hollow octagon, as Goodwood is three sides of what was intended to be an octagon. But Sundridge Park is actually solid, and its north side against the hill contains the offices. After 1796 Nash added the two L-wings at right angles, the east one forming part of the offices, and the west one the billard-room. These continue the style of Wyatt's work so exactly, except that the stucco of the west wing has since been replaced by cement, that they appear contemporary with the main block. The whole effect of the outside is not however as impressive as it should be because, owing to the right angles of the plan and the fall of the ground to the south, it is not possible to see more than half the house at one time.

Internally the plan is one of the most ingenious Wyatt ever devised.

Behind the round room is a circular staircase well. Between this and the reception rooms to the south runs a corridor, from which little domed recesses give access to the rooms. The whole of the ground floor is decorated with most elaborate plasterwork which is in excellent condition. But its effect is unfortunately mitigated by the fact that the building was, until recently, a hotel, and all the stucco work has been painted that uniform coffee-colour which is so beloved of hotels.

The round room has three windows framed in round-headed arches with enriched pilasters, spandrels, frieze and cornice. On the other side these are echoed by three elliptical recessed double doorways with medallions set in festoons in the tympana. The centre one is flanked by twin fluted engaged columns with foliated capitals, the outer ones by single similar pilasters. There is a panelled dado and a rather plain chimney-piece with medallions at the head of the jambs. Above this is a mirror framed in a surround to match that of the windows. The ceiling has a cove enriched with festoons of husks and a central rosette surrounded by eight wedge-shaped panels, of which four contain painted roundels in the centre.

The same dado, window surrounds and overmantel occur in the adjoining rooms. The room to the east has apsidal ends. The eastern apse contains a recess set in a frame like that of the windows, the west one a doorway enriched with two different kinds of mouldings with a broken pediment over and doors of convex curve. The chimney-piece has enriched pilasters and a floral frieze with putti in the centre. The ceiling springs from a narrow cove of thin divisions with a flower pattern and is set in a narrow border of three different kinds of mouldings. In the centre is an oval panel edged with an anthemium border. Round this are grouped four long thin rectangular panels containing central rosettes and between these at the angles four charming small square painted panels of classical figures. At each end above the apse are three further divisions of scroll work, the centre one containing an octagonal painted medallion of a head.

The room to the west of the centre room has only one segmental end containing two shallow recesses. The arrangement of the ceiling is very similar to that of the east room, but the central panel is octagonal, those at the angles irregular pentagons and the other four long thin strips which are painted and not stuccoed. Below the ceiling is a frieze of vases and scrolls. The dining-room beyond the east room has been altered beyond recognition.

The staircase is of the familiar Wyatt pattern: a single flight flanked

66

by sienna-coloured scagliola Ionic columns and branching into two with a half-domed recess in an enriched surround at the half-landing and two more columns on the landing at the head of the stair. The balusters are of brass and of unusual design: a thin hollow oval alternating with a flower. It is lit from above, and round the dome are panels of ornamental plasterwork with sphinxes and rosettes in the lowest portions and a cornice of bows and swags of leaves.

The intricately contrived passage which leads off the staircase has panelled walls enriched with festoons, a frieze of vases and paterae and a scrolled ceiling. The doorcases opening off it are extremely fine. The architraves take the form of bound rods with a medallion above, and the doors themselves have six panels set in concave reeding.

The entrance hall, which balances the dining-room on the west, is octagonal. Opposite the entrance are two recesses flanked by round-headed archways with wide pilasters and semi-circular tympana. At each end are two more similar arches, of which the inner ones are wholly open and the outer ones have similar tympana enriched with scroll-work. The two arches at the south end give into an irregular-shaped cabinet or extension of the hall, those on the north into a curved passage leading to a subsidiary staircase and the billiard-room. This little staircase is a charming piece of work with panelled walls containing two niches and lit by an oval skylight set in a cove with a fluted frieze.

The billiard-room is in the west wing. Its flat barrel ceiling of sunk octagonal or half-octagonal panels joined by ribs of scroll-work is very similar in design to James Wyatt's work, though perhaps of slightly heavier nature, and possibly was by Samuel.

Possibly the most delightful room in the house is the round bedroom in the centre of the first floor. Apart from the fact that the walls have been repainted biscuit colour, which is too dark, this room retains its original colouring, principally green and gold. Above the panelled dado the walls are divided into upright rectangular panels set in reeded mouldings and surmounted by vases. Each is divided into three small sections edged by festoons and scrolls, the top ones containing crossed rods with pineapple heads, the centre ones either baskets of roses, trophies of arms, agricultural implements or musical instruments, and the bottom ones festoons of drapery. The curved door forms another panel of rather similar pattern. The three windows are framed in green pilasters enriched with gilt ornament and surmounted by a similar frieze and broken pediments with vases in their apertures.

67

Above the ceiling frieze of small red and gold circles is a cove with a border of green tongues enriched with gold. The colours of the ceiling are cream, two shades of green, gold and red. The central rosette of light and dark green in a gilt border is set in a diamond of light green patterned with gilt scrolls and having fan ornamentation in the points edged with red and enriched with gold. The outer portions of the ceiling have a cream background and contain three roundels of bas-relief in gilt frames. These have a dark green ground with white figures colour-washed light green. On each side of the roundels are pointed shield-shaped panels of gilt scrolling on a dark green ground. The whole circle of the ceiling is set in a border of red with gold circlets like the ceiling frieze.

There are few better surviving examples of Wyatt's work than this room. The whole house is a very complete example of rich and elaborate plasterwork that was beginning to be replaced by simpler decoration in the seventeen-nineties when this was designed and was rather more typical of about fifteen years earlier.

Between 1793 and 1797 Wyatt was employed by Lord Rous, later Earl of Stradbroke, at Henham Hall, Suffolk; the Elizabethan house on the site having been burned down in 1773. The building which Wyatt substituted was a plain house of three storeys, the ground floor having small windows and the floor above forming a piano nobile. It was nearly square in plan with a projecting centre of three window-bays to the main front. This is surmounted by a pediment and has a Wyatt window with a pediment and a balcony on the first floor placed between two windows in round-headed arcading. At a later date the house was encased in a restrained Italianate disguise by Sir Charles Barry for a subsequent Earl of Stradbroke. Barry added a modillion cornice and balustraded parapet, a loggia along the whole length of the ground floor with a small portico above in the place of the Wyatt window and architrave surrounds to all the other upper windows. But he left intact the Wyatt staircase of a single flight branching into two at the half-landing and a few other features such as the frieze of the library ceiling. These, alas! vanished also when the whole building was demolished in 1953.

Wyatt's stables were undistinguished, but he also built a more interesting dovecot and dairy. The dovecot is a charming little octagonal brick building with pilasters flanking each of the sides and a gay little Gothic lantern, shaped rather like a font-canopy, which formed the birds' entrance at the apex of the room. The dairy was less

33. Liverpool Town Hall

34. Dodington Park

35 and 36. Dodington Church

successful. The central feature was a crow-stepped gable which was repeated above the gable ends, but the whole thing was dwarfed by a gigantic tower quite out of proportion to the rest of the building.

A house to which John Betjeman and John Piper have assigned the date 1795 in their Berkshire Guide is Purley Park, near Reading. This is built of Portland stone and somewhat resembles Hothfield Park, Kent, in style, which would suggest an earlier date. But seen from a photograph in which the difference between stone and stucco is not apparent, the entrance front is rather similar to that of Frogmore House. The house is square in plan, with five windows facing south and five facing east but only three facing north. The entrance front has a square porch supported by two pairs of coupled Doric columns with an iron balcony over it. The centre first floor window is of the Wyatt tripartite variety with a pediment over, and the whole window-bay is flanked by grooved pilasters. These pilasters and a similar window also appear on the north front facing the river, and on the ground floor is a portico but this is of tetrastyle semi-circular pattern with a curved bay of three French windows beneath it. The outer ground floor windows have side strips of fancy glazing and a semi-circular fanlight above, similarly flanked, with a segmental tympanum over the whole. The east front is quite plain. On the west is a service wing of lower elevation. None of the four fronts is very impressive.

The hall has a screen of two fluted Ionic columns opposite the door, but this leads into the main drawing-room with the bow of the north front and not, as usually was the case in Wyatt houses, into the stair-case. The latter is placed to the west of the hall. This has wrought iron balusters of two interlacing ovals with a smaller oval between containing a brass rosette. The main rooms have good plaster ceilings.

The lodges, which are now on the opposite side of the main road to the park, are probably Wyatt's. They are single-storeyed buildings with balancing canted bays containing three ogee-headed windows and roofs of three panels over.

Bowden House, Wiltshire, of which a design was shown in the Royal Academy in 1796, has a central Ionic portico with a saucer dome above it. At each end of the house is a wide pilaster containing an empty niche on the ground floor and an oval panel above. Between these and the portico are scrolled panels on the first floor and below tripartite Wyatt windows with segmental tympana. This must be one of his most successful smaller works. Its façade has an elegance and lightness of touch which is more reminiscent of his early Heaton Hall manner.

Wyatt's last but one great classical country house was Stoke Poges Park, Buckinghamshire. The old house here, known as Pinner House, had been built by Lord Chief Justice Coke in the early seventeenth century. The estate had been purchased in 1760 by Thomas Penn, the second son of William Penn of Pennsylvania. The house not having been occupied for some years, his son, John Penn, in 1789 decided to build a new residence on a site about a quarter of a mile to the south-west. The old building was demolished, except for one wing which still remains and is known as Stoke Poges Manor House.

The first architect whom Penn employed was Robert Nasmith, while Humphrey Repton laid out the grounds. Farington, who was a friend of Penn's, called Nasmith 'a person who had been under Adam and was recommended by Sir George Howard'.[1] Nasmith did not however give satisfaction, and Farington went on to say that 'owing to bad design it [the house] cost Mr Penn £10,000 more than it ought to have done'.[2] Nasmith died in 1793. Penn then called in Wyatt, who commenced work about 1797. Nasmith's work was evidently classical in character. Wyatt therefore had no option but to continue in this vein. But Penn must have been a man of catholic tastes as more or less contemporaneously with the construction of the new house at Stoke Poges he employed Wyatt to build him a Gothic castle in the Isle of Portland called Pennsylvania Castle.

Stoke Poges Park is quite unlike any of Wyatt's other houses. In plan it rather resembles one of Henry VIII's coastline castles and forms a quatrefoil or a square with projections at all four angles. All four façades are exposed. The house consists of a square central block of three storeys with a balustraded parapet and a flat roof, in the centre of which is set a circular lantern. This comprises a fairly large cupola ringed by an Ionic colonnade with a vase standing on the entablature above each column and a dome surmounted by a pepper-box turret. According to Neale's *Seats* this contained an observatory. On each front there is a ground floor projection beyond the main block terminating in the corners in pavilions which break forward still further, those on the east and west front having curved centres. (Plate 61.)

Standing on the south terrace at Stoke Poges Park, the most prominent object in the fine view to the south is the silhouette of Windsor Castle. Even in its pre-Wyatville days this must have been so. Ensconced there, Wyatt clearly bethought himself of the adjoining

[1]*Farington Diary*, 22 Aug. 1797.
[2]*Ibid.*

Frogmore House and reproduced here the main elevation fourfold with slight variations. The effect of the colonnades and wings is very impressive, and it is strange to find Wyatt almost apologising for it. Farington recorded that 'Wyatt would not have placed a colonnade to the aspect which it is but did it from *necessity* in order to join the wings',[1] which were added about 1808.

The south front is the most imposing aspect, though the projection is there the narrowest. It forms an open colonnade of twelve fluted Doric columns with a triglyph frieze and an iron balustrade above interspersed with stuccoed piers. The small square flanking pavilions have one window each set between Doric pilasters. The three centre window bays on the first floor are emphasised by engaged Ionic columns of white marble supporting pediments. The north or entrance front is somewhat similar but is enclosed, and ten Doric pilasters take the place of columns. The wings contain niches for statues flanked by pilasters and surmounted by pediments. On the east and west fronts the wings occupy a greater width of the whole elevation. Each comprises a curved bay of three windows flanked by empty niches. The west front has only two engaged Doric columns in the centre, but the east front has six which are glazed to form a conservatory within.

Stoke Poges Park is much the finest of Wyatt's surviving classical houses. How much of its aspect, if any, must be attributed to Nasmith it is difficult to say. From the entry already quoted in *Farington's Diary* and from the similarity of the elevations to the south front of Frogmore House, there can be no doubt that Wyatt was responsible for the colonnades and wings. It might therefore be assumed that the central block was largely Nasmith's work. But a plain stuccoed building of this nature is not at all dissimilar to some of Wyatt's other houses, and even the cupola, though an unusual feature to find in a Wyatt house, has considerable affinity with the little temple which Wyatt built in the grounds of Heaton Hall. Whatever may have been the respective responsibility of the two architects, the result is a grandiose and monumental conception that also has great delicacy and grace. It is a pity that Wyatt was not more often inspired away from his mostly very plain exteriors to design other houses of similar distinction to this. It is a fine climax to his classical career.

The interior is entirely Wyatt's. The house is now used as a golf club. The hall is an oval room with a frieze of ox-skulls between swags of drapery. It has four semi-circular niches with half-domes and four

[1] *Farington Diary*, 22 Aug. 1797.

71

doorways, of which two are open and two have curved doorcases but flat doors.

The hall leads into a large central staircase. (Plate 28.) This is divided into two by a screen of red marble Corinthian columns. The walls have plaques in bas-relief, probably of Coadeware stone. The chimney-piece has Ionic marble jambs and a frieze of masks. The staircase is not of the usual Wyatt pattern dividing at the half-landing but rises in three flights on one side of the room. Its handrail is of most unusual design and quite unlike any other by Wyatt. (Plate 5.) It has alternately upright panels of ironwork enclosing a floral design or the outline of a lyre and long rectangular scrolls framing either crossed torches or groups of musical instruments. Although Stoke Poges was the only one of Wyatt's houses to be surmounted by a large dome visible from the outside, this is not open to the staircase but is approached from a subsidiary stair starting on the first floor. The main staircase is lit by three large windows flanked by engaged fluted Ionic columns with a frieze of urns, scrolls, gryphons and cherubs, and a pediment over. On the fourth or landing side is a dummy window of similar design and a gallery with a handrail of the same pattern as that of the staircase. Above the cornice of the staircase-well are four large lunette windows set in squinch arches with a central rosette and wide coffered bands at the ends.

The ground floor rooms on the west side of the house were the private apartments of the family and are now occupied by the proprietor of the club house. The centre of the east front forms a conservatory with a flat glass roof. To the south of it is a rather plain room, now the bar, with a frieze and doorcases enriched with scroll-work and mirrors between the three windows of the bow in the east wall.

The *pièce de résistance* of the house was the library, now the club dining-room, which was completed in 1808. This was then 192 feet long and occupied the whole of the south front including the end pavilions. But these have now been partitioned off. They contained little semi-circular apses with small round domes of two tiers of curved lights. The room is divided into five sections by archways shaped like Venetian windows supported on mottled green and white scagliola columns with foliated capitals. The entablature of the arches and the ceiling frieze are decorated with wreaths. The central compartment of the ceiling has an oval of enriched plasterwork encircled by a series of bouquets in festoons and the compartments on each side of it a similar round motif. The long wall is given up to enclosed bookcases

72

set in guilloche moulding. Over each is a half-domed niche of radiating fan pattern and above this a rectangular grisaille trempe l'oeil panel painted by Robert Smirke or his son Richard. In the centre of the middle compartment is a doorway in a round-headed recess and in each flanking section a fireplace. The room is impressive in its scale and proportions but probably lacked, even originally, the vivid colour-scheme which one associates with Wyatt's earlier work and is today in its club décor rather sombre.

Wyatt designed the charming little single-storey lodges with tiny Doric porches flanking the drive. On the west side they are joined to a fine crested iron gate and railing. The bridge across the lake was not Wyatt's and no doubt belonged to Repton's lay-out. But in the park to the north of the house Wyatt designed a column in memory of Sir Edward Coke, at the erection of which George III was most indignant. There is a curious entry in *Farington's Diary* on this subject. Farington wrote that Wyatt thought Coke's monument should be 'designed agreeable to the Architecture of that day—something like the designs of Inigo Jones before he went to Italy—a mixture of Gothic and Roman manners'.[1] No such mongrel composition however resulted. The monument is simply a fluted Doric column faced with Roman cement on a tall square base, holding aloft a drum surmounted by a statue of Coke sculpted by Rossi. It was erected in 1800 and cost £100.

The year before Wyatt had also designed a monument to Thomas Gray in a meadow adjoining Stoke Poges church-yard. This has a stone base and a tall square plinth, now colour-washed, with a sunk panel on each side inscribed with quotations from Gray's works. Above this stands a square sarcophagus on short legs with pediments on two opposite sides and acroteria on the other two sides. It is a massive affair but hardly beautiful. He completed his work at Stoke Poges by rebuilding the Vicarage in 1802, but designed this in mildly Gothic character.

A year after embarking on the erection of Stoke Poges Park, Wyatt began work at Dodington Park, Gloucestershire. This was built between 1798 and 1808 for Christopher Codrington, in whose company Wyatt met his death, and is said to have cost £120,000. A design was shown in the Royal Academy of 1798. Wyatt's building replaced a gabled Tudor house. The grounds had been laid out by Capability Brown in 1764. Miss Dorothy Stroud has pointed out that the sham castle, in

[1] *Farington Diary*, 8 Dec. 1798.

which the cascade between the two lakes is located, must have been Brown's, and not, as previously thought, Wyatt's work. By 1798 Wyatt was well launched on his Gothic progress. It is therefore surprising that he did not use the existence of this Gothic garden building as an excuse to gothicise the house. One would imagine that he must have received specific instructions from his client to stick to his classical vein. This was the first time Wyatt had had occasion to construct a house in a pre-existing landscape of Brown's. He had a great respect for Brown and told Farington that Brown 'possessed great ideas and has laid out many grounds with judgment'.[1] Capability was no more a mannerist than the great masters in painting. 'He had a peculiar way of thinking on the subject of laying out grounds, and it was scarcely possible that it should not produce a style of his own. Many of his imitators have merely copied his "manner", and most of them his defects only, but their imperfections cannot with justice be attributed to him.'[2]

At Dodington Wyatt seems to have aimed at giving the house a very modest place in Brown's landscape. The exterior is quite the most undistinguished of his major works and a great anticlimax after Stoke Poges Park. The chief feature is the massive hexastyle portico on the entrance front with a balcony most unusually placed on the first floor beneath it. But the portico is far too large for and dwarfs the façade from which it projects. The south front has a central feature of four Corinthian pilasters and two engaged columns with a solid panel above the cornice containing an attic room flanked by a portion of balustrading. But this panel only breaks the roof line to no purpose and appears redundant. The east front is the plainest of all, and even its curved bays at each end do not redeem its dullness. The north side has no façade exposed but has a most interesting feature in a curved conservatory or corridor leading to the chapel. Along its concave face this has a two-storeyed gallery with trellised iron columns.

The chapel, which also served as the parish church, has the plan of a Greek cross with a dome in the centre. (Plate 36.) It is lit from this dome and from lunette windows inserted in the segmental arch of each arm of the cross. The interior is one of Wyatt's most outstanding successes. Fluted Doric columns support the pendentives of the dome. These, with the soffits of the arches and the coffered dome itself, are of green and white marble; as is also the floor. The whole effect is one of cool elegance. (Plate 35.) This little chapel is the only one of Wyatt's

[1] *Farington Diary*, 23 Dec. 1798.
[2] *Ibid.*

74

classical churches that survives since the demolition of St Peter's, Manchester, at the beginning of this century.

The hall at Dodington, like that of Heveningham, has two columns at each end forming a screen. These are of the composite order and are made of red scagliola with gilt capitals. The floor is paved with red and black marble divided by brass strips. The ceiling is richly coffered with a rosette in the centre of each panel. The frieze is of paterae interspersed with lions' masks. The end sections of the room behind the columns have coved ceilings supported on red scagliola pilasters and divided into lozenge-shaped panels each containing a wreath and two honeysuckle designs with a luxuriant heap of trophies in the corners.

The staircase is one of the most impressive Wyatt ever constructed. At the entrance stand twin fluted Corinthian columns with a round-headed arch between. Opposite rises a wide single flight divided into two in the usual way at the half-landing. An unusual feature here is a fireplace in a recess. (Plate 34.) The balustrade is of a most elaborate pattern. The total outline of some of the balusters forms the shape of a wide vase, but within this are a variety of interlaced patterns. The first floor landing on two sides of the staircase-well is screened by two pairs of fluted Corinthian columns. The whole is lit from above by means of a square aperture containing giant semi-circular fanlights which is framed in a ceiling of enriched square and rectangular panels.

After the hall and staircase at Dodington the reception rooms are very simple in decoration. The drawing-room has a frieze of winged gryphons facing a tripod, a doorcase of the same motif with scrolled uprights, a plain caryatid chimney-piece and Corinthian scagliola pilasters flanking this. The library has bookcases with a gilded grille rather similar to those which Wyatt designed at Norris Castle in the Isle of Wight and a frieze of scroll-work.

The incidental buildings are all of Wyatt's construction. The stables are undistinguished, as is the Dower House, apart from its domed semi-circular portico. Entrance to the park is by triple gates flanked by colonnades, one of which leads to a two-storeyed L-shaped lodge. Of exceptional attraction is another lodge—a small circular building ringed by a Doric colonnade and surmounted by a shallow dome that echoes the chapel. (Plate 21.)

A house very similar in character to Dodington Park, which Mr Arthur Oswald writing in *Country Life* of the 4th and 11th February 1949 has attributed to James Wyatt, is Rudding Park, Yorkshire. The entrance front has the same double bow, and each of the other fronts a single bow. But all its façades are much less monotonous than those of Dodington Park, to a great extent on account of the superior and much lighter effect of the honey-coloured stone of which Rudding Park is built. The plan of the house with its central staircase of a single flight dividing into two at the half-landing and balusters of two lyre shapes, one inverted, is substantial evidence of such an attribution, and the gateway of the old entrance to the park is almost identical, save for a pediment which it lacks, with the gateway and lodge of Bryanston, Dorset.

About the turn of the century Wyatt built a house at Roehampton for Lord Huntingfield, formerly Sir Joshua Vanneck, the brother of Sir Gerard Vanneck, for whom he had worked at Heveningham Hall. This was originally called Roehampton Grove but is now known as Grove House, Roehampton Lane. It was a modest stuccoed house of which the chief feature today is its fine grounds opposite Roehampton House with a lake to the north of the house. It was greatly enlarged in the late nineteenth century, and only the entrance front remains in its original condition. This is divided into three sections of three windows each, with stone pilasters flanking each section. The wings are topped by a balustraded parapet, the centre, which projects slightly, by a pediment containing a large Coadeware plaque of a female profile set in a wreath. The centre first floor is tripartite with a semi-circular tympanum above the centre light framed in a semi-circle of fan pattern. Above it is a long thin panel of scroll-work flanked by rectangular Coadeware plaques of festoons. The porch has probably been added.

Most of the interior has been redecorated in Edwardian taste. But the staircase and the large drawing-room to the left of the hall, now used as a music-room by the Froebel Educational Institute which occupies the house, remains as built. The staircase is lit by a small circular dome which has at its base a frieze of urns linked by festoons of drapery. The dome is supported on pendentives of fan radiation framed in a wide border of wreaths encircling cameo heads with whole figures at the corners. The balusters of the handrail are of a cast iron pattern more typical of about 1820 and probably not original. The doorcases are of rather heavier design than was usual with Wyatt. The cornices are supported on console brackets, and in the centre of each architrave is a plaque of an urn.

The drawing-room walls above the dado are divided into panels

76

with slightly projecting borders enriched with anthemia and are eared in the top corners. On each side of the fireplace are pilasters decorated with arabesques and rams'-head capitals. The frieze is of wreaths and festoons with groups of trophies over the pilasters. The ceiling has a central rosette encircled by wreaths and set in a diamond bordered by four concave bands of scrolls with roundels of musical instruments in the angles. At each end of the ceilings are four octagonal panels containing oval rosettes. The room has very beautiful mahogany double doors of six inset moulded and reeded panels. The chimney-piece has white marble engaged Corinthian columns set in a surround of sienna-coloured scagliola with a marble plaque of a classical scene flanked by white scroll-work on a sienna scagliola architrave topped by a marble modillion cornice. The room is a good example of the restrained classical style which Wyatt used at the end of his life.

A commission which Wyatt no doubt owed to his appointment as Surveyor General to the Board of Works was for the erection of the Royal Military College, Sandhurst. This dates from 1807-12, and, like Castle Coole, is a product of the Greek revival. It is a long low stuccoed building of two storeys and twenty-eight window-bays, imposing in its monumental dignity. Wyatt skilfully applied to its design the country house motif of a centre and colonnaded wings. The principal feature of the main block is the central Doric portico which, on account of the great length of the building, projects to an unusual depth with return columns at the sides. Any porch of less proportions would have been reduced to insignificance by the vast wall surface on each side of it. It is approached by a flight of steps up which the Adjutant always rides his horse at passing-out parades, though no doubt it was not designed for equestrian access. The tympanum of the pediment contains a cartouche flanked by seated figures of Britannia and Mars. The wings are planned equally skilfully. Again, on account of the immense length of the centre block, they are set back so that their front walls are flush with the back wall of the centre. They thus fall into scale and, when seen from a distance across the lake, appear to have a continuous flush façade, as is normally the case, but without seeming a monotonous length. Each wing is in four sections. A colonnade of two square pillars links the main block to a building of seven windows, and a further colonnade of four similar columns joins this to a smaller pavilion of three windows. In comparison to the unrelieved gloom of most barracks architecture, Sandhurst is a composition of great dignity and even stateliness.

77

One attractive feature consists of the lodges to the north-east of the College, near the modern Staff College. The central rectangular dwelling has an octostyle colonnade in front of it with three columns on the return sides. Spear-headed railings with stuccoed gate-piers link this to further small square lodges which have recessed centres, each containing one window flanked by engaged columns.

On the 3rd February 1811, Farington recorded in his *Diary* that the 'Government has taken the superintendence of the building [Sandhurst] from him [Wyatt] most probably owing to his own neglect'. He was succeeded by Sanders.

Wyatt did not execute any other classical work on the same monumental scale as Sandhurst, and, like Stoke Poges Park amongst country houses, it was a fitting climax to his work. The fact is that he was not impressed by monumentality in architecture. In the same breath in which he condemned St Peter's at Rome he told Farington that he thought 'St Paul's, in London, very defective—window over window, where there is only one storey divides the architecture into little parts, and exhibits a false idea,—as they signify different stories while there is only one.—The three Porticos are the best parts of the architecture but should have been only one range of Pillars instead of Pillars over Pillars. The best effect of these Pillars is from inside of the building, where they come into comparison with the Houses.'[1] He added: 'The Portico of St Martin's in the fields is good, and excepting the windows, the body of the Church is well designed.—The Spire bad.'[2]

As Wyatt did not admire monumentality, Vanbrugh was an architect for whom he had little use. He thought that Vanbrugh's designs 'when executed on a small scale are disgusting and contemptible. Whereas regular architecture can produce beauty on any scale, and the most striking effects on a large scale.—Vanbrugh was undoubtedly a man of talents and strong Ideas, and with a proper education would probably have made a great artist.'[1] Blenheim, he admitted, 'from its size,—projection of Porticos,—Colonnades etc. had great effect and strength of light and shade,—but a "stone quarry" of equal size would also have a great effect.'[2] Capability Brown's setting of the house in the Park he did however admire, without ever being able to make up his mind to what the general effect was due. 'It was not the building, or

[1] *Farington Diary*, 7 Nov. 1797.
[2] *Ibid.*
[1] *Farington Diary*, 22 Dec. 1798.
[2] *Ibid.*

78

the grounds, or the woods or the water, singly, as none of these constituent parts are such as his judgment would approve entirely yet the whole together makes a forcible impression.'[1]

(5.) *Summary*

From a study of Wyatt's general classical work the fact emerges that he had a favourite plan for country houses which he applied whenever space and circumstances permitted. This was to place the staircase in the centre of the house and to group the main reception rooms round it. He even adopted this arrangement in some of his Gothic houses, such as Ashridge. The staircase itself was preferably of the type which begins as a single flight but divides into two at the half-landing. It was lit from a small dome not visible from the exterior of the house. At the foot and head is a pair of columns and on each side of the head a landing with more columns forming a small gallery. Often if the single flight of the stair is opposite the entrance from the hall, there is a screen of columns dividing this end of the room from the staircase itself. But sometimes the screen of columns appears in the outer hall instead.

In the planning of his rooms Wyatt was more practical than most contemporary architects. He was not fond of basements and did not go out of his way to place the offices as far away as possible from the principal rooms. He quite often used the plan of a main building with flanking wings, but the latter were not placed in such a position that their only communication with the centre block was by means of an underground passage, as his contemporaries and predecessors frequently did.

Of Wyatt as a classical architect it can be said, as of Adam, that all his genius was lavished on the detail and elegance of his interiors and far less was shown by his exteriors. His elevations were generally plain to the point of sternness or dullness. Even his contemporaries were conscious of this. C. F. Cockerell said to Farington in 1798 that 'the finishing and decorations of Wyatt are generally beautiful, but his outside designs are blocks of stone'.[2] This is the more extraordinary in view of the great feeling for scenic effects which Wyatt displayed in some of his Gothic houses. It was almost as if he rigorously excluded scenic considerations from his classical work as being suited only to romantic conceptions.

[1]*Farington Diary*, 22nd Dec. 1798.
[2]*Ibid.*, 10th Nov. 1798.

In the alteration and adaptation of existing houses he showed great ingenuity. William Porden, who had been his pupil, said of him that, though he had 'expansion of mind',[1] he had 'great address in inventing and much resource in contriving alterations'.[1]

It is however his interior work that constitutes his chief speciality and claim to fame in the purely classical sphere. It was with a building having virtually no visible exterior, the Pantheon, that he made his reputation. His subsequent career did not prove false to this beginning. His finest rooms are as beautiful as Adam's in detailed invention, delicacy of design, vivid colouring and graceful planning. The respective merits of the taste of any particular period are largely a matter of opinion. But there is a good case for maintaining that the period and style of interior decoration associated with Wyatt and Adam in the seventies and eighties of the eighteenth century attained the highest level of beauty ever reached by English interior design.

[1] *Farington Diary*, 26 Dec. 1804.

CHAPTER V

WYATT AT OXFORD AND CAMBRIDGE

(1.) *Oxford*

WYATT had a very extensive connection with Oxford, for he worked there as early as 1773 and as late as 1809 and altogether dealt with seven colleges.

His first commission came from Christ Church. At the beginning of the eighteenth century the College had erected the stately Peckwater Quadrangle and the Library which formed its south side. The neighbouring medieval buildings of old Canterbury College on the east were considered quite out of harmony with these new productions and were in any case in poor repair. In 1773 the College received a large gift for their reconstruction from Richard Robinson, Archbishop of Armagh and Primate of Ireland, whose portrait by Reynolds in the Hall is one of the most outstanding in the College's fine collection. The north and east sides of the quadrangle, with the Doric gateway of Burford stone in the centre of the latter, were built between 1773 and 1778. There are two drawings of the elevation of the gate signed by Wyatt in the College Library. One such was shown in the Royal Academy Exhibition in 1780. The south side of the quadrangle followed and was completed by 1783. This was also financed by the Archbishop, at whose wish the accommodation provided was reserved for the use of noblemen and gentlemen commoners. In the following year Wyatt and the Archbishop formed part of a house party at Mrs Montagu's who was a cousin of the Archbishop's. The company discussed a suitable motto for the new gate and decided on—though for what reason is not clear—'The fairest way about is the nearest way home.' The whole quadrangle forms a worthy back entrance to Oxford's most imposing College.

Wyatt must also have carried out some alterations or adaptation at the Deanery at this period. In the Victoria and Albert Museum is an album of Wyatt's drawings which contains a sketch for a Gothic door-

81

way at the Deanery. All the drawings in this album relate to work executed by him at least as early as the eighties.

In 1805 Wyatt was again employed by Christ Church, this time in Gothic style. He erected the staircase leading to the Hall beneath the beautiful mid-seventeenth century fan-tracery which is often cited as the last spontaneous manifestation of Gothic architecture in England. Four years later he reconstructed the lodgings of the Regius Professor of Hebrew and the adjoining rooms in the south west corner of Tom Quadrangle after a fire. Wyatt evidently was drawn towards Christ Church, which had given him his first commission in Oxford, for in 1795 he entered his eldest son, Benjamin Dean, there as an undergraduate. Benjamin however did not do well at Oxford, as he ran up so many debts that he went down at his own wish after two years, without taking a degree.

Wyatt's finest production in Oxford was his second work there: the Radcliffe Observatory, which had been begun by Henry Keene in 1770. Keene died in 1776, and Wyatt completed his work; but he may have been called in earlier. The minutes of the Trustees for March 1773 record that another elevation had been submitted to them, and that Keene was required to proceed no farther with the work. This entry may refer to Wyatt, as he was working at Christ Church at the date. But on the other hand he may not have come upon the scene until 1776, when his name was perhaps suggested by the fact that he succeeded Keene as Surveyor of Westminster Abbey.

The plan of the building had been made at the direction of Thomas Hornsby, the Savilian Professor of Astronomy, who was responsible for inducing the Radcliffe Trustees to erect the Observatory. He projected several rooms for fixed instruments upon the ground floor, a room for study above, and over that an occasional observing room; also a house for the Observer.

The plan of the Observatory comprises a central block and two wings, of which one is connected by a further curved corridor with the Observer's house on the east. The wings are of ground floor height only. The central block contains two storeys and has a semi-circular front on the north and a canted bay projection on the south. Above it rises a tower which is the shape of an irregular octagon. (Plate 38.)

By the time of Keene's death the Observer's house and the ground floor observing rooms were finished. Wyatt adopted the plan with very little alterations, and by 1778 the lecture-room on the first floor was roofed in. By 1777 £10,400 had been spent. Therefore, on Wyatt's appointment as architect the Trustees directed that, for the future, only £1,000 should be spent each year. Hence the protraction of operations until 1794, though the building was half finished in 1776. Wyatt's plans were shown in the Royal Academy of 1780.

The upper storey of the tower was almost certainly of Wyatt's design. Hornsby had planned a tower, and Wyatt chose to make it in imitation of the Tower of the Winds at Athens. Both main fronts are decorated with Coadeware stone plaques, with which Wyatt ornamented many of his buildings. Those above the first floor, which consist of the signs of the Zodiac, and the three larger panels on the bowed front, representing morning, noon and evening, were executed by J. C. F. Rossi, the larger panels being from the designs of Robert Smirke. The eight plaques round the tower, which represented the winds, were the work of John Bacon, as was also the globe surmounting it supported by two Atlas figures.

In 1787 Wyatt was asked for an estimate for fitting up the lecture-room and in 1789 ordered to finish it off, with the staircase and rooms adjoining. In 1788 additions were made to the Observer's house. Four years later the erection of the upper room for occasional observation was ordered, and the finishing touch was put to the exterior when the globe was placed on the roof in 1794.

The ground floor of the building contains a hall and on each side an apsidal-ended room intended for the Observer and his assistant. The hall is an irregular octagon, of which each side is flanked by engaged columns supporting a ribbed ceiling of compartments with a diamond panel in the centre. (Plate 40.) The lecture-room on the first floor, later made into a library, is of very plain design. The principal apartment is the observing room above it. This again is the shape of an irregular octagon, of which the wall-space of the four larger sides is entirely taken up by tripartite windows with engaged columns flanking each of the three lights, the smaller sides each containing a single sash window. There is a gallery round the room, above which is a circular dome with moulded ribs and enrichment both of Coadeware stone. (Plate 39.)

By 1794 the cost was already £27,925; but expenditure continued until 1801, when the total was £31,661. In 1797 Wyatt was directed to provide furniture for the Observatory. This comprised a number of mahogany ladders for telescopes and twenty-four chairs fitted with flaps fixed to their backs for writing-desks and intended for use in the

83

lecture-room. These still exist and are some of the few surviving pieces of furniture known to have been designed by Wyatt.

The Observatory represents the very best of Wyatt's classical work. It combines a close attention to detail, which that style demanded, and an excellent effect *in toto*; and it is one of the finest constructions both of its architect and of the city in which it stands.

The University Observatory having retreated to South Africa, the building is now used as a laboratory attached to the Radcliffe Infirmary on the south. Unfortunately its south front now suffers from the too near approach of utilitarian buildings which form part of the Infirmary, but the bowed front facing the garden still preserves the serene aspect of the days before science had become synonymous with defacement.

In November 1783 Wyatt designed the interior of the Hall and Chapel at Worcester which form part of the main building designed by Dr George Clarke of All Souls forty years or more earlier. Five drawings of the Hall, showing the doorway, the ceiling, the east window and the two side walls, and three of the Chapel, comprising the doorway, the ceiling and the east wall, have been preserved in the College Library. Both buildings are amongst the least interesting of Wyatt's works. The Chapel and to a lesser extent the hall, were altered, not for the better, by William Burges in 1864. The stained glass in the Chapel is in any case so dark that it is almost impossible to see by daylight the detail of the ceiling decoration which was the chief feature of the building.

Wyatt's third important work in Oxford was the Oriel Library. In 1786 the College received an extensive and valuable bequest of books from Lord Leigh of Stoneleigh Abbey and decided to erect a new library to accommodate them, with common-rooms beneath, in what was then called the garden but is now the second quadrangle. An elevation and section dated 1787 and signed by Wyatt are in the College Treasury. According to the rather confused accounts kept by the Provost, John Eveleigh, payments of £141 4s., £70, and £50 respectively were made to Wyatt; and in addition the sum of £191 6s. 'for slate and self'. This refers to a method of roof-slating invented and patented by Wyatt, with which the library was roofed. It consisted of slate slabs over which fillets of slate about $2\frac{1}{2}$-3 inches wide, bedded in putty or cement, were screwed down to prevent the entrance of rain. The regular appearance of this type of roofing gained it some celebrity, but it was soon abandoned owing to the constant dislodgment of the putty in which the slates were fixed. The sums mentioned above, apart

37. Oriel College, Oxford. The Library

38. The Radcliffe Observatory, Oxford
(*Country Life Photograph*)

THE RADCLIFFE
OBSERVATORY,
OXFORD

*(Country Life
Photographs)*

39. The Dome

40. The Hall

from the proportion paid for patent rights, no doubt represented Wyatt's usual commission of 5 per cent on the total outlay. He was also paid the sum of £20 for work done in the Provost's house at this time.

The Library at Oriel is a simple dignified building of fine proportions. Even if it is not 'the most perfect piece of architecture in Oxford'[1] as one contemporary called it, it is certainly one of the best additions made to the architecture of the city during the eighteenth century. The front has a rusticated ground floor with five round-headed windows set in arcading and a similar doorway at each end. This ground floor forms a podium on which stand eight engaged Ionic columns rising the whole height of the building above to support the entablature. The whole front is faced with various kinds of Cotswold stone which have worn extremely well in comparison with Wyatt's contemporary Canterbury Quadrangle at Christ Church opposite. (Plate 37.)

The interior of the Library is rather plain, as the whole space from floor to ceiling on three sides is occupied by unornamented bookshelves. The east end of the room forms an apse, and almost the only architectural feature of note consists of the two green scagliola columns which separate this apse from the remainder of the room. An iron gallery runs round three sides of the Library about two-thirds of the way up the walls. This leads at the west end to a small room above the main staircase which is known as the Cedar room, though it is actually panelled in oak. There is an oral tradition in the College that this panelling comes from the east end of New College Chapel, where Wyatt was working at the time when the Oriel Library was built. The removal and use elsewhere of such fittings is certainly something which is not entirely out of character with Wyatt, in view of his similar actions in cathedrals.

Wyatt did not, as at the Radcliffe Observatory, design any furniture for the Library at Oriel. The furniture for the common-rooms beneath was not bought until 1795. The chimney-piece in the east common-room was designed by Richard Westmacott and cost £48 5s. 2d.

The remainder of Wyatt's work at Oxford was of less importance than the three buildings already mentioned and in some cases was, by modern standards, not too creditable to him. In 1779-1780 he redecorated the interior of the Library at Brasenose College and inserted a coved ceiling. In 1789 he remodelled the Library at New College, now called the Old Library, with the Upper Library above it. At the same time he restored the east end of the Chapel there, placed

[1]James Dallaway, *Anecdotes of the Arts in England*.

canopies over the pews and removed the old hammer-beam roof, replacing it with a plaster ceiling. This was taken out by Sir Gilbert Scott in 1877-81. The Hall received the same treatment and was similarly altered by Scott in 1865.

The next College to receive Wyatt's attention was Merton, where he rebuilt the Hall in 1790-4. His work here was once again obliterated by Sir Gilbert Scott in 1872-4. In 1792 Balliol underwent a similar redecoration of the Old Library and a reconstruction of the Old Hall (now the Library).

Lastly in 1792 Wyatt tackled Magdalen College. Together with a builder named Pears who was connected with nearly all Wyatt's Oxford work, he applied the same treatment as at New College, removing the old roofs of the Hall and Chapel and substituting plaster ceilings. He also made a design for a new reredos in the chapel that was not executed. But this was not all the damage that was intended. He found the Cloister Quadrangle to be in very bad condition and planned to pull down the north side and open it out into a wider quadrangle of the width of the New Buildings but not actually connected with them. These were not quite on the same axis as the Cloister Quadrangle, so that the south side of the new extension would have had two window-bays on the east of the old quad and seven window-bays on the west. A drawing of what was intended, signed by Wyatt and dated 1791, which was exhibited in the Royal Academy of 1795, has been preserved in the College Library. (Plate 42.) The new Gothic work was to have been very similar to the old with cloisters occupying the whole of the ground floor, but with thinner buttresses and without the heraldic beasts which are one of the chief features of William of Waynflete's buildings. In the centre of each new section of the north and south sides was placed a tower of four storeys with a gateway and an oriel window above not unlike the old Founder's Tower but flanked by a single window-bay of three storeys in height. At the same time Wyatt made alternative designs for a new main gateway to the College west of the Founder's Tower.

The grandiose scheme however was never executed. In April 1795 Wyatt wrote to Dr Routh, the President: 'I like the idea which has been suggested of taking down the old Quadrangle very much. It is in a very bad state and extremely inconvenient. I am not afraid of undertaking to form a design that shall be perfectly consistent with the Hall, Chapel and Tower. The new buildings will have a good effect by being totally detached, and I cannot conceive other objection than the present inconvenience of not having a covered way to the Hall and Chapel.'

This was the second time in the century that the old buildings of the College had been potentially swept away by adventurous architects whose enterprise was greater than their respect for antiquity. But in each case they were balked by lack of funds. So, in spite of himself Wyatt was saved from adding to the list of his archaeological crimes.

At some period fairly late in Wyatt's life, probably about 1805, there was some question of his doing work at Corpus Christi College. He made a design for the refacement of the south side of the front quadrangle, which is now in the Bodleian Library. But this does not seem to have come to anything. This was the last of his Oxford schemes.

(2.) *Cambridge*

As a contrast to all this work carried out at Oxford, there neither is, nor was, any building of Wyatt's construction or alteration in Cambridge. This is particularly interesting in view of the fact that he is known to have made several designs which were never carried out.

Wyatt's first potential commission was for the construction of Downing College which at the end of the eighteenth century was just emerging into existence under the terms of the will of Sir George Downing who died in 1749. But the college was not actually a legal entity at the time when Wyatt was first called in.

A rough sketch of a plan and elevation for Downing, together with a note in Wyatt's handwriting dated 10th July 1783 setting out the composition of the College, recently came to light in an album of drawings by Wyatt which is now in the possession of the Vicomte de Noailles in Paris. The note is as follows: 'Downing College to consist of —a Master's Lodge to be a complete dwelling wt. a good Library Dining Room and Drawing Room abt. 20 x 30 or rather less—3 Professors 4 rooms each 12 Fellows 3 Rooms each and fourth large enough for a bed—a Hall, Common Room, Library Chapel observatory and Kitchen, Buttery etc. Lodgings for a Cook, Butler Gardiner [*sic*] etc. And 2 sets of spare Rooms[1] Lodgings for Strangers, consisting of 2 Rooms each and a Servts. Room—Porter's Lodge.' The plan of the College showed a court 130 or 160 feet square with a cloister or arcade all round it. The west side or entrance front was occupied by Fellows' lodgings or guest rooms, the south side entirely by domestic offices and the north side facing the garden by the Master's lodgings and more

[1]The word 'Rooms' is crossed out in the manuscript.

87

Fellows' rooms. The principal front was the east side facing the lodge. This was to contain the Library, Chapel and Hall. The Chapel was in the centre and took the shape of a Greek cross with porticoes projecting into the court and on the outer side. A covered passage joined it to the Library and Hall on each side.

The sketch of the elevation does not differ greatly from the finished drawings signed by Wyatt which were acquired by the Royal Institute of British Architects in 1937 and were reproduced in the Journal of the Institute for the 17th October 1938. These drawings show the proposed buildings from different angles and only differ in design as to certain details of the tower and cupola in the centre of the front. But Wyatt actually prepared and submitted alternative versions for the College. These differed in size only. One comprised a complete court with flanking wings on each side and the other a courtyard of three sides only, open on the fourth side. Both were in Roman Doric style, George III having recommended that the building should not be Gothic. The entrance front had a gateway in the centre not unlike Canterbury Gate, Christ Church, Oxford, and pavilions at each end of higher elevation than the remainder with Doric pilasters and either small saucer domes or hipped roofs. But the principal elevation was that of the side facing what is marked in the sketch plan as the Bowling Green. In the centre was a Doric portico with pediment projecting as on the inner side of the court. Above this was a heavy square tower with a smaller round or octagonal cupola set back within this. The design of this tower and cupola differs slightly in the two finished drawings. The flanking portions to the width of the court were much the same as on the entrance front, except that the Hall (and possibly also the Library, though this cannot be seen in the sketch) had round-headed windows rising the whole height of the building with Doric pilasters flanking them. Then, beyond the width of the court, this side of the building was continued in the finished drawings to the extent of ten window-bays of similar design to form the letter L on each side of the main court. (Plate 41.)

Wyatt was not officially appointed architect to the College until 1800, the same year when the Master and Fellows were chosen. He then made a report which speaks of the accommodation to be provided as for 'A Master—Two Professors—Sixteen Fellows and from sixteen to twenty Undergraduates; with a Chapel Library and Hall; Bursary, Muniment Room, Common Room, etc. etc.' The total cost of the building he calculated would be £60,000, including £10,000 for the ornamental parts. The whole would take four or five years to build. Wyatt urged strongly that a site for the College might be found opposite some of the colleges on the river, as he would not there be cramped for space, and might construct four fine façades to a court 250 feet square. As this would have made communication with the town difficult, he was forced to be content with the site actually employed.

Francis Annesley, the Master, passed on Wyatt's plans in 1804 to Thomas Hope, the antiquarian and architectural critic, that he might give his opinion of them. The latter was delivered in a pamphlet printed in the form of a letter to the Master.

'I cannot help repeating that, where, with the estimate given in, such a structure may be produced as would become a lasting ornament to the country, I should be grieved, grieved to the heart to see such a pile arise as . . . I am loth to conclude the sentence. And this would be the case with the material defects I have pointed out, and many lesser ones which I will pass over in silence. I do not see in it one striking feature, one eminent beauty. Neither elevations nor sections convey a single spark of genius to make up for the many faults. Everything in them is trite, commonplace, nay often vulgar. . . .

'The portico is that of the Pantheon in Oxford Street, and however much credit I am willing to give the architect of that temple of pleasure for the inside thereof, though borrowed from a very different kind of temple, consecrated by the Emperor Justinian to Divine Wisdom, yet I much doubt that a man of taste would ever quote its outside portico as one of the fine architectonic productions of our time: why then should the same architect so many years afterwards, not satisfied with repeating its obsolete form in a chapel on the road to Highgate, replicate the same in a most important addition to one of the finest universities of Great Britain? . . .

'It is time that those who make it their business to adorn its' [England's] 'cities and plains, learn their business. It is time to revert to the fundamental principles of an art, the practice of which affords them the yearly means of converting into bricks and stucco so many of its millions.'[1]

Hope's letter throughout is written in a style of egotistical bombast and utter conviction that the writer is the sole man living who possesses either taste or ability. But the letter had little relation to the merits or demerits of Wyatt's design, as Hope so loathed what he called 'the degraded architecture of the Romans' that it is clear than any building

[1]Thomas Hope, *Observations on Wyatt's Plans for Downing College.*

in Roman Doric style would have been ruled out by him from the start.

In spite of its absurdities, this pamphlet undoubtedly succeeded in depriving Wyatt of the commission. The College minutes say nothing of the merits and demerits of his designs; but they do record that these, together with his estimate, were laid before a Master in Chancery, who required an alternative to be submitted by another architect. This was accordingly done by James Byfield. Other designs and estimates were afterwards voluntarily drawn up and offered to the College by William Wilkins, Junior Fellow of Gonville and Caius College, and by two further architects, Francis Sandys and Lewis Wyatt. After being considered by the College, these were also submitted to a Master in Chancery. Those of Wilkins were selected and executed. Wyatt thus lost his first opportunity of building in Cambridge.

Wyatt not unnaturally bore Hope a strong grudge arising out of this fact and prevented him being invited to the Royal Academy Banquet in 1804.

It is interesting to note that, in addition to the three architects whose plans were submitted to a Master in Chancery, William Porden apparently made full designs for building Downing College. These have survived and are now in the Library of the Royal Institute of British Architects. They are in Perpendicular style and had an interesting plan. The residential part of the College formed two large blocks facing each other, each the shape of a letter E without the centre stroke. Between them was to have been a building with the ground plan of a cross which comprised the Chapel with the Hall and Library making the transverse pieces of the cross on each side of it.

Wyatt's second potential commission at Cambridge was from King's. The front court at that period consisted only of the Chapel on the north and the Gibbs Building on the east side. Various plans had been made at intervals during the eighteenth century for the completion of this court but none of them had been carried out, and the south and east sides were still open. Wyatt's commission was to fill in these sides. He exhibited two designs in the Royal Academy of 1796 and a third in the following year. The College still possesses several of his drawings.

The south side was to contain common-rooms, a bursary, a muniment room, a kitchen and offices. At its west end was a building intended to balance the Chapel on the north side of the court and almost exactly copied from it but of slightly lower elevation, about half the length and without the tall turrets at each end. The remainder of the new building was to have had a Tudor Gothic elevation of three

90

storeys and fourteen windows with a castellated parapet above. At the east end facing Trumpington Street was to have been a block continuous with the main north front but separately treated from it in that at its four angles were tall octagonal buttresses. Along the inner face of the whole side except the extreme west end was to have been a projecting cloister with unglazed windows having obtusely pointed heads and eight lights. The south front of this side of the court would have had a central bay.

For the east side of the court facing Trumpington Street alternative schemes were provided. One of these was for a screen not unlike that actually erected by Wilkins in 1822. The other comprised a low two-storeyed building with a taller gateway in the centre flanked by octagonal buttresses carried up to crocketed pinnacles.[1] In either case the cloister of the south side would have been continued round to the chapel behind this façade.

Wyatt did not propose, as Wilkins later did, to gothicise the Gibbs Building on the west side of the court. His designs were not however more fortunate in their reception than those of Hawksmoor or Adam had been earlier in the century. None of them was ever executed. On the 22nd January 1796 the College voted Wyatt £200 for his trouble and as a retaining fee for his future services, but the College accounts do not show any trace that this sum was ever paid to him. Why the plans were never carried out has not been explained. Thus vanished Wyatt's second opportunity of composition in Cambridge.

[1]The former was reproduced in the *Architect and Building News* of the 23rd June 1933, the latter in *Country Life* of the 24th Nov. 1950.

CHAPTER VI

THE RELATIONS OF WYATT AND THE BROTHERS ADAM

WHAT were the relations of James Wyatt and the brothers Adam?

Robert Adam returned from Italy in 1758, and his first dated work occurs in the following year. The brothers very soon became fashionable and for twelve or fourteen years practised the style which is now called by their name without either rivalry or imitation. In fact Sir William Chambers and Sir Robert Taylor were the only two architects who provided any competition whatever against them.

Then suddenly in 1770 to 1772 came a young man of twenty-four to twenty-six, who with a single work became the rage of the fashionable world; and to the indignation of the Adam brothers this same work was executed in a style which they had come to believe their exclusive property. Robert Adam had been thirty when he began to attract attention, and he had achieved fame gradually. James Wyatt was twenty-four when appointed architect of the Pantheon and by this single commission leapt into the most prominent place in his profession. Though Robert Adam still continued until his death in 1794 to receive all the employment that he required or could desire, yet at least he was forced to share with the newcomer in a general way the fashionable practice of architecture in England—for he appears to have kept Scotland very much as a close preserve—and more particularly the employment of the style which he himself executed. The satisfaction which is one of the necessary concomitants of monopoly must have been lost, and his resentment of the intrusion is very understandable.

In 1773 appeared the first part of *The Works in Architecture* by the brothers Adam, to which was attached the extremely self-eulogizing preface which Horace Walpole considered to contain a charge of plagiarism against Wyatt. As Walpole knew both persons concerned, he was in a position which enabled him to understand their words and deeds better than others; and in view of the fact that the book was published so soon after Wyatt's appearance on the scene, the issuing of it in its entirety, and not only a few phrases of the preface, may have been motivated by a desire to counteract the new force working against the Adam influence.

But there was almost certainly no specific accusation in the book with regard to anything more definite than the general style. Hunt[1] relates, without crediting the tale, that a certain nobleman reported to the King that, before leaving England, Wyatt had been employed as a clerk in the office of the brothers Adam. He had thence pirated the design of the Pantheon, and slunk clandestinely away to Italy. By this story the King was prevented from noticing Wyatt until he was informed of its falsity by Richard Dalton. The reason assigned to the whispering of the nobleman was a special interest in the speculations of the Adams, or more likely, thought Hunt, that he was himself deceived. There was no foundation whatever for such a rumour. Wyatt was only fourteen when he left England and could hardly have been in any office before that age; in addition to which it is known that when he visited Italy he accompanied the Earl of Northampton. The most probable explanation is that no such rumour was ever spread.

All that can be said, then, is that the Adams were, quite naturally, jealous of Wyatt as an interloper and deliberately inserted in the preface of their book, as a place where it would receive considerable notoriety, an implication of imitation—for it cannot be called anything stronger—against him, in the hopes that it would deflect back to them some of the patronage and prestige that they felt that they had lost.

Mr James Lees-Milne in his book *The Age of Adam* says that there is no apparent authority for assuming that the Adams were jealous of Wyatt as an interloper. But I still think that, Wyatt being so much their most formidable competitor, the fact that their *Works in Architecture* appeared in 1773, immediately after the opening of the Pantheon, in itself points to the fact that Adam was thinking principally of Wyatt when he complained of his innovations being copied by other architects. This is greatly strengthened by Horace Walpole's remark that Adam in his preface 'seems to tax Wyatt with stealing from him',[2] but would still be the case even without this.

At some period after the publication of the first instalment of *The Works in Architecture* there appeared under the pseudonym of 'Roger Shanhagan, Gent.' a pamphlet entitled *The Exhibition; or a Second Anticipation, being Remarks upon the Principal Works to be Exhibited*

[1]T. F. Hunt, *Archittetura Campestre*.
[2]Walpole to The Rev. William Mason, 29 July 1773.

Next Month at the Royal Academy. This was really written by Robert Smirke at the period when he was a pupil of Wyatt's, though unfortunately it is undated. Very little can be gathered from the comparison of the list of works criticized in it and the catalogues of the Academy. A view of Wynnstay in Denbighshire was however exhibited by Wyatt in 1785 and in 1788; so perhaps the pamphlet was composed in one of those years? All that portion of it which concerns Wyatt is a covert attack upon Robert Adam and an attempt to prove the superiority of his rival. It would justify a little quotation.

'Mr Wyatt seems to be the only architect who knows the full value of columns. When he is not confined by circumstances, we seldom see them in his buildings elevated upon high basements or ranged order upon order, and never do they lose their effect in a crowd of embellishments. They are always the first objects which catch our attention, and always appear to be usefully employed. We must likewise praise him for his management of windows. . . . These and other excellencies might justify me if I placed this artist the first of his profession, but he also claims our praises for his contrivance and for his taste in decorating private apartments. . . . In all the works of Mr Wyatt, the style of the interior is totally different from that of the exterior. On the outside he is simple, plain, and bold; within light, fanciful and elegant. . . . In the decoration of private apartments he gives full liberty to his elegant fancy, and amuses the eye with every vanity of form, proportion, and colour, that by harmony and contrast can give pleasure. His ornaments are never of inelegant shapes, nor lavished with vulgar prodigality, nor too minute to be seen, nor so predominant as to engross our attention. We are never pained by lines violently contrasted, nor perplexed by a harsh opposition of glaring and discordant colours, but a timely repetition of the same form preserves variety from confusion, and one mild prevailing colour softens every brighter tint into its own sweetness.'[1]

This all sounds very much like special pleading, and in spite of Smirke's tribute, it is unnecessary, even if it were possible, to attempt to prove the superiority of Wyatt to Adam. Both men practised the style common to them in a way which pleased their contemporaries, and each had his admirers. Walpole, though he had been an admirer of Adam, came to prefer Wyatt's work. All those who employed Adam, and many others besides, no doubt thought him superior. But, although he was a great architect, he was probably not such a great architect

[1] Roger Shanhagan, *The Exhibition.*

94

as he himself would have liked to have people believe. He spent several years abroad, drawing and measuring the extant examples of the architecture of antiquity and studying the works of Piranesi and others which appeared between 1740 and 1778. When he returned to England his actual achievement was to apply this store of knowledge to the interior decoration of town and country houses.

Exactly the same is true of Wyatt. He spent six years in Italy, drawing, measuring and studying the same buildings and works. In exactly the same way as Adam, we are told that he rejected the Italian style for the simplicity of the Roman and returned to England with a serious acquaintance of ancient architecture and a portfolio of drawings.

Whether he returned with the definite intention of applying what he had learnt to domestic English architecture, or whether he came to this resolution during his two years of apparent unemployment at home when he saw with what success the Adams were working, it is impossible to say. The latter would certainly give a much greater Adam flavour to Wyatt's work. But this was of much too high a quality to be a mere copy; and in either case, the point to grasp is that both men went to the same quarry for the origin of their work. Adam was the first to introduce the style into this country, and for that reason, and also because he devoted his whole life to its interpretation, it is rightly called 'the Adam style'. Wyatt came later into the field, and towards the end of his life his classical work was influenced by the Greek revival. He also gave a very considerable proportion of his attention to serious Gothic work, in which Adam indulged very little. So he is to a lesser extent identified with the style than Adam was.

No doubt each of them practised it with his own particular peculiarities, and an experienced critic of the work of both can possibly distinguish one from the other. But it is a mistake to say that all work unassigned to any definite architect which is below the standard that Adam usually produced must therefore come from the hand of Wyatt. As large numbers of Adam's designs have survived and are to be seen in Sir John Soane's Museum, while comparatively few of Wyatt's are known to exist, it is very likely that unassigned work does belong to the latter. But to attribute to him all that is of an inferior standard, just because of its inferiority, is to accept without examination an appreciation of him which has been handed down for generations and is not necessarily correct.

There is one very curious entry in the *Farington Diary* which concerns this matter of the connection between the Adams and Wyatt. On 4th

January 1804 Farington noted, on the authority of Benjamin West, that Wyatt had told the King that 'there had been no regular architecture since Sir William Chambers—that when he came from Italy he found the public taste corrupted by the Adams and he was obliged to comply with it'.[1]

There is no satisfactory explanation of this remark. In the first place, if Wyatt really admired the rather heavy type of house that Chambers favoured, it is extraordinary that throughout the forty-three years of his practice as an architect he did not build more in this style himself. Secondly when in 1783—ten years after the opening of the Pantheon—he constructed his own house in Foley Place, which he occupied for thirty years, it was in the style which, according to this remark, he professed to despise that he designed it. It is quite inconceivable that he should have done so if this really was his opinion. It should be remembered that the remark was not noted by Farington until 1804, by which time Robert Adam had been dead ten years and Wyatt himself was no longer designing houses in his early manner. It possibly represented a reaction from the taste which had only recently gone out of fashion. The repudiation may too have been something in the nature of a reply to the challenging and boastful charges of the Adams. It is also possible that the statement became a little twisted in the process of passing through several hands before it reached Farington's journal; for Wyatt told the King, who told West, who told Farington. Apart from these possibilities the remark just cannot be explained at all.

There is one further consideration dealing with the general problem. The Adam brothers' second claim to notoriety lay in the fact that they were the first English architects who continually executed designs of furniture and even small details such as inkstands and candelabra. Their predecessors had occasionally laboured at such accessories: they made a speciality of them. The number of cases in which Wyatt designed furniture for houses that can definitely be identified is very small—in fact only Heveningham Hall, Suffolk, and the Radcliffe Observatory, Oxford. But an album of drawings of furniture recently came to light at the Hotel des Ventes at Paris which can certainly be assigned to Wyatt. The album is now in the possession of the Vicomte de Noailles. In addition to wall panels and permanent fittings of that kind, it contains designs for urns, vases, candelabra (Plate 43), grates, bracket clocks, a stool, a chair in what might be called the Chippendale

[1] *Farington Diary*, 4 Jan. 1804.

manner, an occasional table, settees, and a wall-mirror. One of the most interesting is for a bracket clock with three different designs for the base arranged on flaps that can be turned back. (Plate 44.) The only drawing which bears any clue as to the house or client for which or for whom it was made is of a wall-mirror, on which the words 'Wm. Drakes Esq., Grosvenor Sqre.' are written in pencil. The existence of these sketches shows that Wyatt must have designed much more furniture than is generally supposed. No doubt much of it was dispersed when the houses for which it was made passed out of the ownership of their original families, and it cannot on that account now be identified. But Wyatt cannot have specialised in furniture design to anything like the extent that the Adams did.

The same album also contains a number of drawings of tombs and memorial wall tablets. No doubt Wyatt received commissions for several of these. But besides the monument to Thomas Gray at Stoke Poges only six of Wyatt's memorials have been identified.

Circumstances made Wyatt necessarily less attentive and thorough than the Adams. He was one, instead of four. His practice was large, and he was not methodically minded. He did not labour at designs but left others to work them out. The sphere of activity of his sub-ordinates must therefore have been larger.

So it would seem that the Adam brothers' greatest point of superiority lies in their preoccupation with general detail. Wyatt was, as a rule, too busy and too erratic to give time to this, though, when he did, he was as successful as anyone could wish. They really were geniuses in infinite painstaking: he in brilliant ideas. Unfortunately for his reputation, in the style in which they all worked the former capacity was bound to lead to greater success.

The work of the Adams and of Wyatt meets in a curious way in one room in England. This is in the Library at Shardeloes, Buckinghamshire. This house had been built by Stiff Leadbitter in 1758 for the William Drake of Grosvenor Square, for whom the design of the wall-mirror in the Vicomte de Noailles' album was made. The majority of the interior decoration at Shardeloes was carried out by Adam between 1751 and 1766. This included the library. Drawings of the bookcases, chimney-piece and ceiling have been preserved in Sir John Soane's Museum. The design for the ceiling was actually executed by the stuccoist, Joseph Rose. The 'Shardeloes Papers', edited by Mr G. Eland, show that Wyatt also worked in the house between 1773 and 1775. One of Wyatt's accounts preserved in the muniments of the house proves that he employed Biagio Rebecca to paint the still extant green and white frieze in imitation of bas-relief round the top of the Library walls, for which Rebecca was paid fifty guineas and Wyatt his usual 5 per cent of the cost of the work executed. This combination in one room of work designed by both Adam and Wyatt must make the Shardeloes Library one of the most interesting rooms in England, perhaps unique.

William Drake seems to have been quite unable to make up his mind whether he preferred Adam or Wyatt as an artist, since in 1782 he employed Adam again and a few years later Wyatt once more. In 1785-6 the latter designed a pavilion for the pond garden at Shardeloes, in 1789 some garden houses, none of which survive, and possibly also the orangery which still stands. Another design, probably never carried out, which can be attributed to Wyatt is a sketch for a Gothic tower intended to act as a sheep-fold. He also, in 1779, planned alterations for William Drake to another house named Stainfield which the latter owned and which was burned down at the end of the century. He carried out work too in Drake's house in Grosvenor Square, though the number of this house has not been identified. Nor was the nature of the work specified in the account.

Of the personal relations of Wyatt and the Adams we know next to nothing. Wyatt is reported to have said that in early life he had never spoken to any one of them. By 1789 they must have met, as in that year he and Robert Adam were associated together on the committee of architects which reported upon the state of the buildings at Westminster. In 1791 Wyatt, together with George Dance, Henry Holland, and S. P. Cockerell, agreed upon the names of those whom they should ask to become foundation members of the Architects' Club. These included that of Robert Adam. We must conclude, therefore, that by this period, which for Adam was the end of his life, the jealousy of the latter and the assumed scorn of the former had been softened down into some sort of mutual respect.

CHAPTER VII

THE RESTORATION OF CATHEDRALS

(1.) *Lichfield*

THE ten years from 1787 to 1797 form the intensive period into which is concentrated all the ecclesiastical restoration ever executed by Wyatt, save at Westminster and Windsor. The cathedral at Lichfield in his native Staffordshire was the first in which the work planned by him was actually carried out and to some extent serves as the model for all his treatment of English cathedrals.

As Wyatt was seldom on the spot, he engaged a Mr Potter to act as superintendent of the repairs in his absence. This gentleman was succeeded in his post by his son who was thus obviously in a position to know the real nature of Wyatt's work at Lichfield and to speak authoritatively about it. This second Mr Potter, in reply to certain attacks upon Wyatt made in *The Staffordshire Advertiser* of 1861, contributed a letter dated 5th December stating the official view of the matter; and one cannot do better, when considering the alterations at Lichfield, than quote frequently from this letter which is printed in Hewitt's *Handbook to Lichfield Cathedral*.

First of all it is essential to give a rather dull list of the actual alterations undertaken by Wyatt. He partly rebuilt the two spires; erected the two great buttresses of the south transept; raised the roofs of the external aisles; took down five divisions of the stone roof of the nave and replaced them with plaster; restored the doors and windows throughout; renovated the floor with grey and white marble paved lozengy; replaced broken columns, capitals, and bases, and restored their mutilated parts; scraped the walls and roof and coloured them stone colour; new glazed the windows; designed the pulpit, reading desk, and pews, and renewed the appearance of the stalls; lastly he carried out certain changes in the choir.

These latter were: to unite the choir and Lady chapel by pulling down the reredos erected in 1677, to block up the four easternmost arches of the choir, north and south, which alone were still open, by

99

erecting a plain walled screen flush with the inner arches of the choir; and to transfer the high altar to the end of the Lady chapel.

These alterations in the choir caused far the largest storm of criticism. But it happens that we have definite proof that Wyatt was not responsible for them. Stebbing Shaw, in his *History of Staffordshire*, tells us that before 1788 the inhabitants of the close had, after morning prayers, to proceed to the nave where they met the citizens of the place, who had come to hear the sermon. When the sermon was ended, all intending communicants had to return again to the choir to receive the Sacrament. 'This circumstance was attended with many inconveniences; it was therefore thought better to enlarge the choir to its present uncommon length' [1798] 'by throwing it and St. Mary's Chapel into one.'[1]

This step was taken by the definite orders of the Dean and Chapter to avoid this awkward procession and retrogression. The choir was not large enough to hold the congregation, and no one seems to have thought of transferring the clergy to the nave. So there was no other solution but the inclusion of the Lady chapel in the choir.

This necessitated the removal of the reredos. As this was put up in 1677, it was classical in design; consequently, in 1788, there was no one who could be found to defend its existence in a Gothic church. Underneath it, however, was discovered the original screen erected by the executors of Walter de Langton in 1321. It had been much mutilated and defaced during the Civil War; hence the imposition of the second screen. Both were removed. Mr Potter says: 'Mr Wyatt was opposed to the removal of the original: nay, he was most ardent for its restoration.'[2] Certainly his restoration of it would have pleased those who criticized its destruction very little better; but it is fair to notice that Wyatt did not wish to sweep it away. The need for accommodation proved stronger, and the screen was taken down. Wyatt then did what he considered second best to its restoration where it was, by repairing the decay with Roman cement, and applying part to form a new altarpiece and part to form a new organ screen.

As regards the walling up of the choir Mr Potter wrote: 'The most objectionable part, perhaps, of the alterations in this portion of the edifice consisted in building up the pier arches, thus separating the aisles from the choir, and pewing the vacant spaces on either side between the stalls and the lady chapel. I cannot say how much Mr Wyatt was

[1]Stebbing Shaw, *History of Staffordshire*.
[2]Letter to *Staffordshire Advertiser*, 5 Dec. 1861.

41. Design for Downing College, Cambridge
(*Reproduced by kind permission of the Royal Institute of British Architects*)

42. Magdalen College, Oxford. Design for the enlargement of the Cloister
Quadrangle
(*Reproduced by kind permission of the College*)

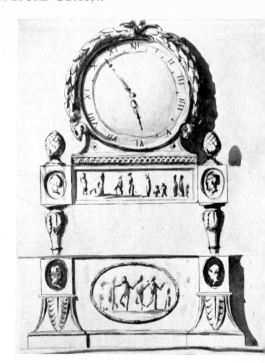

43. Sketch for a Candelabrum
(*Reproduced by kind permission of the Vicomte de Noailles*)

44. Sketch for a clock with three different versions for the base
(*Reproduced by kind permission of the Vicomte de Noailles*)

45. Candelabrum in the dining-room at Heveningham Hall
(*Country Life Photograph*)

46. Design for a day-bed at Heveningham Hall
(*Reproduced by kind permission of the Hon. Andrew Vanneck*)

responsible for the latter, but I do know for a fact that he was strenuously opposed to the former.'[1] This erection of a side wall was an essential portion of the whole scheme and no architectural blunder of Wyatt's or of anyone else's; nor aimed at the enhancement of the length of the church. It was executed by the direct order of the Dean and Chapter with the object, as the Verger told Richard Gough in 1800, of giving the congregation a reasonable degree of warmth.

Mr Potter concludes his letter thus: 'Wyatt may have been guilty of errors of judgement, or his taste may not have had the true Gothic ring' [1861!]; 'but let us not continue to abuse him for the deeds of others. *De mortuis nil nisi verum.*'[1]

One of the necessary results of these changes in the choir, the removal of the pews from the nave, very much pleased Richard Gough when he visited the cathedral in 1800. In the few cases in which a similar effect can now be seen, such as Ely, the spaciousness of the church is certainly shown up to the best advantage in the manner intended by the medieval builders.

The two buttresses put up to strengthen the south transept were much criticized by contemporaries. One correspondent of *The Gentleman's Magazine*[2] went as far as to suggest that they should support a statue of the architect and of the person who ordered their erection (presumably the Dean, but the writer was too timid to say so!); in order that posterity might see who was responsible for such monstrosities. Yet these buttresses were of the same size as those which they replaced and were imposed upon the old foundations. Their colour was offensive, but this has been toned down by exposure.

The substitution of plaster for stonework in five groins of the nave was necessary, as the clerestory walls appeared to be unable to bear the weight they had to sustain. As they showed evident signs of yielding considerably from the great lateral pressure, there was no remedy but to replace the stonework with lath and plaster. A more substantial restoration would have required the rebuilding of the clerestory walls. What was actually done was a wretched alternative, but the funds were insufficient for any more satisfactory measure.

There was in fact no fund adequate to the ordinary repair of the cathedral. The Dean and Chapter were forced to have recourse to an appeal to the clergy of the diocese after a precedent set by Bishop Hacket in 1660. £5,200 was subscribed; and as the amount of the

[1]Letter to *Staffordshire Advertiser*, 5 Dec. 1861.
[2]'W.W.', 1 Jan. 1796, Vol. 66, Pt. 1, p.98.

estimate was £5,950, the Dean and Chapter lent £1,800 as a debt upon the fabric. Of the estimated £5,950 Wyatt probably received five per cent, which was his normal charge. A correspondent of *The Gentleman's Magazine*, urging that the money would have been better spent in the augmentation of clerical stipends, asks: 'Or would a prelate or dignitary be more reluctant to add £20 per annum to the comfort of a poor brother and his family, than to give £500 or £1,000 in a lump to a whimsical architect who were better employed in keeping things in their places, than in pulling them to pieces, and putting the wretched fragments out of place?'[1]

When the alterations at Lichfield were finished in 1795, Wyatt's friends held that he had made the cathedral 'simply purely Gothic',[2] because every ornament that he had added was taken from some other part of the church. His enemies contended that, instead of restricting himself to one order, as it was then called, of Gothic, or of substituting a new one, 'he has borrowed a bit from one era and a bit from another till he has blended them all in an inconvenient, unpleasing arrangement'.[3] Both were true and were only different ways of saying the same thing.

Probably Wyatt did his best restoration work at Lichfield. In his early work he was less sweeping and he appears to have been closely supervised here. Yet there was plenty of scope, as the cathedral was in a very bad state at the time. It had suffered sadly from the Puritan disorders and had been thoroughly repaired by Bishop Hacket at the Restoration. Since then nothing had been done. Wyatt worked here very thoroughly and seems to have done nothing indefensible for which the blame is his alone. It is interesting to note that one of his most persistent defenders in *The Gentleman's Magazine*, a Mr Robinson, states that the alterations met with 'the unqualified approbation of the late Sir William Chambers, whose place at the Board of Works is so *deservedly* filled by Mr Wyatt'.[4]

(2.) *Salisbury*

At Salisbury Wyatt was called in at the instigation of the Bishop, Shute Barrington. He made a thorough survey of the cathedral, probably in 1787 as in that year he exhibited in the Academy a drawing of an altar-piece and screen 'intended to be executed at Salisbury

[1]'Viator', 21 Oct. 1795. Vol. 65, Pt. II, p.924.
[2]*Gentleman's Magazine*, 9 Dec. 1795, Vol. 65, Pt. II, p.999.
[3]*Ibid.*, 31 Dec. 1795, Vol. 65, Pt. II, p.1074.
[4]*Ibid.*, 16 April 1796, Vol. 66, Pt. I, p.299.

Cathedral'. His estimate was for £4,000. The Bishop, who had just spent several thousands in repairing his palace, contributed £500, leaving the remainder to be found by public subscription. The survey was not submitted to the Dean and Chapter until two years later. On 26th August 1789 the *Chapter Acts Book* records: 'The Lord Bishop of Sarum, having caused the contracts and plans for the Altar Piece and Improvements of the Cathedral Church to be laid before the Chapter, and the same having been inspected and considered, after due Deliberation—Resolved, that this Chapter do approve of and authorize his Lordship to carry the same into execution, viz. to make new Canopies to the Stalls, to build a new Pulpit and Bishop's Throne, to put new iron rails to the Communion, with coping thereon, and set new blue stones to receive same, to put two wainscot Screens across the aisles, to lay blue paving stone in the Lady Chapel, in squares to be cut out of the old grave stones, and enrich the side Walls according to the Drawings, to clean and colour the Church from the east end of the Transept, to clean and varnish the Stalls, to fit up the Morning Chapel, and to make the Screen to the western side of the Organ Loft according to Mr Wyatt's plan. Mr Wyatt having reported the Beam in the Choir to be useless in support of the Building, Resolved and ordered that Mr Wyatt do take it down.'[1]

The major part of this quotation clearly represents the instructions Wyatt received before making his survey, but the incident of the beam shows that Wyatt was just as able to make suggestions of the repairs necessary as either the Bishop or the Chapter to give directions.

Other things were done besides those included in the quotation. The north and south porches were taken down, the south door near the Verger's house stopped up and another opened near the Chapter vestry, the chapels in the transept opened out, and a large number of alterations carried out at the east end of the church.

Again it was the treatment meted out to the part of the church east of the crossing which was most deprecated by critics. The choir and the Lady chapel were thrown into one, as had been done at Lichfield, but without apparently the existence of the cause that gave rise to it in the former instance. For this purpose the reredos was destroyed and the high altar transferred to the far end of the Lady chapel.

The idea of this fusion had not originated with Wyatt at Lichfield and does not seem to have done so either at Salisbury, since in the first place he had planned to fill with tracery the three arches which

[1]*Chapter Acts Book*, 26 Aug. 1789.

separated the choir from the Lady chapel and the chapels on each side of the latter. During the first half of 1788, before Wyatt's plans had been submitted to the Chapter, the Bishop gave them to his friend William Gilpin, Vicar of Boldre in the New Forest, with a request for his comments thereon. Gilpin had made a special study of Gothic architecture from an untechnical point of view in connection with his books about various parts of England 'relative to picturesque beauty' and was considered to be quite an authority on the subject. He was particularly interested in Salisbury as he held the Prebend of Beaminster Seconda in the diocese and had subscribed a whole year's income of his prebend to the restoration fund. Gilpin approved Wyatt's plans with the exception of this insertion of tracery in the arches behind the high altar. He considered that this was 'a nugatory'[1] and 'inharmonious ornament'[1] and 'was destroying a great beauty; for the view of the pillars etc. of St Mary's Chapel through the great arch was both a very beautiful piece of perspective and gave space to the Choir'.[1] As the result of the representations made by Gilpin to the Bishop this proposal was suppressed. Gilpin wrote that 'Wyatt had the candour to be convinced' of the justice of what he had pointed out, and so it looks as if Wyatt then went one better and introduced the plan followed at Lichfield of throwing the choir and Lady chapel into one as being a still more effective way of giving a fine view of the pillars of the Lady chapel through the great arch.

The Lady chapel itself Wyatt reported to be unsafe. In the erection of the chapels on either side of it, buttresses and supports had been removed; in fact Wyatt expressed surprise at the temerity of the builders. Price, in his survey fifty years earlier, had said that the building of tombs into the walls of the Lady chapel had weakened the whole. The demolition of the flanking chapels enabled the walls to be strengthened outside, and the injurious tombs were removed to the nave.

The chapels on either side of the Lady chapel, known as the Hungerford and Beauchamp chapels, have already been referred to. They had been much defaced by the Puritans and, as they were never used, had been suffered by the Chapter to remain unrepaired. Consequently they were reported by Wyatt to be in a very dilapidated and unsafe condition. This was, of course, loudly denied in the usual

[1]Unpublished letter dated 3 July 1788 from the Rev. William Gilpin to the Rev. Clarke, kindly communicated to the Author by Gilpin's great-grandson, the Rev. E. Geoffrey Benson.

manner by John Carter and all the antiquaries. So it is a little difficult to establish the exact truth; but it seems more probable that they were much decayed if they had not been renovated since the Civil War.

Yet they could have been given a new lease of life if they had met with favour in the eyes of the authorities. But the point was that their destruction was welcomed by nearly everybody. Together with two separate porches, they were the only portions of the church not in the same uniform style. The porches were Norman and had been brought from Old Sarum. They too were taken down at this period. But the Hungerford and Beauchamp chapels were Perpendicular additions. The antiquaries regarded them historically, but most of their contemporaries aesthetically. Now already Perpendicular was considered a debased kind of Gothic; and thus the majority of persons welcomed their demolition as the restoration of the pervading pristine harmony, in much the same way as we might now find the aesthetic effect of a church improved by the removal of a Victorian vestry, although a piece of history would vanish with it.

In addition to these considerations, the repair of the chapels would have been exceedingly costly, whereas the sale of their materials would realize a fairly large sum. It was recognized that something had to be done to them. To restore them would have been an additional drain on the funds, to pull them down an additional asset. So the Dean and Chapter needed little support from the architect to resort to the latter. Finally the consent of the descendants of the founders was obtained, and the destruction was decided on.

According to his usual habit, Wyatt united pieces of these chapels in a patchwork screen made to support the new organ given by George III in his capacity of a 'Berkshire country gentleman', Windsor being then in the diocese of Salisbury. The screen which it replaced was contemporary with the cathedral and was only discarded because it was 'so injudiciously situated as to hide the lower part of the pillars'.[1] The substitution aimed at enhancing the lofty spring of the four principal arches of the tower. This was probably the most unjustifiable part of Wyatt's work at Salisbury.

The three chapels situated behind the site of the high altar in 1788 contained nearly all the important tombs of the church. These were now removed and ranged in orderly rows underneath the arches of the nave. The interior of all these tombs was examined, and a few rings and other relics extracted; but remarkably little was found, that of

[1] William Dodsworth, *Guide to Salisbury Cathedral*.

St Osmund being completely empty. These tombs had necessarily to be moved somewhere, and the rearrangement seems now to us a very reasonable and tidy measure.

But that was not how it appeared to contemporaries. They did not regard the effect. It was the sepulchral interference to which they so strongly objected. The eighteenth century found monuments of the utmost sanctity. Without being in any way curious as to design or inscription, these were the object of as much attention, especially from antiquaries, as the building in which they stood; and most guide-books of the period devote a quarter of their text to the minute description of their form and the repetition of their epitaphs. So it is not to be wondered at that these transplantations and 'ghoulish explorations' were anathema to those who held such views, and the architect who directed them a sacrilegious profaner of the dead.

Further, the Lady chapel was repaved with squares cut out of the flat gravestones of unimportant persons, of which the inscriptions were indecipherable. Richard Gough's drawing of the Hungerford chapel before its destruction shows this to have been full of those stone slabs piled up against the wall. Wyatt received all the blame for the supposed uprooting of these stones, but evidently he was not wholly responsible, as many were already out of place, and their employment was another piece of economy.

When attention was turned to the roof of the choir, it was found to be decorated with certain paintings over which a furious controversy raged. The archaeologists maintained that they were coeval with the building, their opponents that a close inspection revealed, beneath them, lines drawn in imitation of brickwork, as could then be seen on the roof of the nave. Richard Gough concurred in the latter view so far as to say that they dated from the end of the fifteenth, rather than from the thirteenth, century. Drawings of them were made for the Society of Antiquaries, and the whole was then effaced; the arches and ribs being coloured like the original stone, the ceilings and walls a little lighter. Whether this measure improved the appearance of the church, as seems very likely, or not, the old decorations were probably worth saving, whatever their age; and one cannot but regret their disappearance.

Salisbury had possessed a campanile contemporary with the cathedral, which stood at the north-west corner of the close. As no repairs had been undertaken on it since the Civil War, it was in a very dilapidated condition, and in 1758 the Chapter ordered the two uppermost stages, the spire and the tower, to be removed, and the remainder finished off neatly. They found it 'neither useful nor ornamental' and so ruinous that it could not be repaired 'without a much greater expense than the present state of the fabric fund will admit of'.[1]

When these, the best parts of the tower, had been removed, the remainder was still less useful or ornamental. It had lost its bells and it blocked the north-west view of the cathedral. Curiously enough, those critics who disliked the removal of the belfry claimed that this was the least interesting view of all; those who favoured it, that it was the most pleasant. On the whole, the demolition of the rump of the tower was regarded with indifference.

In 1787 the Chapter ordered an estimate to be made for the materials of the belfry. This amounted to £846: a proportionately large sum, when compared with the £3,300 acquired by subscription. In March 1790 the clock and bells were removed to the cathedral, the building pulled down, and the materials sold. It is clear that the measure was prompted by financial, rather than aesthetic, considerations; and it is certain that Wyatt was not responsible for the destruction, although it has been often laid to his charge.

There are other instances from the same cathedral and at the same period of objects being sold to relieve the strain on the funds. In November 1791 and May 1792 the lead from the roof of the cloisters was sold and replaced by slate, according to an estimate of Wyatt's; and the balance was appropriated to the repair of the cloisters. Likewise in December 1792 and in January 1793 the brass eagle and two spare bells were sold for the benefit of the fabric fund.

But nothing similar was true of the glass. The history of its removal is fragmentary, incomplete, and confused. The *Chapter Acts Book* contains several entries with regard to various sections of the cathedral glass, but it always speaks of its transference from one window to another, and not of its destruction. Yet C. Winston, in a paper, *The Painted Glass of Salisbury*, delivered to the Archaeological Institute in July 1849, says: 'The most woful destruction of painted glass appears to have taken place during Mr Wyatt's "restoration" of the cathedral; when in the words of my informant, whole cartloads of glass, lead, and other rubbish were removed from the nave and transepts, and shot into the town ditch, then in course of being filled up; whilst a good deal of similar rubbish was used to level the ground near the chapter-house.'[2]

[1] *Chapter Acts Book*, Nov. 1758.
[2] *Memoirs of Wiltshire and Salisbury*, July 1849.

Unfortunately Winston does not mention who this authority was; but he does confirm the latter part of the statement by the evidence of one William Rangier, glazier to the cathedral, who dug up the head of a figure and some pieces of painted glass near the chapter-house. The first part has also been substantiated by the discovery of glass on the site of the town ditch. Yet we know that lead was not thrown away, as its value was too well known. Besides this evidence, there exists also the letter of John Berry, glazier to the cathedral, who speaks of beating to pieces 'the fine painted window at Sarum' for the value of the lead.[1] But that was dated 16th June 1786, which was before Wyatt came to Salisbury.

The conclusion of all this is that some glass was destroyed before, and some during, Wyatt's activities at Salisbury. It cannot be proved that he was responsible for the havoc, though most lovers of the cathedral are inwardly convinced that he was. Yet it is only fair to note that a verger of Salisbury has confessed that all bad deeds in the cathedral are attributed to Wyatt, which is wholesale condemnation on the strength of an attributed bad reputation. On the other hand it is equally impossible to prove that Wyatt was not responsible for the destruction. The majority of it happened during his restoration and probably was of his execution. But he was seldom on the spot, and much must have been done without his knowledge and consent. So there is really no satisfactory conclusion at which one can arrive.

Turning from the real or attributed crimes of this architect, we come to consider an improvement for which we owe him much gratitude, little of which has been paid. Thanks to him, there exists no more beautiful close in England than Salisbury. Previously the avenues were indifferent and, in bad weather, impassable; for water off the roof ran into open gutters leading into a large ditch, where it stagnated. Wyatt constructed a large circular underground drain to carry off this water, raised and levelled the whole area of the churchyard, made new gravel walks and removed the gravestones.

The extent of the restorations at Salisbury seems to have been wider than elsewhere; and the criticism aroused was certainly greater, though this was more due to the juxtaposition of monuments than to anything else. Among his contemporaries Wyatt found few defenders. The only important name is that of William Dodsworth, Verger of the cathedral, who has to his credit a history of the see and a guide to the cathedral. The former was really written by Henry Hatcher, a

[1]Fifth Report of Historical MSS. Commission, MSS. of Miss Conway Griffiths.

108

knowledgeable archeologist of the period, from information supplied by Dodsworth; and the latter may have been similarly composed. John Milner and Richard Gough professed to believe that the architectural portions of this were actually written by Wyatt himself. But, as they advance no evidence for their theory, it cannot be entertained.

Generally speaking, how much of what was done at this period was due to the architect, and how much to the Chapter and, in this case, to the Bishop? On 24th August 1789, Horace Walpole wrote to Richard Gough: 'I shall heartily lament with you, Sir, the demolition of those beautiful chapels at Salisbury. I was scandalized long ago at the ruinous state in which they were suffered to remain. . . . I am sorry that I can only regret, not prevent. I do not know the Bishop of Salisbury even by sight, and certainly have no credit to obstruct any of his plans. Should I get a sight of Mr Wyatt, which it is not easy to do, I will remonstrate against the intended alterations; but probably without success, as I do not suppose he has authority enough to interpose effectually: still I will try.'[1] This quotation reveals the subordinate position occupied by the architect. His influence lay in his survey, in which he could and did make suggestions. But after that, he had to do as he was told. Consequently, except in certain cases such as the belfry, where we know the Chapter to have been the sole agent, the blame is bound to be shared between the Chapter, the Bishop, and the architect.

(3.) *Hereford*

The cathedral of Hereford seems to have been in an even worse condition at the end of the eighteenth century than her sisters. In 1786 the tower at the western end of the nave collapsed, crushing the western arches. The Chapter does not appear to have been very solicitous about the deplorable state of their fabric, for Wyatt was not called in to attend to the damage until two years later.

He shortened the extent of the nave by one bay, making thus a completely new west front of his own without a tower. The old Norman clerestory and triforium had been slightly damaged by the fall of the tower. Wyatt most unsuitably rebuilt them in Early English style in imitation of their counterparts at Salisbury, where he was also working at the time. This eighteenth-century imitation accords very ill with the massive Norman arcade beneath it. Wyatt also revaulted the nave and raised the level of the floor.

[1]Walpole to Richard Gough, 24 Aug. 1789.

John Britton strongly reprobates these alterations,[1] whereas he says nothing unfavourable of Wyatt's work at Lichfield and Salisbury; and they are bound to have given the nave rather an eighteenth-century Gothic appearance. But the west front at least had to be rebuilt, and it is almost certain that later generations would not be any more pleased with the result, had the reconstruction been entrusted to anyone else among Wyatt's contemporaries, though some of the latter might have been better satisfied. It was entirely rebuilt a second time by J. Oldrid Scott in 1908.

The great spire was removed from the central tower, and battlements erected with crocketed pinnacles at the angles. The close was levelled, and the gravestones removed, 'in the presence of an assembled multitude, who could not refrain from venting their grief at this outrage offered in a civilized country to the memorials of their relations, many of them erected at no little expense, part of which had been paid for the use of the ground'.[2] The case certainly seems a hard one for the individuals concerned.

The Gentleman's Magazine also tells us that 'Mr Wyatt endeavoured very much to lengthen the choir at Hereford Cathedral, as he has done at Lichfield'[3] and Salisbury. Evidently the authorities forbade it.

When operations were begun upon the nave, the director of the works erected scaffolds from the ground below the groining, instead of suspending them from the timbers above. As a result, when one stone was removed, the whole collapsed, killing three men and injuring five others. Wyatt had wished to take down this roof, rather than allow it to fall down, because it would have been cheaper and easier and because he wished to re-use the stone. But as he was not himself present, he was not able to ensure that this could be safely performed.

Richard Gough was right when he said with pardonable exaggeration: 'But as, if all the critical cases of health were committed to the care of one physician, it would be impossible for him to do justice to, or to save, all; so, when a single architect undertakes every parish church and cathedral in the kingdom, and besides attending to the desperate cases, where immediate help is required, amuses himself with hazarding adventurous criticism in the alterations and new modelling others which, at most, want only new furbishing up, the consequences must be, as in the present case, a neglect of the more important matters.'[4]

[1] *History and Antiquities of the Cathedral of Hereford.*
[2] *Gentleman's Magazine*, 24 June 1797, Vol. 66. Pt. II, p.607.
[3] *Ibid.*, 27 Sept. 1795, Vol. 65, Pt. II, p.785.
[4] *Ibid.*, 5 March 1790, Vol. 60, Pt. I, p.217.

There exists no evidence for assessing the respective responsibility of the Chapter and the architect for the work done at Hereford. The *Chapter Acts Book* contains no reference to Wyatt. We must assume, therefore, that he was called in to perform certain definite repairs, beyond which he was not allowed to go. But the form and design of them must have been entirely his concern; consequently the greater part of the interior of the nave as we see it today is his work.

(4.) *Durham*

When Wyatt was actually called in to attend to the needs of Durham Cathedral is not absolutely certain. *The Dictionary of Architecture* gives 1775 as the date—on what authority I have been unable to discover—but it seems most improbable. The first definite date at which we find him in connection with the cathedral in 1795. The Bishop, Shute Barrington, had been translated hither from Salisbury in 1791. As we know that it was he who introduced Wyatt to Salisbury, it was certainly he who brought Wyatt to Durham at any time between 1791 and 1795. At the same time Wyatt designed for the Bishop the Gothic screen and the inner gateway to the south front of Bishop Auckland Palace.

The whole of the east front of the cathedral was rebuilt at this period and, not being approved, was taken down and again reconstructed. The Perpendicular tracery in the lower windows of this front was removed, and so destructively that the mouldings and panellings were destroyed. The round window in the east gable was replaced by one of new design. All the stained glass was removed from the east windows, on the plea that it made the church too dark, and was allowed to lie in baskets unheeded until in 1818, after much had been stolen, the rest was replaced. As regards the other portions of the cathedral, two or three inches were chiselled away from the outside surface of the walls because they were very worn; the north door was rebuilt, and the porch removed.

A great deal more than this was planned. Wyatt thought of demolishing Bishop Hatfield's tomb with the throne over it and Bishop Neville's reredos, to unite the fragments in an organ screen at the entrance to the choir. He hoped to throw into one the choir and the chapel of the nine altars situated behind it, raising the level of this chapel to that of the choir, and transferring the high altar to the extreme east end. A scheme was also made to superimpose upon the tower an octagonal structure with pinnacles and flying buttresses, which was itself to support a tall spire. None of these projects was realized and all probably received their death-blow in 1796.

At a Chapter meeting on 20th November 1795 it was ordered that the chapter-house, 'being pronounced by Mr Wyatt to be in a ruinous state, be taken down by Mr Morpeth under contract, also that a new room be erected on the same site according to the plan given in by Mr Morpeth'.[1] The demolition took place early in 1796, and thus vanished the only other surviving Norman chapter-house in England besides that of Bristol. The Dean, who afterwards disclaimed any share in the transaction and asserted that he had not even been consulted, was actually present at this meeting.

Carter automatically affirmed that the building was not ruinous at all. His statement cannot be believed because he never allowed that any ancient edifice was in danger of collapse; but it is sufficient to prevent one from putting much faith in the contrary verdict. In all probability, by the phrase 'in a ruinous state', was meant 'in too ruinous a state to be repaired without a much greater expense than the funds could, or the Chapter would, meet'.

The destruction of the Galilee chapel was likewise planned; not, however, because of its decay but because Wyatt desired to make a carriage road from the castle to the west door of the cathedral and round into the College. The step was sanctioned and the chapel unleaded, when the Dean, who was also Bishop of Coventry and Lichfield, arrived to keep his annual residence in the summer of 1796 and stopped the work. Carter had drawn attention in the Society of Antiquaries to the disappearance of the chapter-house and to the proposed similar fate of the Galilee chapel. Such a clamour had been raised there that the Dean, who had sanctioned both measures, became alarmed and withdrew his permission for the destruction of what could still be saved. So his later boast that he saved the Galilee was a piece of monstrous conceit. If anyone was responsible, it was Carter. All Wyatt's other plans were probably cancelled at this same moment.

Durham certainly represents the very worst of Wyatt's cathedral repairs, and his activities there are incapable of being defended. When called in to do a certain task, or when supervised, he could and did produce very satisfactory results. But when left on his own he often ran riot, as in this instance, in a manner which one is bound to deplore. As the havoc intended was greater than the havoc wrought, for once it is true to say that gratitude is due to those who hampered his movements.

[1] *Chapter Acts Book*, 20 Nov. 1795.

(5.) *Summary*

From Wyatt's general treatment of cathedrals the fact emerges that the ideas which he applied to them were very limited. He seems to have had a certain formula which he presented on every occasion and which was adopted in varying degrees. This formula was: to throw the choir and the chapel behind it into one by pulling down the reredos; to transfer the high altar to the extreme east end; to make the floor of the cathedral a uniform level throughout; to remove the organ screen and replace it and the altar-piece by a patchwork composition of his own formed of old pieces taken from elsewhere, generally from the reredos; and to drain and level the close. Local needs were also attended to in each case, but this was the substantial plan for universal application where permitted.

Its existence to a certain extent helps us in the division of responsibility between Wyatt and the Dean and Chapter. Anything within the list certainly originated with Wyatt alone, except the enlargement of the choir at Lichfield and Salisbury. As to the rest, the Chapter must have some share in the praise or blame.

The usual procedure was for the Chapter to instruct him as to certain things which they required carried out and then to request him to survey the cathedral and report his opinion of what needed attention. This was submitted to them, and the suggestions approved or rejected. Then, and not before, was work begun.

After making his survey, Wyatt almost certainly left the city; and his subsequent visits were very infrequent. The Chapter did not encourage his reappearance, as he charged five guineas a day for attendance and half-a-crown a mile while travelling, in addition to five per cent of the whole expense of the repairs; whereas they had his plans and his name, which was all that they especially desired. Consequently in Wyatt's absence a good deal may have been done without his knowledge or consent. Different effects may have been due to the ignorance or negligence of the foreman left in charge, who was usually the clerk of the works permanently employed by the Chapter and so quite subservient to any alterations in plan proposed by them in Wyatt's absence.

It happened that at the end of the eighteenth century nearly all the cathedrals in England were in a very stricken condition. After the Restoration substantial repairs had been undertaken; so thoroughly in fact that little had needed attention for a long time after. But the authorities had relied on this restoration for too long and had let things drift until there was an accumulation of decay. Wyatt, in his survey, reported all the corrosions and damaged parts, which the Chapter was only too pleased to demolish, if encouraged. Their fabric funds were slender or non-existent; to repair the breaches in the walls made greater breaches in their finances; to raze the decayed portions to the ground and dispose of their materials actually increased their resources. Also, the encouragement was forthcoming—from Wyatt.

He undoubtedly admired Gothic architecture but seems to have had a regular and classical mind which fitted ill with the irregularities of Gothic. Small additions were excrescences that could be, and were, well nipped off. Ruinous chapels it was easier and neater to pull down than to patch up. In spite of his artistic temperament, he had tidy ideas. But these were carried out at the expense of archaeology, and he obviously had no antiquarian conscience. The age of a building was not a sufficient title to respect, and it had to be, as well, useful, ornamental, and sound; if not all these, it was probably not thought worth saving.

Secondly, long contact with the cathedrals did not augment his respect for their age. Rather, he began to work upon each with moderation and as more and more crumbling stone was revealed, as the survey or the work proceeded, he became increasingly ruthless and destructive in much the same way as when sorting an accumulation of old objects the process leads to more and more rejections as it continues. Most of the rebuilding had, as its object, increased safety; and there was no motive of rebuilding the old work in a purer style. That was a later and a worse development.

Wyatt's reputation as 'the Destroyer' was manufactured very soon after his death and has clung to him ever since. It was created largely because the nineteenth century disapproved so strongly of the way in which the eighteenth century treated Gothic, as they disapproved of everything that the eighteenth century produced. We also disapprove of the way in which the eighteenth century treated Gothic, but we disapprove as much, if not more, of the way in which the nineteenth century treated it. But this has not prevented us from accepting ready-made the damnation of Wyatt, prepared, nourished, and entertained during the nineteenth century.

He has suffered from misattribution of the sins of others, from a gross enlargement of his own, and from a complete belittling of his ability. He stands out from the early days of the Gothic revival as the one personal and known figure, who is used as the scapegoat for the sins of the whole body of contemporary and successive 'innovators'. Very few of these hostile critics are aware that only four cathedrals in England suffered from what they are pleased to call his 'ravages'. If this is compared with the number restored by Sir Gilbert Scott in the nineteenth century, it will be seen to be a very moderate list. In Wyatt's own day these alterations were discussed as a matter of 'taste'; now, as a matter of archaeology; and Wyatt certainly cannot be acquitted of antiquarian irreverence. But at least we can know exactly what he did, and why. We should also remember that to whichever of his contemporaries, were it Carter or the most ardent of the antiquaries, had been entrusted the same buildings and the same tasks, though our list of complaints would have been different, we should not have today any higher opinion of their labours.

CHAPTER VIII

THE INCIDENT OF THE SOCIETY OF
ANTIQUARIES

IN May 1797 Wyatt was proposed for election as a Fellow of the
Society of Antiquaries. His sponsors were the President, Lord Leicester,
Lords Hertford and Harcourt, Edmund Ferrers, Robert F. Greville
and L. Pepys. At first sight his candidature is apt to seem rather odd
to us as, quite apart from his traditional character of archaeological
disrepute, one wonders what his qualifications would be. But at this
period less specialized historical or prehistorical knowledge was in
general required for membership than today, and it was quite a
common occurrence, as in the case of Wyatt himself, that one man was
at the same time a Royal Academician and a Fellow of both the
Society of Antiquaries and the Royal Society. Henry Holland and
William Wilkins had both been elected Fellows in the preceding year.

At the time when Wyatt was proposed for election his cathedral
undertakings were either still in progress or just completed and were
fresh in everyone's mind. Consequently a great storm arose within the
Society. His enemies argued that his abilities were 'confined to the
Grecian orders and to profane buildings', and that as to Gothic he was
'but half learned, which is worse than being totally ignorant' and 'has
not an idea of the nature and uses of a cathedral church'.[1] His activities
had led to the destruction of tombs (the old apotheosis of monuments
once again!) which it was the business of the Society to protect. His
election would show approbation of this work and deny their own title
to be called antiquaries.

The ballot was held on the 29th June. Wyatt received sixteen white
balls and eleven black balls and was not elected. The leading part in the
opposition against him was played by John Carter who had undertaken
for the Society a survey of Durham cathedral contemporaneously with
Wyatt's restorations there. At the very meeting when Wyatt's name was
voted on, but apparently after the ballot took place, Carter read a

[1]*Gentleman's Magazine*, 2 Aug. 1797, Vol. 67, Pt. II, p.638.

47. James Wyatt
    by Ozias Humphrey

48. Unidentified drawing in
    the Victoria and Albert
    Museum

49. Sheffield Park

50. Sandleford Priory

paper on the subject of Durham cathedral in which he stated that the Galilee chapel had just been wantonly destroyed by Wyatt for no other reason than to make a carriage drive round the cathedral. This actually was not true but was quite an innocent mis-statement on his part as, unbeknown to him, the chapel had been reprieved at the last moment after he had left Durham.

Carter celebrated the triumph of Wyatt's rejection by the Antiquaries in a letter to James Moore and his wife, preserved in the Ashmolean Museum, which was written in doggerel verse of ineffable badness. Wyatt's friends however were not in the least daunted by his rejection. At the very next meeting his name was re-submitted, this time backed by fifteen supporters including the President, Lord Ducie, Sir Joseph Banks, Joseph Farington and both Daniel and Samuel Lysons.

This led to a pitched battle in the Society. The ballot was fixed for the 7th December. John Milner prepared and submitted a paper, to be read in November, on the late innovations in Salisbury cathedral. Wyatt's friends secured a postponement of its reading on the grounds that it would influence the election, which was just what its sponsors intended it to do. It was in fact never read and was returned to the author in July 1798.

Meanwhile the storm burst at the meeting of the 9th November. The Minutes of the Society and the account given by Farington, who was present, do not quite concur in the order of the proceedings. But apparently a Fellow named John Thomas Groves drew attention to the fact that Carter's previous statement as to the destruction of the Galilee chapel at Durham was not correct since it was at the date of speaking still standing. Carter then rose and made a long explanatory statement, in the course of which he said that if this had been the only building in the actual or threatened destruction of which Wyatt had been involved, he would apologise for having mentioned Wyatt's name in the matter. But as it was not, he would not do so. Thomas Astle, who claimed to be the oldest Fellow present, then rose and said that he had never before witnessed such a proceeding and considered Carter's conduct most improper. He proposed that no thanks be returned for the communication which Carter had made. Samuel Lysons seconded this. The President intervened to say that he 'extremely condemned'[1] Carter's conduct, and the meeting concurred, for it was officially recorded that the Secretary be directed to return no thanks for the communication received.

[1] *Farington Diary*, 9 Nov. 1797.

Carter's party did not let the matter rest even there, as at the meeting on the 7th December, at which the ballot took place, there was a further rumpus, though the Minutes do not refer to it. While the ballot was taking place a letter from Lysons was read, no doubt in support of Wyatt or in condemnation of Carter. Sir Harry Englefield moved that no thanks be returned for this. The Duke of Norfolk supported him. Carter 'attempted to speak'.[1] When the King was told of this incident he jokingly called it a popish plot. The President, Thomas Astle and a barrister named Mingay opposed Sir Harry Englefield's motion, and thanks were in fact accorded to Lysons for his letter. Meanwhile the ballot had been concluded. There had been a record attendance of 163 out of a total of 600 Fellows. 142 voted in favour of Wyatt's admission and only 20 against. He was therefore elected.

[1] *Farington Diary*, 7 Dec. 1797.

CHAPTER IX

WORK AT WESTMINSTER

WYATT was appointed Surveyor of Westminster Abbey in 1776; but we do not hear of any work being undertaken until 1789, with the exception of temporary arrangements for particular events such as the Handel Festival in 1784 and the installation of the Knights of the Bath in 1788. The post involved the repairs, not only of the Abbey itself, but of all the buildings at Westminster.

In 1789 a Committee of the House of Commons was delegated to inspect all the buildings adjacent to Westminster Hall and the two Houses of Parliament and to report how they might best be secured from the danger of fire. It is very difficult to picture the general scene at Westminster before the fire of 1834. The buildings were of vast extent and of diverse character; but there was neither plan nor system. All the offices of the important functionaries of the country were jumbled together round the Parliament house in an indescribable hotchpotch of confusion, together with the offices of the legions of placemen, holding both functioning posts and sinecures, who were such a feature of the eighteenth century. Many of them lived upon the premises, in which case their house, stables and other appurtenances were included in the medley. Lastly there were several coffee-houses actually neighbouring upon the official buildings. All these erections were of different dates, sizes and component materials; so it is not remarkable that the Committee thought that 'some great and noble Plan ought to be adopted; Conformable to which, public Buildings ought to be erected, not only substantial and convenient, but also of a Magnificence suitable to the Dignity of this Country'.[1]

Plans of such alterations would have cost £2,000. Therefore, before commanding such, the Committee took the opinion of the most eminent architects of the country upon the existing buildings. Their report must have been very enlightening and is worthy of considerable attention.

[1] *Journals of the House of Commons*, 22 July 1789.

Of the large and important rooms, the House of Lords, the Prince's Chamber, and the Painted Chamber they thought incapable of useful repair. The House of Commons and the Court of Requests might stand for many years but they were very exposed to the risk of fire from their surroundings. The buildings east of the House of Lords might fall down at any minute and would cost more to repair than to rebuild. All the rest were partially composed of timber and a menace in themselves.

The report ends thus: 'We beg leave to submit to this Honourable Committee That, from the very circumstantial Detail we have entered into, of the State of the various Parts of the Buildings, which the Committee requested we might examine, it is almost superfluous and unnecessary to declare our unanimous opinion that the Hazard they have been, and still are, exposed to from Fire is so great that we cannot help being astonished at their having so long and so happily escaped, (with but one late fortunate exception), from the most imminent Danger. Unprotected by Walls of either Brick or Stone, connected and joined together by boarded and Lath and Plaistered Partitions, with Iron Bars to defend the Windows of the most consequential Offices, which serve to attract the Lightning, to the Destruction of their valuable Contents; by Funnels and Chimneys running up in old decayed Piers, in the very bosom of the combustible Materials, in many of which, Fire from a neglected Chimney might consume the Whole; without the Possibility of bringing sufficient Water to extinguish the Flames, such Aid being hitherto overlooked, or deemed unnecessary, and not more than One Engine kept near the most essential offices in this Kingdom.

'All of which is humbly submitted.

'Robt. Adam. Geo. Dance. J. P. Cockerell.[1] Hy. Holland. John Yenn. John Soane. Robt. Browne. Thos. Tildesley. John Woolfe. John Woolfe Junr. Robt. Adam for Robt. Mylne. Thos. Fulling. Chas. Alexr. Craig. James Wyatt.'[2]

This is a list of very eminent names. Sir William Chambers was omitted, but 1789 is rather past his prime. Also Nash does not appear in it, as it was before his name was well known. Otherwise it appears to be comprehensive, and in view of the strength with which the opinion was expressed, it is surprising that so little was done about it. After 1806 a Committee of the House of Commons met to improve the

[1] A mistake for S. P. Cockerell.
[2] *Commons' Journals*, 22 July 1789.

amenities of Westminster, with power to buy up buildings in the neighbourhood, but they do not appear to have achieved much.

In 1800 repairs and alterations began on the larger Parliament buildings. The House of Lords was moved from the site of the Royal Gallery to the Court of Requests to which Wyatt gave a Gothic interior. Soane also prepared plans for a new House of Lords. Farington records an interesting utterance of Mrs Soane's on this subject of most unwifely disloyalty: 'Mr Soane was not to be compared with Mr Wyatt as to ability but had taken more pains than Mr Wyatt therefore his designs might be more eligible.'[1] They were not considered so, and Wyatt's were executed. The Peers sat in the new chamber till the fire. In view of the augmentation of members of the House of Commons due to the Act of Union with Ireland more accommodation had to be provided in St Stephen's Chapel which contained the Commons. It was this necessary undertaking which first gave rise to all the criticism of the alterations at Westminster.

The most important name in this connection is that of John Carter. In 1789 he began to write for *The Gentleman's Magazine* a series of articles entitled 'The Pursuits of Architectural Innovation' under the pseudonym of 'An Architect'. They were continued until his death in 1818 and altogether amounted to two hundred and twelve separate articles, apart from many letters inserted in the same numbers under his own name and feigning to be from another hand. But the general plan of discussion of the reparation lately undertaken upon ancient buildings became subjected to particular animosity, and the whole series of articles became largely a continual stream of criticism of so malignant a nature that it is really abuse poured out almost entirely upon Wyatt.

The style of the articles is curious, for it is both artificial and cryptic. Carter throughout conceals his identity with his own pseudonym 'An Architect' and, when speaking of those letters contributed under his real signature, he refers always to the author as 'my friend, J.C.' When, however, he becomes really worked up by his subject he signs himself, in a quixotic manner, 'The Red Cross Knight'.

As far as Wyatt was concerned, it was the alterations at Westminster that formed the chief cause of and target for abuse. In due turn, Carter visited and spoke of the cathedrals on which Wyatt operated, and he duly fumed at what he saw and through what he reported. But Westminster was the centre of the storm because Carter himself lived there and so could often inspect the proceedings.

[1] *Farington Diary*, 29 Mar. 1801.

Sometimes he refers vaguely to 'the innovators', but as few names are given, this is nearly always a concealed cut to add to the many open attacks made upon the unfortunate Wyatt. Carter's vehemence appears to have had no effect whatever upon the object of his wrath, and his voice rises almost to frenzy as he perceives his own impotence.

Wyatt himself never broke through the silence. His only answer was to exclude Carter from admission to view the progress of work at Westminster; and one cannot help comparing, most favourably to him, this dignified silence with the hysterical screams of his adversary.

Whatever the subject of Carter's monthly discourse, he always came back in the end to the same topic, and the refrain was ever Wyatt the Vandal, Wyatt the Destroyer. If Pugin invented the title of 'the Destroyer' and applied it to Wyatt, Carter had previously drummed in the idea for at least thirteen years and with such violence that Wyatt's chief defender could write with complete accuracy: 'For years he has been exposed to the persecution of a party and defamed by the malevolence of an individual: if ever he should feel his professional credit injured by this malevolence, assuredly he will apply to the laws of his country for redress.'[1] Carter did in fact go about as far as the law of libel permitted and throughout with such a disgusting pose of assumed virtue that he might well have been the predecessor of Pecksniff.

Finally, the way in which he pursued Wyatt almost to the gates of hell, as he thought and hoped, is ludicrous to a degree. Thus he quoted from Wyatt's obituary in *The Gentleman's Magazine*: 'Revived in this country the long forgotten beauties of Gothic Architecture from monastic and baronial structures and to collate from their character and ornament: these he translated to structures of his own design with additional grace and symmetry and richness of decoration.'[2] As it stands, with much omitted, this quotation is nonsense. Carter's comment was: 'Reflecting on these lines, it will be no very great difficulty to account for the alterations and "additional grace etc." (otherwise inaccuracies and false imitations) attempted in the renewal of the sculptures in Henry VII's chapel, as well as the monastic detail before cited.—Surely there is a fate, according to Sir Henry Spelman, attending the meddling with ancient religious piles: therefore I still warn those who have the care of such relicks of art always to bear in mind the good Knight's manifestations.'[3]

[1] *Gentleman's Magazine*, 2 March 1811, 'An Old Correspondent', Vol. 81, Pt. I, p.231.
[2] *Ibid.*, Nov. 1813, Vol. 83, Pt. II, p.442.
[3] *Ibid.*, Nov. 1813, Vol. 83, Pt. II, p.448.

The crux of the matter seems to have been, as 'An Old Correspondent' pointed out: 'Mr Carter complains that between Altar and Communion-table he is unemployed. I am sorry for it,—his talents are unquestionable, and I sincerely wish that they were better employed than they are at present. If we had a single fabric of his construction, every artist whose work he has criticised would be a critic in return.'[1] The writer evidently did not know of the chapel built for Bishop Milner at Winchester, or, if he had, might well have had something to say about Carter's own ideas of Gothic. His few actual works seem to have been as unknown to his contemporaries as they are to posterity. But he was partly or wholly responsible for the Duke of York's country house, Oatlands in Surrey and for Midford Castle, Somerset.

There must have been a flavour of jealousy at Wyatt's quantity of engagements and his own unemployment. There may have been more than that. In Carter's own obituary in *The Gentleman's Magazine* in 1818, the reviewer of his life states that he had been told by a friend that, forty years ago, Carter had been employed by Wyatt as the superintendent of the men who did his work. If this story was true, perhaps something lies in the history of this their connection and of its termination which would account for the vindictive hatred borne by Carter towards Wyatt.

A more moderate man than Carter could have advanced intelligent criticism of the activities at Westminster. But by lashing every particle of the enterprise with unmitigated condemnation he destroyed the value of those censures that were reasonable.

It is now time to consider what actually was done to give rise to all this criticism. In order to make more room in St Stephen's Chapel the panelling supposed to have been put up by Wren in 1707 was removed. There was revealed beneath it some medieval wall-paintings supposed to be contemporary with the chapel. These were quite ruthlessly and most unnecessarily destroyed, as their erasure cannot possibly have provided more space. So this was an act of vandalism that deserved all the ill that was said of it.

But condemnation must pause there. Almost all the rest of what was executed in any of the buildings, except the Abbey itself, was mere external repair undertaken to secure the buildings and render them weatherproof. In view of the parlous condition in which they were reported to be by the list of architects quoted above, it was absurd to maintain, as Carter did, that such measures were unnecessary; and

[1]*Gentleman's Magazine*, May 1808, Vol. 78, Pt. I, p.415.

had any one of them collapsed, he would himself have been the first to dilate upon the neglect of those whose business it was to look after the fabric.

So much for the repairs to the old palace at Westminster; now as regards the Abbey itself. Here, it was especially Henry VII's Chapel which was in a decayed condition. In 1793 the Dean and Chapter had undertaken a gradual repair of the roof and in 1803 had ordered Wyatt to complete the restoration of a small portion of the building over the east window in order to ascertain how great would be the cost of a total repair. But the outbreak of the fire in the main body of the church had involved them in an unexpected expense of nearly £4,000 mainly spent upon renewing the vaulting of the central tower.

Altogether, between 1787 and 1807, £28,749 had been spent upon general repairs. Consequently the Dean and Chapter felt that the exterior repair of Henry VII's Chapel lay beyond their means and accordingly in 1807 petitioned the House of Commons for a grant of £1,000 per year and of £1,000 in the initial year to meet the new demands upon their funds.

A Committee of the House examined Wyatt and the Chapter Clerk to prove the truth of the statement of the petitioners. Wyatt had surveyed the chapel to ascertain exactly what repairs were necessary. The exterior facing was injured, and the ornamental repairs must extend to the whole of the outside. The windows were decayed and propped with timbers; and the flying buttresses and octagon turrets in a dangerous state. An estimation of the cost of ornamental repairs was difficult, but about £10,400, it was thought, would be the amount; that of the necessary repairs, £14,800.

A precedent existed for a national subsidy to the restoration of the Abbey in the thirties of the same century, when £4,000 a year was voted. In this new instance the House granted £2,000 to the petitioners in 1807 and, with the exception of 1809, annually accorded a grant of varying sums until Wyatt's death, though he did not live to see the work completed.

The financial arrangements were superintended by a Committee of the Commons, and the architectural character of the work by the Committee for the Inspection of Models for National Monuments which was composed of Sir Charles Long, the Marquess of Stafford, the Marquess of Buckingham, Lord Aberdeen, Sir George Beaumont, Thomas Hope, R. Payne-Knight, John Flaxman, Thomas Banks, and Sir Richard Westmacott. The work seems to have been very carefully executed, with attention to both the safety and character of the building. We know that Flaxman and Stothard thought it very proper work.[1] Presumably the rest of the Committee agreed with this, as it had come under their supervision. Their number included Thomas Hope who was by no means disposed always to give credit to anything connected with Wyatt. In fact there is a general consensus of opinion, apart from Carter, that the work was well worthy of respect.

Carter was led into making grave errors concerning the architects whom he criticized by attributing to them motives which they did not possess. This was partly due to his own standpoint. He reverenced and admired all old buildings for their antiquity itself and deprecated any interference with them whatever. Therefore, thought he, those who tamper with them must automatically prefer and consider superior all new work to the old. 'Nothing but devotion to Novelty and hatred of Antiquity governs all these undertakings',[2] he wailed. Nothing was ever more untrue. Wyatt had no hatred of antiquity as such. He genuinely admired Gothic work, and the fact that he so often re-used in other compositions old stonework that had been removed shows that he was not devoid of archaeological leanings, however mistaken may have been the idea to which these gave rise.

The buildings were all in a bad state at this date, and the repairs were instituted for specific reasons. It was just because so much needed attention that a certain amount of havoc was wrought. For, if he had no dislike of antiquity as such, he certainly stood in no awe of it and dared to question its excellence. So it was in the progress of the work that the ruthlessness arose.

[1]*Farington Diary*, 24 May 1811.
[2]*Gentleman's Magazine*, June 1807, Vol. 77, Pt. I, p.533.

CHAPTER X

ORIGINAL GOTHIC CONSTRUCTION

(1.) *Early Works*

VERY early in his career Wyatt turned his attention to Gothic architecture. He designed a ruin or folly at Milton Abbey, Dorset, for Lord Milton about 1775.

But his first complete house of which the exterior was Gothic was Sheffield Place, now called Sheffield Park, Sussex, which he built for Gibbon's friend John Baker Holroyd, Lord Sheffield. A print of it appeared in Watts's *Views* of 1779. Wyatt exhibited in the Royal Academy of 1771 an elevation of a house intended for a nobleman in Sussex which, as far as I know, has never been identified. It is at first tempting to conclude that this was Sheffield Place. But Holroyd was not created Lord Sheffield until 1781, and so this cannot be the case. It is more likely that the house was newly completed when Watt's *Views* appeared. In 1776 Capability Brown laid out the magnificent grounds of Sheffield Place, and Wyatt's work there was presumably contemporary with this. There was an older house on the site, but it had no Gothic connections. No evidence exists to show who was responsible for the decision to gothicise the new building. It is faced with Roman cement. The entrance front looks north. This has two storeys of seven square-headed sash windows with stepped dripstones and a castellated parapet. The outermost window-bays are flanked by pilasters, between which the cornice is carried up to form arches over the attic windows. Above each is a stepped gable crowned by tall pointed finials at the apex and angles. The bays on the ground floor and the porch are later additions. (Plate 49.) This front has a very thin Gothic disguise to its basically symmetrical and classical conception.

The east front is slightly more irregular. To the north it has a square projection with a pierced parapet surmounted by similar finials at the angles and fleurs de lys in the centre. Then comes a central bay of three windows with a battlemented parapet. The principal feature of this façade is the third or southernmost projection which is very elaborately treated. On the ground floor it has a tripartite sash window with three separate ogee-headed tympana. Above this is what appears to be a tall pointed church window of six lights with a simple rose in tracery at its head. In actual fact this window is entirely a sham. Only a few panes of it light a small room now a bathroom. The remainder cannot be seen from the inside at all. No better example of Wyatt's unfamiliarity with Gothic construction at the period could be found. Above the window is another stepped gable, but this time a pointed niche is set at the base of each of the three surmounting finials.

The south front, which is the least interesting of the three main façades, is much more typical of the Gothic work that Wyatt came to execute at a later date in his career and has some affinities with West Wycombe Park amongst other houses. Its main portion has a central feature one storey higher than the remainder of the front, set between octagonal turrets capped by machicolation. The end window-bays have a miniature version of this treatment with buttresses instead of turrets and a small round window in the embattled parapet. Some of the dripstones over the windows are square-headed, some stepped and some ogee-headed. To the west is a recessed service wing of which the design roughly repeats that of the main front but with two evenly spaced emphasised features instead of three.

Inside, a passage with groined plaster vaulting leads to the central staircase. This exactly follows the plan of most of Wyatt's staircases in his classical houses but is a curious mixture of Gothic and classical detail. At the foot of it is a pair of solid five-sided columns forming a screen of three pointed arches opening off the passage. The stair begins as a single flight and divides into two at the half landing. The bannisters have plain uprights. On the first floor each of the three open sides of the staircase well has four clustered wooden columns with leaf-shaped capitals, and the fourth side similar half-columns. The doors leading off the landings have pointed heads and quatrefoils or other Gothic decoration. There is a frieze with a design of acanthus leaves set in ribbed recesses. The staircase is lit by a small circular dome with a cove beneath it and ribbed squinch arches at the corners.

Gothicisation did not penetrate beyond the staircase, passage and landings. The principal rooms are the library, the saloon, the dining-room in the south-east corner of the house, later a drawing-room, and the Winter drawing-room to the north of this. The library has open book-shelves now painted in imitation of graining but originally white. The white marble chimney-piece has a frieze of fret-pattern which is repeated in the doorcases. The original dining-room has an apse at the west end containing two niches filled with shelves and surmounted by ribbed semi-domes. The frieze of the ceiling and of the doorcases consists of a series of oval mouldings framing lions and sphinxes alternately. The ceiling is a most unusual one. It was no doubt intended to suggest a Tudor design but is an attractive mixture of Tudor and classical detail. It has bold mouldings or ribs which form a pattern of interlaced circles. Within these are quatrefoils, each of which contains four beautifully-moulded plaster sprays of roses with abundant leaves. Between them are diamonds set between four sprays of tulips. As far as I know, Wyatt designed nothing else at all like this ceiling in any house throughout his career.

The most remarkable work in Sheffield Park is however to be found in a bedroom on the first floor known as the Prince's room. This occupies the central bay in the east front. The walls are plain, except for a gilded cornice of stylized trees and leaves alternately. But the ceiling, painted by Charles Cotton the elder R.A., is exceptionally beautiful. Its principal feature is a wide cove with a biscuit ground, on which a series of the most vivid and delightful figures of lions, tigers and leopards, each set in festoons, has been painted. This cove is carried round the bay. As in the case of the original dining-room ceiling, this is unique amongst Wyatt's houses. In each angle of the cove is radiating fan ornamentation which Wyatt often used in such a position. The flat portion of the ceiling has a central oval containing a rosette within a diamond. The surround of this and of the other painted panels has a pale pink background with a most delicate encircling festoon of ivy leaves. At each end is a polygonal painted panel displaying two cherubs springing from cornucopiae. In the bay is a similar painting of two female figures standing beside a rams'-headed tripod. These three panels are much more similar to work in others of Wyatt's houses and are not nearly so outstanding as the cove of the ceiling. The chimney-piece is rather reminiscent of Wyatt's Etruscan work, as it is of white marble painted and not treated in an architectural fashion. The jambs and frieze have a pattern of dull red sphinxes set in black diamonds with red borders. In the place of capitals are ram's-headed tripods, and what would normally be the cornice has a row of black stylized trees. The doors of the room have six reeded panels in a similar surround.

It is interesting to note that Benjamin Henry Latrobe, who had a successful architectural career in the United States, executed some minor alterations at Sheffield Park. His principal English works, built before he emigrated to America in 1795, were Hammerwood Park and Ashdown House not far away. Maria Josepha Holroyd's letters record that in the previous year, Latrobe pulled down the partition between her father's bedroom and dressing-room and also planned to open up the great pointed window which is only a sham. But this latter project was never carried out.

No doubt Wyatt designed the principal lodge at Sheffield Park on the Lewes to East Grinstead road. This is a rather charming little building. The four-centred carriage archway is set between slightly recessed dwellings of one room on two storeys with a pointed window on the ground floor of each and a round opening above with a window of quatrefoil design in it. Over the whole is a form of miniature machicolation and a parapet. The archway has a pair of most beautiful wrought iron gates of fleur de lys design with an overthrow in the head of the arch.

The Fletching lodge is a small octagonal tower of three storeys with a vice staircase and on one side of it a two-storeyed addition and on the other a four-centred castellated archway across the carriage drive.

Wyatt's work at Sheffield Place leaves no doubt as to his unfamiliarity with Gothic construction at this early date. But in its unpretentious unreal manner the house has considerable charm and was a more successful work in its Gothic characteristics than Sandleford Priory, Berkshire, which followed it.

This was built for Elizabeth Montagu, the Queen of the Blue Stockings, about 1780. Mrs Montagu's husband, Edward Montagu, had purchased the Priory about 1730, but it is very doubtful whether there then remained any of the monastic building founded for Augustinian Canons in 1200, apart from the chapel. This stood detached from the house at the back. Edward Montagu does not seem to have done anything to the house during his lifetime. He died in 1775, and his widow soon embarked upon an extensive building programme. Her first enterprise was the construction of Montagu House in Portman Square, which was begun in 1777. Three years later she set about altering and enlarging Sandleford Priory. There is nothing to show why she did not on the second occasion employ James Stuart, who was the architect of Montagu House. Instead her choice fell upon James Wyatt. It is more likely than that he was recommended to her by her cousin Richard Robinson, Archbishop of Armagh and Primate of

Ireland, who between 1773 and 1783 financed the construction of Canterbury Quadrangle at Christ Church, Oxford, of which Wyatt was the architect.

Mrs Montagu's letters only refer to the two large rooms which Wyatt added to the house. But there is little doubt that at the same time he disguised the old house by the superimposition of its present Gothic façades. There is no evidence to show whence originated the idea of this transformation. Mrs Montagu was acquainted with Horace Walpole but was certainly not one of his intimate friends. It is not likely that the idea of gothicising her house originated with her. It is much more probable that the name and monastic origin of the building caused Wyatt to suggest it to her.

The west or entrance front presents just such a façade as a country gentleman or builder who was attracted to the then dawning fashion of Gothic might have elaborated for himself with the aid of a book of designs. It is a straight-forward classic composition to which a few Gothic frills have been added. It is not at all dissimilar to the north front of Sheffield Park but even more classical beneath its Gothic skin. The two window-bays at each end project and are surmounted by embattled gables which masquerade as pediments. Angle buttresses flank these projections and are carried up into crocketed finials. The centre portion of the front has a castellated parapet. This is raised to a greater height over the centre window-bay, which also projects. No attempt has been made to gothicise even the glazing bars of the round-headed sash windows. But the doorway is unusual. It is flanked by narrow lights and has a four-centred head containing a narrow fanlight of similar shape with thin trefoil-headed divisions. (Plate 50.)

The south front reveals the full extent of Wyatt's ignorance of Gothic ideas at this period. This is a wing forming an ordinary curved bay of three windows, which is flanked by buttresses surmounted by crosses. On the first floor between is an iron balcony following the curve of the bay. The windows here are casement windows with four-centred heads and small pointed panes. This wing contained the library on the ground floor. The east front facing the garden is a hopeless muddle. There are three projections, one containing a recessed balcony and the other two blind window-spaces, the centre one being of an elaborate design with a pointed head set in a be-pinnacled gable. This is even more futile than the window at Sheffield Park which lights nothing.

Inside, the Gothic work was confined to the outer and inner halls. The former has a plaster ceiling edged with a border of Gothic design and a frieze round the top of the walls imitating machicolation. On each side of the door leading into the inner hall are niches with triple ogee heads. The inner hall itself is curiously divided into two unequal portions. The main section of the room is quite plain but at the south end opposite the doorway is a strip, perhaps intended to give the effect of a screens passage, which has elaborate imitation fan-vaulting in plaster.

The best part of Wyatt's work at Sandleford consisted of the additions which he made for Mrs Montagu. These actually preceded his transformation of the exterior. He converted the ruined chapel of the Priory, which stood detached from the house to the north east, into a large 'eating-room' as Mrs Montagu called it, by the insertion of a false ceiling below the barrel vault. Mrs Montagu was fortunate in the concentrated attention—most unusual for Wyatt—which he gave to the matter. In June 1781 she wrote that he had 'converted the gloomy chapel into a charming room with such expedition that it is now complete and fit for use'.[1] She called it 'my reformed chapel—for what has been taken from the owls, the bats, the rats and mice, to be dedicated to the sober use of sober society and a temperate dinner, preceded and concluded by a grace, may rather be esteemed reformed and purified than polluted and debased'.[2] The south windows, she said, 'will command a very gay and rich prospect, and will give me all the splendours of a summer when I am inclined to the allegro; when I am more disposed to the penseroso, those windows may be shut against the garish day and a large Gothick window be thrown open.'[3] There is incidentally no sign of this 'Gothick' window, as the large east window is a triple sash window surmounted by an immense segmental fanlight. The decoration of the room is of the simplest possible: a plain classical frieze, overdoors and marble chimney-piece. Sandleford Priory is now a girls' school, and the room is used as a gymnasium.

Wyatt next joined the new eating-room to the house by the construction of an octagonal drawing-room. Here he was not able to keep up his expedition, and one of Mrs Montagu's letters mentions delay in the arrival of blue tiling for this room. Apart from this tiling, the drawing-room exists today substantially intact as Wyatt designed it and is one of his most charming rooms. It is decorated in cream picked out in

[1] *Mrs Montagu: Her Letters and Friendships*, by Edward Blunt.
[2] *Ibid.*
[3] *Ibid.*

gold. It is made up of eight round-headed compartments flanked by pilasters with a frieze of paterae and a semi-circular tympanum over each compartment containing a circular panel of bas-relief. Pendentives and squinch arches with soffits decorated with rosettes support an oval semi-dome edged with an anthemium design in gold. On the south side are three sash windows, in the centre compartment facing them a marble chimney-piece decorated with Wedgwood plaques, and in the east and west sides doorways flanked by Corinthian columns which lead into small rectangular lobbies. (Plate 24.)

Apart from the insertion of a bed alcove in Mrs Montagu's bedroom and the gothicisation of the outer and inner hall, which has already been mentioned, this was the limit of Wyatt's work within Sandleford Priory. But he was still employed there in 1786, and the transformation of the exterior no doubt followed the construction of the two additional rooms. From 1781 onwards Mrs Montagu had been employing Capability Brown to 'lead the View from the East window of the Eating-room

> Through arched roof of twilight Groves
> And Shadow brown that Sylvan loves,'[1]

and to improve the whole of the grounds. It was presumably to harmonise with Brown's new landscape that the façades of the house were arranged in their new Gothic outline.

Wyatt's last commission for Mrs Montagu was in 1793 when he added to her house in Portman Square two nurseries for the family of her nephew who inherited the house on her death in 1800.

After Sandleford Priory Wyatt's next Gothic work was Lee Priory in Kent for Thomas Barrett. This was built between 1782 and 1790. An album containing a few of the working drawings for the house is in the Victoria and Albert Museum. Barrett was a friend of Horace Walpole, and it has usually been held that it was Walpole who introduced Wyatt to Barrett and, with this commission, first turned Wyatt's attention to Gothic. The Gothic façades of Sheffield Park and Sandleford Priory, however, effectively disprove the latter point. James Elmes, writing in *The Civil Engineer and Architects' Journal* for 1847, alleged that it was George III who first suggested to Wyatt that he should make a Gothic design. But this has still less foundation in fact, as Wyatt was not in touch with the King during the early years of his career. It is not however necessary to find a specific introduction of Wyatt to Gothic design as this was sufficiently in the air for any prominent archi-

[1]*Mrs Montagu: Her Letters and Friendships*, by Edward Blunt.

51. Lee Priory

52. Frogmore House. The Ruins
(*Reproduced by gracious permission of H.M. The Queen*)

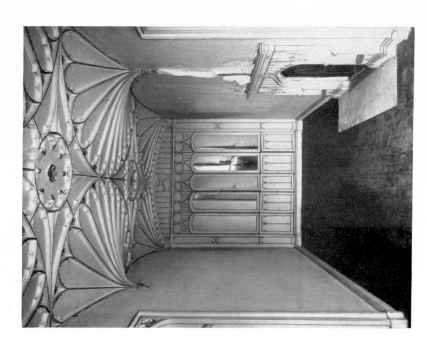

54. The Strawberry Room

LEE PRIORY

53. The Library

tect to be fully cognizant of the possibility of buildings in such a style and to have adopted it at his own instigation. Mr Christopher Hussey has suggested that, as Wyatt was a pupil of W. Atkinson before he went to Italy, and as a York architect named Thomas Atkinson, possibly a member of the same family, designed the Gothic features of Bishopsthorpe for the Archbishop of York in 1765, Wyatt might even have studied Gothic before he went to Italy. This is not impossible, but it does not seem likely in view of the extremely amateur nature of his Gothic work at Sheffield Park and Sandleford Priory. If he had been studying Gothic buildings for nearly twenty years, these would surely have been of a very different character.

There is a possible connection of some interest between Sandleford Priory and Lee Priory. Edward Blunt in his Life of Mrs Montagu[1] quotes a letter written to her in 1777 by Lord Nuneham, the son of Horace Walpole's friend, the Earl of Harcourt. In this Lord Nuneham says he will ask his father to give 'Mr Barret' a letter of introduction to Walpole. Edward Blunt conjectured that this referred to William Barrett, the Bristol surgeon and antiquary. But it might equally well have referred to Thomas Barrett to whom, as a friend of Walpole's, the earliest surviving reference in Walpole's letters is in 1780. If so, then it might equally well have been Mrs Montagu who introduced Wyatt to Barrett, though it is perhaps more probable that Walpole did so.

Wyatt's own introduction to Walpole had come about as early as 1772 but had nothing to do with architecture. Walpole was then engaged in bringing out an edition of the papers and letters of the poet, Sir Thomas Wyatt, with a preface giving an account of his life. So he wrote to James Wyatt to enquire if by any chance the latter was descended from Sir Thomas. The letter is in the British Museum. As it has not, I think, been published before, it is worth giving in full.

Strawberry Hill,
July 26 1772

'Sir,

I beg your pardon for asking you perhaps an impertinent question. It is whether you are descended from Sir Thomas Wyat, who lived in the reign of Henry VIII. I am employed in collecting materials for his life, and very solicitous to find out some of his family. I know that some years ago there did live in Charterhouse yard an

[1] *Mrs Montagu: Her Letters and Friends.*

old Mr Wyat, who was the Representative of the family and had portraits of his Ancestors, which I should be very happy to discover. You have so much genius and merit yourself, Sir, that it can be of no consequence to you whether you are related to that family or not. No man with such talents as yours wants to be distinguished by the Lustre of others. My anxiety you see is founded solely on my own business, and I trust you will excuse my making the application to you—nor was I sorry to take the opportunity of telling you how extremely I admire your taste, and how much I am, Sir, yr. Obedient

Humble sert.

HOR. WALPOLE.'

A copy of Wyatt's reply to this letter has also survived, though a small piece has been torn off the bottom left-hand corner.

Newport Street.

August 1st 1772

'Sir,

The Loss of the best of Fathers, an acct. of whose Death I received on Tuesday last, prevented my answering your very obliging and polite letter as soon as I wished.

I cannot but regret the want of Materials to furnish me with the means of giving you that intelligence you seek for—my pursuits having been of a different nature, the Knowledge I have of my family is derived from Oral Traditions only, and goes no farther back than my Great-Grandfather, who, as I have been told, was a Farmer in Staffordshire, where I myself was born, whether therefore we are Descendants of Sir Thos. Wyatt or not is a subject I am not acquainted with or be assured, Sir, the [?knowledge] of having contributed the least matter [?as the subject of y]our pen, could have been exceeded by nothing [?but your appro]bation of the Works of

Sir,

yr. most obt. hble. servt.

JAMES WYATT.'

There is no reference to the two men having met before 1784, when Walpole mentioned in a letter to the Earl of Strafford that Wyatt had been at Strawberry Hill. But this was probably not their first meeting.

Even if Walpole did not introduce Wyatt to Barrett, it is certain that he suggested the gothicising of the old house at Lee by calling one room 'the abbot's study'. He thought that the position had 'a tranquil cheerfulness that harmonises with the house, and seems to have been the judicious selection of a wealthy abbot, who avoided ostentation but did not choose austere gloomth'.[1] Wyatt made several plans, some Gothic, some classical, of which the former were selected by Barrett because they evidently appealed to him more than the more conventional designs. (Plate 51.)

The medievalism of Lee Priory was however entirely affectation— the fantasy of a moment brought to birth by a mind that had been led to connect Gothic as a style with certain particular associations or emotions.

There was an old house on the site but this had no monastic origins, The title of 'Priory' was only attached, like the fairy on the Christmas tree, to add realism to the effect of the transformation. Wyatt incorporated part of the old building in the new house. The subsidiary staircase, for instance, dated from the early eighteenth century, and the cellars were probably much older. Until Mr Reginald Turnor's book on Wyatt appeared in 1950 it was generally assumed that Wyatt's house in its turn had been completely destroyed in the eighteen-sixties when Sir Gilbert Scott greatly enlarged the house. Besides adding a vast wing on the east side, Scott encased the whole of the exterior in red brick with a diaper pattern and placed a large tower above the dome of the library. This proved too heavy a load for the dome to carry and had to be demolished in the present century. But within the nineteenth-century brick shell much of Wyatt's house remained intact until the whole building was demolished in 1954. On the ground floor the chief survival was the outer hall which had a coffered ceiling with a pattern of rosettes and a fireplace in an alcove with a recess on each side, of it, all three having imitation tracery in plaster at their heads. It is interesting to note that gothicism stopped short at the dining-room door. Wyatt's version of this room, which Walpole called magnificent, remained intact, but it was a classical interior of a simple chimney-piece and overdoor both containing a plaque of a few figures in Greek dress. The drawing-room and the staircase of delicately carved dark oak were remodelled by Scott.

The most important rooms of the Wyatt house were to be found on the first floor, including the famous library which was the chief feature of Lee Priory and was called by Walpole 'a prior's library that does such honour to Mr Wyatt's taste'.[2] This was an octagonal room

[1]Walpole to Mary Berry, 17 Oct. 1794.
[2]Walpole to Mary Berry, 28 Sept. 1794.

with an elliptical traceried dome, above which were originally a gallery and lantern containing stained glass, surmounted by a spire. The spire, lantern and gallery were however removed to make way for Scott's tower. Each side of the octagon formed a ribbed recess flanked by clustered shafts which supported the tracery of the dome. The walls were painted pale blue with the ornamentation picked out in darker blue and red. If original, this colour-scheme was an application of classical 'Adam' decoration to Gothic subject-matter which succeeded because the latter was entirely fanciful and unrealistic in conception. But it may possibly have dated from Scott's time. The library shelves which filled most of the recesses were surmounted by ogee-shaped cusping all along the top and coloured in the same manner as the walls. One recess contained the fireplace which was enclosed in a sort of cupboard composed of cinquefoil-headed panels to harmonise with the walls. (Plate 53.)

The library was entered through a rectangular ante-room with a ceiling of imitation fan-vaulting in plaster, in the centre of which was a circular or 'rose' panel which was glazed to give light. The ante-room was lined all round with shelves or cupboards similar to those in the library itself. An entirely inappropriate ecclesiastical touch was provided by the existence of a stoup to the right of the door on entrance.

Walpole was in raptures with the whole room when he saw it. He wrote to Mary Berry: 'For, to me it is the most perfect thing I ever saw, and has most the air it was intended to have—that of an abbot's library, supposing it could have been so exquisitely finished three hundred years ago.'[1] The only defect he considered was the chimney-piece which was not distinguished enough. He regretted that Barrett had not forced Wyatt to place over the fireplace the Mabeuse which Barrett had recently purchased, thereby bringing this central feature into greater prominence. The library at Lee seems to have borne more resemblance to the closet at Strawberry Hill than to the Library there. Walpole thought that both his closet and Barrett's library had an undoubted air of survival, whereas the rest of his house every true Goth must perceive to be 'more the work of Fancy than imagination'.[2]

The other important survival of Wyatt's house on the first floor at Lee Priory was the 'Strawberry room'. This was a small rectangular closet so called because of its resemblance to much of the interior of

[1] Walpole to Mary Berry, 17 Oct. 1794.
[2] Ibid.

Walpole's house. The ceiling, like the ante-room of the library, was of imitation fan-vaulting in plaster with the detail picked out in gold. There was a fireplace to match with an ogee-shaped opening, and the end wall facing the window was panelled with five narrow strips of mirror set in a fancy Gothic design of ogees, cusped circles and cinquefoil heads. In its unpretentious, unrealistic way, this was a charming little room. It is no wonder that Walpole thought it 'a delicious closet too, so flattering to me'.[1] (Plate 54.)

The house at Lee, when completed, was so decked out in fancy dress that the lovers of Gothic thought it had the real flavour of the genuine article. The chief vistas showed a small convent which had not suffered demolition but had been adapted to the requirements of a modern secular household. Walpole wrote in 1785: 'I have seen over and over again Mr Barrett's plans, and approve them exceedingly. The Gothic parts are classic; you must consider the whole as Gothic modernised in parts, not as what it is—the reverse',[2] though even the latter was not strictly true. On another occasion he wrote: 'It is the quintessance of Gothic taste exquisitely executed. I wish William of Wykeham was alive to employ and reward Mr Wyatt,—you would think the latter had designed the library for the former,—it has sober dignity without prelatic pomp.'[3] He was in fact so enthusiastic that he felt Strawberry, if not the parent of Lee, would have been jealous of it. He called it 'a child of Strawberry, prettier than the parent, and so executed and finished'.[4]

This phrase reveals both the strength and weakness of eighteenth-century Gothic. Its practitioners applied to their Gothic interiors all the ideas of decoration with which they were familiar in classical styles, merely introducing shapes which were to be found in genuine Gothic buildings, such as ogees, cusping, trefoils and cinquefoils. Walpole must partly have understood this, for he wrote of Lee: 'the Gothic parts are classic'.[5] The results were, in a sense, far more Gothic than anything that the Middle Ages ever produced and would certainly have made medieval people stare. But it is precisely these fanciful and unrealistic trimmings which give the very early buildings of the Gothic revival their attraction in our eyes. They neither are nor try to be replicas of

[1] Walpole to Mary Berry, 28 Sept. 1794.
[2] Walpole to George Hardinge, 1785.
[3] Walpole to Hannah More, 25 July 1790.
[4] Walpole to Mary Berry, 28 Sept. 1794.
[5] Walpole to George Hardinge, 1785.

original Gothic buildings but are rather what the eighteenth century thought Gothic architecture ought to have looked like. They include, however, such major anomalies as the placing of a spire on top of a dome, as in the Library at Lee. The association of Gothic with certain fixed emotions, such as melancholy, also produced odd results, for instance the introduction of stained glass into most rooms in spite of the fact that it can seldom have had a place in the secular or domestic portions of monastic buildings in the medieval period.

If Lee Priory was superior enough to make Strawberry Hill jealous, as Walpole thought, had the latter not been its parent, wherein did this superiority lie? In 1788 Walpole wrote to Barrett: 'But Mr. Wyatt has made him' [Mr Mathew] 'too correct a Goth not to have seen all the imperfections and bad execution of my attempts; for neither Mr Bentley, or my workmen, had studied the science, and I was always too desultory and impatient to consider that I should please myself more by allowing time, than by hurrying my plans into execution before they were ripe. My house is therefore but a sketch by beginners, yours is finished by a great master.'[1]

This passage does not mean that Wyatt had for many years been studying Gothic. Before working at Lee he had in all probability had very little experience of Gothic architecture. If he had, the new house at Lee would surely have been very different. But the practice of architecture was the professional occupation of his life, and he had been responsible for the whole of Lee. Strawberry, on the other hand, was designed in bits and pieces by the Strawberry Committee, none of whom had any professional acquaintance with architecture. But both houses belonged to the rococo school of Gothic and were bound together in spirit, date, association and relations of kinship.

When Walpole wrote in his *Anecdotes of Painting*, 'Mr Wyatt at Mr Barret's at Lee, near Canterbury, has, with a disciple's fidelity to the models of his masters, superadded the invention of a genius', he was carried away by a gush of admiration. But when he wrote, 'Mr Wyatt, if more employed in that style, will show as much taste as he does in the Grecian',[2] he was far nearer the truth and quite prophetic.

Walpole's enthusiasm for Lee naturally gave him the wish to satisfy Strawberry's jealousy by employing Wyatt there; and it is almost certain that he did so. As early as 1774 the offices had been projected and plans drawn up by James Essex, which were duly paid for in 1777.

[1]Walpole to Thomas Barrett, 5 June 1788.
[2]Walpole to George Hardinge, 1785.

For some reason or other they had never been erected, and in 1784 Essex died. So we find Walpole writing to Wyatt in 1789: 'I have determined at last to build my offices next spring, and wish much to have them executed under your direction. I know how much you are deservedly employed; but whenever you have a morning to spare, I shall hope you will bestow it on me here, and if you will take a bed here, I shall be more glad.'[1] The offices were erected in the next year, as Walpole planned, at the cost of £1,855. Though Wyatt's name does not occur in the accounts, it is to be assumed that he superintended their construction.

Another commission that might have come to Wyatt through the instrumentality of Walpole was for the rebuilding of Arundel Castle, Sussex. Writing to Mary Berry on the 16th August 1796, Walpole mentioned that he had recommended Wyatt to the Duke of Norfolk for this work two years before. But the rebuilding appears to have been carried out by Francis Hiorne of Warwick, and the Duke of Norfolk spoke against Wyatt's election to the Society of Antiquaries in 1797. So it is unlikely that Wyatt was employed at Arundel. In either case almost the whole of what was then done was obliterated by the reconstruction a century later by Charles Alban Buckler.

Contemporary with Lee Priory was the commencement of Wyatt's work at Plas Newydd in the Isle of Anglesey, though this is only partly a Gothic house. An old building existed here which had already been gothicised. Wyatt incorporated this in his enlargement, giving the main block a classical plan of a bowed centre and flanking bays. On to this conception he sprinkled a few Gothic details such as a castellated parapet (since removed), pointed windows with dripstones, and octagonal buttresses on each side of the central feature. The interior, which dates from 1795, is wholly classical, except the hall which was not carried out until 1811 and may be the work of Wyatt's assistant, Joseph Potter. The stables are a charming piece of Gothic fantasy. (Plate 63.)

To this same early period of Wyatt's Gothic work belongs one venture which never materialised. This was for the enlargement of Slane Castle, County Meath, an Irish fortified house above the River Boyne. A series of drawings signed by Wyatt and dated 1785 and 1786 are to be found in the National Library of Ireland in Dublin. These apparently came into the possession of Francis Johnston, who succeeded Wyatt as architect at Slane Castle, and are now part of the Murray Collection

[1] Walpole to James Wyatt, 31 Aug. 1789.

of Johnston's drawings which have been loaned to the National Library of Ireland by the Architectural Association of Ireland.

The elevations are rather reminiscent of Adam's treatment of Syon House and show a plain rectangular building with a castellated parapet and square-headed sash windows surmounted by dripstones. The entrance front facing north-east was to have had a central portion flanked by narrow square turrets. Its chief feature was an attic storey with small round windows and machicolation below it. Beyond these turrets were narrow recessed portions containing no windows, and the front terminated in a further pair of wider but more squat towers. All four turrets contained loop lights. The north-west and south-east fronts were even plainer. They contained five and seven window-bays respectively and were flanked by low towers. The only light touch was provided by a row of small round windows lighting the second storey. There is no drawing of the south-west front, which would suggest that this was a pre-existing part of the house. But from the plan of the basement which has survived we can tell that it had a projecting bow in the centre containing the dining-room on the ground floor and the kitchen beneath it. This plan is curiously headed 'Of no use whatever J. Wyatt Oct. 1785' in Wyatt's handwriting. He also made several other notes on the plan, one of which cannot now be read as part of the paper has been torn away. Another contained elaborate details for the arrangement of the passages and staircase from the basement to the dining-room in such a way as to keep the smell of cooking—that great eighteenth-century bugbear—out of the house.

At some other time Wyatt made a rough sketch for a Tudor Gothic house that probably also was in Ireland as it was made for an Irish peer, Lord Courtown. This was for a square building with octagonal turrets at the angles and projections of higher elevation on two of the fronts, one rectangular and one semi-circular. The plan was the same as Wyatt used in so many houses, namely a series of reception rooms arranged round a large central staircase with a screened passage on one side of it.

(2.) *Milton Abbas and other Churches*

Contemporaneously with much of the foregoing work Wyatt built his first church. This was at Milton Abbas in Dorset. In 1771 Joseph Damer, Lord Milton, who was created Earl of Dorchester in 1792, commissioned Sir William Chambers to rebuild Milton Abbey. The new house took the form of a complete courtyard in which the great monastic hall, erected in 1498, was very skilfully made into the centre of one side. All the main elevations were treated with a mild Gothic disguise to their basically classical arrangement. They were in fact Chambers's only excursion into the realm of Gothic. The great abbey church was left standing, detached from but adjoining, the house on the south side. Why Chambers did not complete the internal decoration of the house is a mystery. But Lord Milton was a quarrelsome man, and it is likely that there was a disagreement between them. At any rate during 1775 and 1776 Wyatt made a series of drawings for the decoration of most of the principal rooms in the north, west and south wings of the house, which were duly carried out. Some of the drawings have survived and are now in the Library of the Royal Institute of British Architects, but one of them, for the ceiling of the north-west tower bedroom, has been detached from the others and is in the Victoria and Albert Museum. Most of the interior work in the house can be identified with these drawings, though some of the rooms have ceilings or chimney-pieces which are clearly by Chambers.

Two of the most charming rooms are small hexagonal ante-rooms, one above the other in the centre of the west front. The lower has a coved ceiling, the upper semi-circular panels and pendentives alternately surrounding a diamond-shaped ceiling containing a rosette. The frieze of the doorcases in this room and of the ceiling in the adjoining rooms are of sphinx pattern which reappears in the ceiling itself and in the jambs of the chimney-piece. The next bedroom has an equally charming frieze of cherubs, the dining-room one of alternate vases and anthemia. The pictures in this last room are set in enriched plaster frames. The white marble chimney-piece has a central panel of a ram's head flanked by swags.

In the grounds Wyatt also designed a Gothic ruin or folly, the drawing of which, preserved in the Library of the Royal Institute of British Architects, might easily be the work of a modern stage designer. The building no longer exists.

At the time when the house was rebuilt the village of Milton Abbas was clustered round the Abbey which had served as the parish church since the Reformation. Lord Milton removed the whole village to some distance away from the house in order to provide the facilities for Capability Brown to landscape his park. Until recently it was usually thought that the new village was laid out by Sir William Chambers. But Miss Dorothy Stroud in her book on Capability Brown has shown that this was not so. The lay-out of the thatched cottages of uniform

141

façades, spaced at even intervals facing each other along the single village street which climbs a gentle hill, was Brown's work. Chambers did however build the Vicarage in 1771. When the move was made, Lord Milton, with the consent of the ecclesiastical authorities, appropriated the abbey church as his private chapel and therefore built another parish church in the village street. This was erected in 1786 and is said to have been built of materials from the abbey barn. Wyatt was certainly the architect of it. The interior can no longer be seen as he designed it. The chancel was rebuilt and enlarged in 1887 and a south aisle added at some time in the nineteenth century when the west gallery was removed. But the exterior survives more or less intact. It is built of rosy-tinged ashlar in nominally Early English style but is actually little more than a plain rectangle with 'church-warden' Gothic windows. The tower at the west end is however a pleasant eighteenth-century variation on a medieval theme with its castellated parapet and crocketed pinnacles at the angles. The almshouses opposite the church are dated 1779, but are said to have been built in 1674 and re-erected here presumably under the supervision of either Wyatt or Brown. They are not much of a credit to either.

Between 1789 and 1791 Wyatt also restored the Milton Abbey church. It is a little difficult to know exactly what this restoration comprised, as he was followed by Sir Gilbert Scott in 1865. But he seems to have carried out his usual cathedral ideas of tidying up the tombs and removing inner partitions, using some of their component parts to form a new patchwork rood-screen.

About three years after he designed Milton Abbas church Wyatt embarked upon a far more important ecclesiastical commission. This was the rebuilding of East Grinstead church, Sussex, of which the tower had collapsed in 1785, reducing most of the church to ruins. The walls were demolished, but Wyatt very cleverly incorporated some of the octagonal concave columns of the nave arcade into the new building. This is built of sandstone ashlar, locally quarried, in Perpendicular style. It comprises a nave with aisles, a chancel with north and south chapels, a tower at the west end and a south porch. The nave has a clerestory of round windows. The windows on the outside are flanked by buttresses rising to points resembling miniature gables. But the chief feature of the exterior is the very fine battlemented Perpendicular tower. The whole building is an exceptionally good one for the end of the eighteenth century and is far more characteristic of a church built about twenty-five years later. It compares very favourably, for instance, with Decimus Burton's neighbouring Holy Trinity, Tunbridge Wells, which dates from 1827, and is worthy to rank with Barry's St Peter's, Brighton, of 1824-8. Unfortunately the churchyard is so small and so closely surrounded by other buildings that it is practically impossible to photograph the church. The building cost £30,000 and was not completed until 1813 owing to the difficulty of raising funds. Some of the money was derived from a church brief.

Wyatt's next Gothic church was designed for his native village of Weeford in Staffordshire in 1803. But he did little more than provide the plans, and its construction was actually supervised by his brother Benjamin who was then living at Sutton Coldfield. It is evident from the character of the building that very little money was available and that the design had to be the simplest possible. The Early English style was therefore chosen. The plan is cruciform, but the only real feature externally is a square turret at the west end surmounted by a most un-gothic octagonal cupola with a pointed spire. The interior is equally plain, but the crossing has ribbed vaulting in stone.

At about the same period—the date has been given as both 1803 and 1810—Wyatt built Hafod church (Eglwys Newydd), Caernarvonshire. This was unfortunately consumed by fire in December 1931 and has since been rebuilt, but Wyatt's tower survives.

In March 1808 the Parish of Hanworth, Middlesex, where Wyatt had his own country house, decided to rebuild their old medieval church. He provided drawings in 'English Gothic', and the new church was completed in the year of his death. However, it pleased the succeeding generation so little that it was demolished in 1865 and replaced by the present building in what they no doubt considered a purer style.

(3.) *Fonthill Abbey*

During the first half of the nineties Wyatt seems to have undertaken no original Gothic work except an artificial ruin at Frogmore for Queen Charlotte in 1792, but he was then in the midst of his restorations at Salisbury, Lichfield, Hereford and Durham cathedrals as well as St. George's Chapel, Windsor, Milton Abbey, Dorset, and New College, Merton, Balliol and Magdalen Colleges at Oxford. All these were concentrated between 1787 and 1797. This work and the experience of outstanding original medieval work derived from it entirely transformed his own original Gothic style from the rococo work of Sandleford and Lee Priories, which were associated in spirit and fact

143

with Strawberry Hill, into the far more realistic splendours of the romantic period.

This brings us to the most important of all Wyatt's Gothic enterprises, Fonthill Abbey, Wiltshire, of which the first version was actually begun in 1796, though it had been under consideration for some years before. (Plate 56.) Its begetter, William Beckford, was in most respects the client of whom every architect must dream but is never destined to meet. He had inherited from his father, Alderman William Beckford, Lord Mayor of London, an income derived mainly from West Indian plantations amounting to between £100,000 and £120,000 a year. From his earliest years his mind had been so full of oriental imagery that no conception, however wildly romantic, seemed to him too fantastic to be capable of realisation. As he grew older, he lost none of his interest in the flamboyance of the east and even came to refer to himself as 'The Caliph' in allusion to the principal character in his oriental romance, *Vathek*, which he had written in French at the age of twenty-two.

Fonthill House, which Beckford inherited from his father, had been rebuilt in 1755 after a fire. The architect of the building does not seem to be known, though Farington, in 1797, wrote in his *Diary* that it was 'finished, if not designed by Adam and must have cost £100,000'.[1] Its chief features were the Grand Apartment, paved in Italian marble and with a ceiling painted by Andrea Casali, and the Egyptian Hall or Turkish Chamber, which perhaps gave rise to some of Beckford's oriental fantasies. In 1789 Beckford employed Soane to insert a gallery in the house. Wyatt also carried out some work there. He designed a ceiling for the Egyptian Hall, a chimney-piece for an ante-room and a fishing seat in the grounds by the lake. But whether this was before or contemporaneously with his work on Fonthill Abbey is not known.

What brought Wyatt into touch with Beckford is also unknown. But it is possible that the introduction came through the Courtenays of Powderham Castle. Wyatt made additions to the north wing at Powderham Castle, but the date of his work there is not given in Wyatt Papworth's article in the *Dictionary of Architecture*. It was presumably executed for the second Viscount Courtenay, who died in 1788, as his son and successor lived mostly abroad after that date. Beckford was frequently at Powderham Castle from 1779 onwards. The Courtenays were amongst his closest friends, and it was his violent affection for Lord Courtenay's young son, William, which flared up into a

[1]*Farington Diary*, 7 Nov. 1797.

scandal in 1785 and caused Beckford to retire to the continent for the next five years. Farington in 1794 said that it was about a month before this incident that Wyatt first went to Fonthill. It is not at all impossible that Beckford, on one of his visits to Powderham, may have met Wyatt or have been favourably impressed with his work there.

But it was not until 1790 that Beckford conceived any idea of a Gothic building at Fonthill. In that year he commissioned Wyatt to design a ruin on the highest point on his estate, known as Stop's Beacon. Even at this stage in the proceedings Wyatt in his usual manner neglected to give the matter proper attention and had to be given an ultimatum to appear at Fonthill with the designs within ten days from 23rd October, since Beckford was again about to leave for the continent. On account of this absence nothing further was done at the time. Rutter's *Delineations of Fonthill and its Abbey* rather humorously says that 'it was perhaps to the very excellence of the original design that we may ascribe the cause of its not being carried into effect'!

When Beckford returned in 1793 he gave orders for a wall twelve feet high to be built round the whole seven-mile circumference of his estate to keep out the hunt which he had on one of his solitary rides unexpectedly found trespassing upon his domains. In November 1793 Beckford left again for Lisbon. There seems to have been some question of Wyatt designing him an oratory to form part of his house San Jose de Ribamar overlooking the Tagus. On 10th April 1794 he wrote to Wyatt: 'My appetite for honouring St Anthony you see is still so keen that I cannot live without a little tid-bit of a sanctuary to stay my stomach till the moment arrives when by the permission of Providence and Mr Wildman' [Beckford's agent] 'I may carry your magnificent plan for the chapel upon Stop's Beacon into execution.'[1] This had however to wait until Beckford's return in 1796.

At this time Farington recorded that Wyatt was going to build Beckford a tower 175 feet high and made a sketch of it in his *Diary*. It was to contain a room for Beckford's occupation 60 feet above the ground. Wyatt thought Beckford intended to be buried at the top of the tower. 'Mr Beckford asked how he should get up to his first floor 60 feet high. Wyatt said he should have a staircase to a hall with four fireplaces in it up which staircase he might drive a coach-and-four and turn in the hall.'[2] This is interesting as it was evidently the origin of a

[1]The Hamilton Papers in the Register House, Edinburgh.
[2]*Farington Diary*, 20 July 1796.

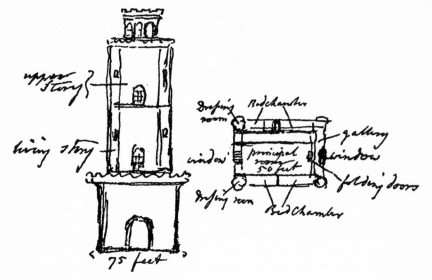

Sketch in *Farington's Diary* for a tower at Fonthill. (Original in Windsor Castle Library. Reproduced by gracious permission of H.M. the Queen.)

rumour that was much repeated concerning Beckford's mysterious house.

Actually Wyatt was instructed to make designs for a structure 'which should contain a suite of rooms small but amply sufficient for the enjoyment of a day whether of sunshine or shower',[1] whose external characteristics were to be that of a convent partly in ruins and partly perfect. The plan produced bespoke the survival of the chapel, the parlour, the dormitory, and a small cloister. This comprised the section of Fonthill Abbey which was later called the Fountain Court, with St Michael's Gallery on the east side terminating at its north end in a great octagonal tower which was designed to form the chapel. Designs were shown in the Royal Academy of 1797 and 1799.

Farington speaks of Beckford having planned to endow the Abbey and have a 'cathedral service to be performed in the most splendid manner the Protestant religion will admit'.[2] The gallery was to be filled with British pictures. Beckford, having abandoned his idea of being buried at the top of the tower, had chosen the gallery as a last resting-place befitting a great patron of British artists. It was to lead to

[1]Rutter, *Delineations of Fonthill and its Abbey.*
[2]*Farington Diary*, 16 Nov. 1798.

a 'Revelation Chamber'[1] wainscoted in ebony with a floor of jasper. The walls would be five feet thick with recesses to contain coffins. The room would only be viewed through an iron grating, Beckford's own tomb being exactly opposite the entrance, on the spot occupied by the altar in the final design!

Yet in spite of the prospective scale of the new buildings, they were still to form part of the decorative effect of the landscape and were not intended for permanent habitation. Just as in the earlier half of the eighteenth century the grotto had been the chief feature of garden architecture, so Gothic ruins had come to be thought the most decorative ornament—a development of the Gothic fashion which coincided and was much connected with the rococo school of medievalism. Hence Beckford chose an eminent position for the site of his central exhibit, that it might show to greater advantage.

Although the exterior must present the appearance of both sham antiquity and decay, nevertheless the building had to be in reality a sound and perfect construction, as its second purpose was to serve as a place of excursion for a sophisticated picnic. Just as George III breakfasted in the ruins which Wyatt had built for the Queen at Frogmore in 1792, so Beckford desired an immense pavilion where he and his household might spend an occasional day or which they might visit just in order to take a meal. The building at Frogmore was plain in construction and moderate in size, as befitted the simple style in which the Royal Family lived. But Beckford demanded a gigantic ruin to express his extravagant romantic personality.

The style was to be Gothic because all ruins were Gothic and because, in particular, the windows and compartments afforded Beckford opportunities to blazon the arms of the various European families, either extinct or still surviving, from which he and his daughters were descended. So there was little share left for the architect in the choice of the style.

The work proceeded in spurts. When Beckford was absent Wyatt, unsupervised, relaxed his attentions. During the first six months of 1799 Beckford was in Portugal, and little was done. On his return he was so indignant at the lack of progress that he managed to induce Wyatt to transfer five hundred workmen to the Abbey from Windsor Castle, where Wyatt was also working.

To increase the speed of construction and as no residence was intended, the materials used were timber and cement. But in May 1800,

[1]*Farington Diary*, 22 Dec. 1798.

before the fastenings of the tower could be completed, attaching it to the base on which it was erected, a sudden gust of wind blowing upon a heavy flag hoisted upon a pole fixed to the summit shook the tower with such force that the whole structure collapsed. The fall was however so self-contained that not a single part of the main building was damaged or the smallest ornament injured. When told of the disaster, Beckford regretted that he had not been on the spot to witness the fall and commanded another tower to be commenced at once. He wrote to Sir Isaac Heard on the 21st May 1800: 'We shall rise again more gloriously than ever, provided the sublime Wyatt will graciously deign to bestow a little more commonplace attention upon what is supposed to be his favourite Structure. The Crash and the Loss sound magnificently in the Newspaper, I neither heard the one nor feel the other.'[1]

But this was not the tone he used to Wyatt, on whom the full burden of his wrath fell. To the plea that Wyatt was prevented from giving greater attention to Fonthill by the public work in which he was involved as Surveyor-General to the Board of Works, Beckford replied: 'I should be extremely sorry to express in its fullest and deepest extent my surprise at this the very ———[?] delay of yr. journey to F. The Fall of the Tower has certainly not shaken your Reputation so much as this last disappointment my Faith in yr. promises of future attention. This is a woeful beginning of reform. I should presume by yr. total silence about the sneers in the Morn. Chron., which have been repeated in a different shape, that yr. indifference at least is immoveable. You give me much greater credit for boundless good humour than I deserve. It is not in the power of ordinary persons to ruffle it, but you, not being of that description, should not carry the experiment too far. I am somewhat sore in consequence of the late tumble and this new rub in my present convalescent state I confess is almost too much for me. Notwithstanding my respect for the Privy Council and the absolute necessity I am to suppose of your personally presenting the plan required I cannot help feeling this dereliction of my councils in the severest manner. I feel it with such acuteness that unless state affairs allow you to bestow that exact and so solemnly promised attention long laid by which the building by its size and importance demands and which sincere friendship may possibly be allowed to merit I must renounce the Abbey and my works and order every account concerning it to be closed immediately.'[2] For once these reproaches seem to have had some

[1] The Hamilton Papers.
[2] Undated draft in the Hamilton Papers.

55. Early design, unexecuted

56. The north west front

57. The Farm

58. The House

effect with Wyatt, and in the succeeding months he really superintended the progress of the work.

So great was Beckford's impatience for the completion of the building that relays of workmen were employed throughout the night as well as the day and seven days of the week. Neither the demand for labourers in the harvest season nor for the operations at Windsor Castle, nor the disapproval of the King had any avail to temper Beckford's haste. All through the early stages of the winter of the year, during a spell of intense cold when it was necessary to maintain huge fires to warm the workmen at their task, four hundred and sixty hands were employed in order that the building might be ready for Nelson's visit on 23rd December 1800. On that night all Beckford's guests drove by torchlight through the grounds from the old house to the Abbey, where they were entertained to a magnificent feast, after which Lady Hamilton danced before the company.

Soon after Nelson's visit Beckford had the idea of enlarging the house, and plans were made for King Edward's Gallery, to balance on the north St Michael's Gallery. But he was no more an easy client to deal with than Wyatt was an accommodating architect, and as fast as the plans were made or even partly executed, Beckford took a dislike to them and had them altered. In 1802 he had a sudden fit of economy when a decision of the Court of Chancery deprived him of a West Indian estate which had produced an income of about £30,000 a year. No further work was done until 1805.

In that year Beckford equally suddenly conceived the idea of permanently inhabiting the new building. This necessitated that, for the first time, durability should be considered. So the whole building was surveyed and stone substituted for the timber and cement throughout. Some of the outbuildings of the old house were demolished to provide the materials.

Wyatt was still playing truant, for on one occasion George Beltz, the Portcullis Poursuivant, who was a consultant of Beckford's, enquired: 'Is Wyatt at the Abbey? He has been lost for a fortnight.'[1] But when discovered he seems for once to have given satisfaction, as that year Beckford also wrote of him as 'at the head of an army of workmen and anxious for a wonder to get on'.[2] This mood persisted even into 1806 when Beckford wrote again that 'Wyatt has but just left

[1]Guy Chapman, *Beckford.*
[2]J. W. Oliver, *The Life of William Beckford.*

me after displaying the greatest abilities and taking the greatest pains'.[1]

The move was made in 1807, and the old house demolished with the exception of the garden wing.[2] Beckford had never liked it. He called it 'a lump of mediocrity . . . in an uncommonly bad situation',[3] or 'a pilgrim's lodge'.[4] Wyatt protested at the proposal to demolish it on the grounds that 'much blame would be thrown on him as adviser'.[5] But Beckford characteristically replied with the advice that Wyatt should pay as little attention to what the world said as he did.

Work on the Abbey continued with even greater zest. In September 1808 Beckford wrote: 'The number of workmen was last week trebled . . . viz. 46 plasterers, 22 labourers scaffolders etc. in proportion. The din, the hubbub, the stir, the dust, the rattling of boards, the swashing of buckets, the vociferation for lime and plaster were never equalled except at Babel.'[6] But Wyatt, he told another correspondent, 'Se conduit pire que jamais. Il arrête tout et je crois qu'il ne se passe pas une semaine sans qu'il est lui-même arrêté.'[7]

By the beginning of 1809 the scaffolding was removed from the tower, and no further advance was made for three years. But the abbey was still not complete. Beckford had some thought of continuing the work in 1811, but wrote to Wyatt on the 23rd December: 'Dear Sir, my engagements not allowing me to wait your arrival any longer I must desire you will have the goodness to defer your journey. It is not without much regret I renounce the satisfaction I had so long promised myself of receiving you here, but being induced from many considerations to postpone all extensive plans of improvement, I feel this renunciation less sensibly.

> I am, dear Sir,
> Yr very obdt. servt.
> WILLIAM BECKFORD.'

In 1812-13 however the eastern transept was added, which was to have been joined to the south wing by a kitchen court or south-east quadrangle. Wyatt's death prevented the execution of this. Jeffry Wyatt superintended the completion of the east transept, but Beckford

[1]J. W. Oliver, *The Life of William Beckford*.
[2]This wing was incorporated in a later house built on the site, but the whole was demolished in 1921. The only existing remains of Fonthill House are the gateway of the Park.
[3]Letter of the 28 Nov. 1806 to the Marquess of Douglas in the Hamilton Papers.
[4]*Ibid.*
[5]*Farington Diary*, 6 Nov. 1797.
[6]Draft letter of 11 Sept. 1808 in the Hamilton Papers.
[7]Draft letter of 19 May 1808 in the Hamilton Papers.

never issued the final order. The building alone cost him £273,000, and by 1820 his finances had come to a crisis. Two years later he was lucky enough to find a purchaser who paid £330,000 for the house with most of its contents, or £270,000 for the house alone. This was a rich doctor named Farquhar who had made a vast fortune in India by selling powder to the Government. Beckford proceeded to instal himself in two houses in Lansdown Crescent, Bath, where he lived until his death in 1844.

Soon after he left Fonthill he was summoned to the death-bed of the man who had acted as clerk of the works there. The reconstruction of the house in stone had been pressed on with the same insane haste; and the foreman, whether from dishonesty or from anxiety to speed up the operations, had never seen that the inverted arches, described in the specification as solid foundations for the tower, had been provided, although large sums had been paid for them. At last he gave Beckford the untimely warning that the tower might fall at any moment.

This caution was passed on to the new owner, Farquhar, who thought that it would last his lifetime. He was mistaken. The tower collapsed for the second time on the 21st December 1825. It involved in its ruin all the portions of the abbey to the south and west of it except the Great Entrance Hall. Farquhar disposed of the property in three lots, that containing the remains of the house passing to John Bennet, one of the Members of Parliament for Wiltshire. The east and west wings were subsequently demolished. What survives today is only the north end of the north wing. This consists of the Lancaster Tower and the rooms to the north of this, or the Vaulted Corridor, the Sanctuary and the Oratory on the principal floor, with the Lancaster State Bed-Chamber above, and on the second floor of the tower the Upper Lancaster Room, which was used as a billiard-room. The interior of these rooms contains no sign of their former glory.[1] Another house called Fonthill Abbey in baronial Gothic style was built by William Burn for the Marquess of Westminster 1847-52 on the estate about half a mile away. This was demolished in 1955.

For the collapse of the tower, both Beckford through his absurd haste and the clerk of the works through his dishonesty were primarily responsible. But Wyatt cannot be held altogether blameless. Contrary

[1]On the first floor is a model of Fonthill Abbey before the tower fell. Beckford refers to such a model in one of his letters (draft of the 28th Nov. 1806 to the Marquess of Douglas in the Hamilton Papers). Can this be the original?

to his usual custom, he spent much time at Fonthill, drawing and superintending building operations. It was certainly the duty of the clerk of the works to see that the materials specified, ordered and paid for, were received and employed; but, as Wyatt was often on the spot, he should himself have investigated important details such as the laying of the tower foundations a little more closely. In December 1806 Farington noted that, four years previously, the abbey had already cost £242,000; and added: 'He' [Beckford] 'showed that Wyatt by his negligence and inattention had caused him an unnecessary expense of £30,000.'[1] If this was so, there was still the greater neglect to follow.

During Beckford's occupation of the house, no visitors had been admitted even within the grounds. The twelve-foot wall, erected mainly to secure the exclusion of the hunt, was used to keep out the curious also. Most country houses were open to be viewed in the absence of their owners. Fonthill was a notable exception. The scandal in which Beckford had been involved in 1785 prevented many of his county neighbours from visiting him. Few besides the members of his household had ever penetrated into the abbey. This, together with the attitude of suspicion with which the average individual regarded any Gothic building, combined to make Beckford's house the object of great wonder and eager curiosity.

The stories that were told about it, however extravagant, such as the idea of driving a coach-and-six up inside the tower, were actually credited. A typical example of the awe with which the enterprise was viewed can be found in William Gilpin's *Observations on the Western Parts of England*. In 1798 he wrote: 'I have been informed that Fonthill hath been much improved; particularly that a Cathedral hath been built of the full dimensions of a genuine one. As Mr Wyatt was the architect, it must be a noble edifice; and if it be properly stationed, it must be a grand decoration.'

When, therefore, the house and grounds were thrown open to be viewed just before the impending auction, people flocked from all quarters to inspect them. As the majority had formed preposterous ideas of what they were about to see, they were bound to be disappointed.

Now this admission of the public did not take place until Wyatt had been dead ten years. Critics of the house, therefore, did not find the same necessity or tendency to eulogise him; for already his reputation

[1] *Farington Diary*, 14 Dec. 1806.

was beginning to wane. Most of them vented their disappointment by disparaging his share in the creation of the house as compared with that of Beckford, who was still living. They remembered that Wyatt had not been limited by Beckford as to expense or expanse of the house and they condemned the result as disproportionate to the opportunities provided. There were a few, however, who lavished unstinted praise upon the building.

Fonthill was not really a house but a vast piece of scenic design intended to dumbfound the beholder by its colossal proportions. The plan was that of a huge cross, 312 feet long from north to south and 270 feet from east to west, in the centre of which rose the great octagonal tower which was 276 feet high.[1] The first design, of which several sketches survive,[2] showed a lofty pointed spire above the tower. The unsuitableness of this for a building within sight of Salisbury Cathedral probably caused the spire to be abandoned quite early in the proceedings. (Plate 55.)

The whole of the west wing was given up to the state entrance. The gable of the wing was surmounted by a tabernacle containing a statue of St. Anthony by Rossi with a cross fleury above. Below, a lofty pointed arch gave into the vestibule or Great Entrance Hall. This was originally built as the Refectory, as the dining room was to be called on account of the supposed monastic character of the building. Over the doorway was a minstrels' gallery. It was in the Refectory that Nelson was entertained to dinner in 1800. But in spite of the fact that a huge fire of scented coal was kept burning night and day, it proved impossible to heat the room, which is not surprising when one remembers that it was 68 feet long and 78 feet high. In 1812-1813 it was therefore converted into the principal entrance, and in the place of the fireplace a wide flight of twenty-two steps was constructed at its east end leading to the Great Octagon or Grand Saloon.

This was the centre of the whole building and no less than 120 feet high. It was originally intended to be the chapel. Rutter's *Delineations of Fonthill and its Abbey* called it 'the loftiest apartment which domestic architecture can present, probably in the world'. Eight piers composed of clustered demi-columns, with eight tall narrow arches eighty feet high, constituted the lowest storey of the octagon. Four of these arches communicated with the main wings of the house. Samuel Rogers, after

[1] c.f. the spire of Salisbury Cathedral is 404 feet high.
[2] There are two in the Library of the Royal Institute of British Architects and one in the Victoria and Albert Museum.

FONTHILL

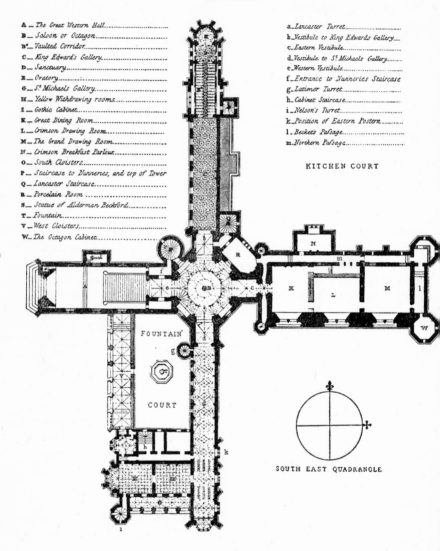

KITCHEN COURT

FOUNTAIN

COURT

SOUTH EAST QUADRANGLE

154

his visit in 1817, wrote that the doors were overlaid with violet velvet covered with purple and gold embroidery. The other four arches held recesses containing tall windows of stained glass with scarlet curtains below these. Above the arches was a gallery approached by a great circular staircase in a turret in the north-west angle of the cross ground-plan. The gallery communicated with four small sitting-rooms with bedrooms over them. The sitting-rooms looked into the Octagon through an arcade which was not glazed but only curtained. These rooms were called the Nunneries on the supposition that in some convents the nuns' choir was situated in a gallery above the public congregation. The bedrooms over the Nunneries Rutter's *Delineations of Fonthill and its Abbey* called 'the highest we should think in the world'. Above the gallery the fan-vaulting sprang from the capitals of tall shafts in the angles of the Octagon to support the lantern.

The Octagon was flanked on the north and south by the two long galleries which together composed the whole length of this axis of Fonthill. That on the south was called St Michael's Gallery. It was 112 feet long terminating in an oriel window flanked by buttresses. It also served as the library, since the recesses between the windows were filled with bookshelves. The ceiling had elaborate plaster fan-vaulting springing from angel-headed corbels. The windows were filled with stained glass of heraldic designs illustrating Beckford's noble ancestry. At the south end of St. Michael's Gallery a series of rooms projected west and was connected with the Great Entrance Hall by a covered cloister. This comprised the extent of the original building and formed a complete quadrangle known as the Fountain Court from the fountain which stood in the centre of it. The most important rooms in the south-west wing were the two Yellow Drawing-rooms. On the first floor was a room known as the Oak Library which was used by Wyatt as a drawing office and was sometimes referred to as 'the board of works'.

The north or King Edward's Gallery was 68 feet long. Beyond it were three compartments opening out of each other which were known as the Vaulted Corridor, the Sanctuary and the Oratory respectively. The Gallery took its name from Edward III, from whom Beckford and his wife were both descended. A portrait of the king hung in the place of honour over the chimney-piece. Round the top of the walls was a frieze containing the arms of seventy-two Knights of the Garter from whom Beckford claimed descent. The ceiling was of oak reticulated in square and lozenge-shaped panels containing heraldic emblems. The upper parts of the windows were filled with stained glass. The Vaulted Corridor was intended to give the effect of a sort of ante-chapel. It was vaulted in oak with gilt mouldings. There were no windows, but on each side were three pointed doorways with perforated bronze doors that communicated with recesses resembling confessionals. The Sanctuary and the Oratory were approached by steps up from a lower level at their south end. Their walls were covered with crimson damask. The plan of the Oratory formed five sides of an octagon. In each angle rose a slender gilt column, from whose capital sprang a fanwork reticulation of burnished gold spreading upward over a ground of deep crimson. At the intersection of the mouldings in the centre was a richly gilt boss, from which a chased golden lamp was suspended. Each of the five walls of the room contained a lancet window of four compartments filled with stained glass. At the north end, on the spot which formed the culminating view-point along King Edward's Gallery, was an altar covered with a Persian carpet, on which stood a marble statue of Beckford's favourite saint, St. Anthony of Padua, by Rossi, flanked by lofty candelabra containing giant tapers.

The east wing was the last part of the building to be erected. It was added in 1812 and 1813 and was in fact never completed. It was intended to contain a vast baronial hall commemorating Beckford's and his wife's descent from all the baronial signatories of Magna Carta of whom any issue was surviving at the date when Fonthill was built; and also a library and chapel. The room adjoining the Great Octagon formed the Great Dining-room after the Refectory in the west wing had proved impracticable and had been converted into the Great Entrance Hall. But this was only used on state occasions. Beckford normally took his meals in the Oak Parlour below one of the Yellow Drawing-rooms in the south-west wing. This suffered from the disadvantage, not unknown in the eighteenth century, of being 'the furthest apartment from the kitchen'![1]

Beyond the Great Dining-room were two Great Drawing-rooms. In these three rooms was housed the greater part of Beckford's fine collection of pictures. At the end of the wing were an octagonal and a series of other cabinets. The wing was joined to King Edward's Gallery by another cabinet called the Porcelain Room in the angle between the two wings.

The State Bedroom and a narrow gallery were situated over King

[1]Rutter's *Delineations of Fonthill and its Abbey*.

156

Edward's Gallery. But of the bedroom accommodation in general Rutter's *Delineations of Fonthill and its Abbey* said that 'all the Abbey, with all its towers, furnishes but about eighteen bed-rooms, thirteen of which, from their almost inaccessible height, their smallness, their want of light and ventilation, from one or all of these causes combined, are scarcely fit for their intended use; and of the other five, not one has a dressing-room'. Beckford himself occupied a small room known as the Chintz Boudoir over the north end of St Michael's Gallery.

The offices were in the basement. But here again all pretence of practicability had been sacrificed to effect. The windows were principally loop windows admitting a very inadequate amount of light. There were no means of baking, washing or brewing within the building, and these functions had to be performed in an outhouse. The kitchen was originally in the sub-octagon but was later moved to the east wing. It was a vaulted and groined apartment of 'truly monastic' character with numerous appendages 'such as would have suited a lordly abbot in the most hospitable days of our ancient ecclesiastical establishments'.[1]

Wyatt evidently designed some furniture for the house. In 1797 Farington recorded that there were to be 'four cabinets of £500 value in the Gothic taste',[2] and at another time that Wyatt had designed two frames for Beckford's Claudes.[3]

What were the merits of Fonthill? The small portion that remains shows how much Wyatt had learnt about medieval buildings from his cathedral restorations since he designed Lee Priory for instance. The work was in every way realistic, not fanciful, and the detail was good. But its main qualities were scenic, however. Gilpin was right when he said it was likely to be a 'grand decoration'.[4] It was the *pièce de résistance* of the landscape architecture of the grounds. Standing up on an eminence looking right across to Salisbury Cathedral, it was intended to produce a spectacular scenic effect and, as the greatest Gothic production of the eighteenth century, to shout defiance at its medieval rival. In all this it was eminently successful. The effect was both planned and achieved; but the greater the distance at which it was viewed, the greater the effect. The secrecy had increased the celebrity but it led to disappointment because it had encouraged high expectations and also because parts of the building itself may not have

[1]Britton's *Graphic and Literary Illustrations of Fonthill Abbey.*
[2]*Farington Diary*, 6 Aug. 1797.
[3]*Ibid.*, 7 Dec. 1799.
[4]Gilpin, *Observations on the Western Parts of England.*

borne close inspection. The tower, for instance, probably looked as insecure as it proved to be.

Moreover, the incongruity of living in a house of which the central hall was one hundred and twenty feet high struck forcibly. The discomfort and inconvenience of residence must have been enormous. This was because the idea of residence itself was conceived too late. Had it occurred earlier, something might have been done to fuse comfort and splendour, though the attempt would probably have detracted from the original aim. But as it was, the latter was patched up, late in its existence, to make habitation possible. The result was bound to be failure. The two ideas were probably incompatible at any time, but at that stage in the proceedings the attempt was ludicrous. Hence the inevitable collapse.

Nevertheless, as a work of art with a magnificent scenic aim, Fonthill was both a splendid construction and a successful composition while it stood; and, in addition to this, it taught Wyatt many useful lessons which he was not to forget.[1]

To the same period as Fonthill (1796-1800) belongs the work done by Wyatt at Windsor Castle for George III. This was almost all obliterated by his nephew Sir Jeffry Wyatville's later reconstruction of the Castle for George IV. *The Dictionary of Architecture* includes in Wyatt's list of works Wycombe Abbey, Buckinghamshire, which was rebuilt for Lord Carrington about 1798. This is not at all typical of Wyatt's work but is far more reminiscent of Jeffry again. One is tempted to think that if James took the credit for the work, Jeffry may have been the shadow architect who actually designed it. The house is built of ashlar set in galleting, and the stone is said to have been quarried locally from Denner Hill near the road from High Wycombe to Hampden. There is also a local tradition that stone from the same quarry was used in the reconstruction of Windsor Castle. If this is true and related to Wyatville's work there, it would have some bearing on the latter's possible responsibility for the design of Wycombe Abbey. But it might equally well refer to Wyatt's work for George III which was replaced by the later reconstruction.

Between 1796 and 1805 Wyatt built the old Royal Military Academy,

[1]Fonthill cannot be said to have inspired many buildings, but a definite echo of its tower can still be seen in the tower of Hadlow Castle near Tonbridge. This was built for Walter Barton May about 1825, but I have not been able to find any reference to the architect. It is purely a scenic construction which is a landmark for miles around. It accentuates the tremendous height of the Fonthill tower, as the tower of Hadlow Castle, which appears considerable on the spot, is about 170 feet high, whereas the Fonthill tower was no less than 280 feet in height.

Woolwich Common, for the Government and designed it in more or less Gothic style, though he used the purely classical motif of a central block and wings joined by colonnades. The central building is Tudoresque and comprises a hollow square of brown brick with octagonal turrets at the four angles surmounted by ogee-shaped cupolas. The castellated parapet between these is raised in the centre to contain a clock face. The central porch contains an unusual doorway set in a sort of window effect containing two tiers of four lights. The colonnades are of Roman cement and have seven four-centred archways each, with castellation above. The wings are again of brick and are simply plain blocks with a projecting centre carried up to contain an extra storey with a castellated parapet over the whole. Beyond them are further colonnades of four arches each, but if these led to outer contemporary wings, the latter have been rebuilt in modern times.

The centre Tudor block with its ogee cupolas is quite a picturesque composition, but the wings are extremely dull, and the effect of the whole is not striking. The building is not now used as a military academy and has rather a forlorn air. But it can never have had anything of the monumental splendour of Wyatt's classical Royal Military College at Sandhurst.

He also worked at the Royal Artillery Barracks at Woolwich. The east half of the mess or main building had been erected in 1776-1782. The west half is an exact replica of this, which was completed in 1802 and may have been executed under Wyatt's supervision. The two blocks are joined by a handsome stuccoed triumphal archway consisting of a tall round-headed carriage entrance and two pedestrian openings, all flanked by Doric columns and topped by a high panelled parapet with projecting portions above the columns, on which stand some fine trophies and a royal cartouche in the centre. This archway may well be Wyatt's. A rough sketch of Wyatt's jotted down on the covering paper of a letter has survived, marked 'sketch of column for the colonade [sic] before the Barracks at Woolwich'.[1] The bottom portion of the column was to be of stone and plain, the remaining two thirds of wood and fluted with a Doric capital. This column does not fit the triumphal arch just mentioned, as the sketch shows the end of a pediment above the column. But it might relate to the new riding-school which Wyatt built at Woolwich Barracks in 1802 and which a local guide-book describes as having been a replica of an ancient temple. The existing riding-school at the Barracks however is an

[1]Now in the possession of the Vicomte de Noailles.

almost featureless building of stock brick with lunette windows and buttresses.

(4.) *Norris and Other Castles*

At the turn of the century Wyatt tried his hand at castle building in the style that Nash used so widely at approximately the same period. His first and most successful venture, Norris Castle, East Cowes in the Isle of Wight, which was built for Lord Henry Seymour, had a definite Nash inspiration. Its estate adjoined Nash's own country house, East Cowes Castle, and the house was begun in 1799, only a year after Nash commenced operations at East Cowes Castle. Norris Castle's other neighbour was the then unknown Osborne House belonging to the Blanchford family, which Queen Victoria was to purchase in 1845.

Lord Henry Seymour was the second son of the first Marquess of Hertford, for whom Wyatt had worked at Ragley Hall and Sudbourne Hall. Farington describes Lord Henry as 'an able man and a scholar, shy but on acquaintance agreeable'.[1]

Norris Castle is much more dramatically situated than either East Cowes Castle or Osborne and, like Fonthill, is another example of how well Wyatt understood the composition of scenic effects. It is placed half-way up a gentle slope overlooking the Solent and is a prominent landmark in our time to all transatlantic liners sailing from Southampton which pass it at very close range. (Plate 58.)

The castle is composed of three sections. The residential portion at the east end is dominated by a round tower of four storeys, behind which is a rectangular block with a castellated parapet, and is balanced to a certain extent by a lower square turret at the south-west corner. Beyond this is the service wing of one storey only on the south front but two on the north owing to the slope of the ground. This is symmetrically designed with a squat projecting tower in the centre. The east section is made up of the stables which are all part of the building without a break and communicate with the house internally. They form a complete courtyard now glassed over. The façades are symmetrically arranged with square projecting towers at the angles and in the centre of the north and south fronts, and a castellated parapet over the whole. At the east and west ends of the castle are great projecting semi-circular bastions which form small terraces. The austerity of the building is offset by sash windows with ordinary

[1] *Farington Diary*, 7 Nov. 1797.

glazing bars, those in the principal portions of the house having round heads.

The interior is very plain. The principal feature consists of a completely circular room on four storeys in the round tower. There is no simulation of Gothic decoration except for a rather half-hearted attempt to imitate vaulting in the hall and a chimney-piece in the library on the ground floor of the round tower. This room also retains its original bookcases which are divided into tall thin panels of which the heads are faintly reminiscent of Gothic motifs, but they are not very impressive and are somewhat of a forecast of early Victorian decoration in the strict sense of the expression.

Of equal interest to the house are the farm buildings at Norris Castle. These are about a quarter of a mile inland to the south-east. They are so disposed as to give the effect at a distance of the curtain wall of a medieval castle and are another piece of purely scenic construction. (Plate 57.) In the centre of the main front facing west is the bailiff's house. This is a small rectangular block with a tiny imitation turret in the centre. It is a small version of the stables. On each side of the bailiff's house a curtain wall links this to a square gateway with castellated parapet, beyond which another portion of wall joins these to slightly larger and higher square towers containing workmen's cottages of two storeys and one window on each floor. Beyond these again is a curtain wall broken by another gateway, this time with gate piers only and no arch. In the angles of the front are square turrets which are purely ornamental and contain nothing. Behind this façade the whole of the farm-yard is paved with stone blocks and backs onto the kitchen-garden which is separated from it by a plain wall. The curtain wall of the mock castle surrounds the latter as well as the farm-yard, and the kitchen-garden is entered on the north side through a gateway in a turret in the centre of this side which is of the same design as the angle towers.

All the subsidiary buildings of the Norris Castle estate are of castle derivation. One of the lodges is a small circular tower of three storeys, (Plate 22) and the other a small rectangular building not unlike the bailiff's house. Even the boat-house has a castellated parapet.

In 1800, the year following the construction of Norris Castle, Wyatt built Pennsylvania Castle, Portland, for John Penn, the grandson of the founder of Pennsylvania, for whom he was working at the same time at Stoke Poges Park, Buckinghamshire. It is traditionally said that the site was chosen by George III when he was riding over the

161

Royal Manor of Portland with John Penn, who was the Governor of Portland. On completion, the Castle was formally opened by the King's daughter, Princess Elizabeth. It is built of Portland stone on a foundation of rock. It is a less spectacular version of Norris Castle with a round tower of only two instead of four storeys. The windows are casements, and those on the ground floor French windows glazed to imitate church windows of Perpendicular style. In 1802, also for John Penn, Wyatt rebuilt Stoke Poges Vicarage in a simple castellated Gothic manner.

Two wash drawings have survived amongst those in the album possessed by the Vicomte de Noailles of a castellated house somewhat in the style of Norris and Pennsylvania Castles. The plan shows an L-shaped addition to a small square pre-existing building. The main wing consists of a 'Cloister Hall' and greenhouse running parallel and joining the eating-room to a circular drawing-room in the tower which forms the main feature of the elevation of the house. There is no clue to the identity of the house except that one of the rooms is marked 'Sir John's Room' on the plan.

Between 1801 and 1811 Wyatt carried out for the 11th Earl of Pembroke work at Wilton House which was Gothic in character. The house as it was left by Inigo Jones and John Webb was, and still is, a hollow square with the centre portion of the east front, then the main entrance, dating from before the fire of 1647. Wyatt pulled down and rebuilt the north and west fronts. The former, as rebuilt by him, contained bedrooms, offices, a dining-room and a hall replacing the former great hall. Wyatt transferred the main entrance to the centre of this side, raising the level of the ground so that the front door opened directly on to the piano nobile. To it he added a Gothic porch. Round the entrance he constructed a forecourt by enclosed walls imitating single-storeyed buildings which are divided into bays, two on each side projecting and three recessed, but not actually containing any rooms. The courtyard was completed by Sir William Chambers's triumphal arch surmounted by a statue of the Emperor Marcus Aurelius which Wyatt removed from the summit of the hill in the park on the south side of the house, where it had been erected in 1755. On each side of the arch he added single-storeyed lodges with balustraded parapets which were connected to the archway by curtain walls forming loggias on the inner side. This makes a very impressive entrance to one of the finest houses in England and is still as Wyatt designed it. But the north front of the house has been again altered in the present century to give it a more classical look in harmony with the east and south fronts. A balustraded parapet has been substituted for castellation. Square-headed casement windows have taken the place of Wyatt's pointed windows on the ground floor and the sunk panels containing roses above them. The Gothic porch has been removed.

The new west front contained a library seventy feet long and a chapel. The interior of the library has been 'ungothicised' by the present Earl of Pembroke. But some of Wyatt's work can be seen in the exterior of this wing. Its arrangement is not symmetrical. The centre is of two storeys with a large oriel window approached by steps across the forecourt. On each side of this is a three-storeyed portion, of which the north section has pointed lancet windows. The whole is surmounted by a castellated parapet.

The old main entrance in the east wing became henceforward only a garden door. Above the surviving Tudor portion of the house Wyatt added an octagonal wooden clock turret surmounted by a small cupola with an ogee-dome and a weather vane. Inside and approached from this entrance he designed the Gothic Hall (a separate room from the front hall in the north wing which is also faintly Gothic in style). This has a ribbed plaster ceiling. Out of it leads the staircase on the south side, which replaced the 'Geometrical' staircase designed by Inigo Jones. This is comparatively small in scale for such a large house but is of the common pattern of a single flight dividing at the half-landing. The balusters are of cast iron shaped like twisted cord. The doorways at the head of the stair have obtusely-pointed heads.

In 1801 there was no connection between one wing of the house and another except through the rooms. To obviate this disadvantage and also to house Lord Pembroke's collection of statuary, Wyatt built a two-storeyed cloister or gallery all round the inner courtyard of the house. This is of slightly lower elevation than the main building and is surmounted by a castellated parapet. It is faced with Roman cement to match the Chilmark stone of Jones's work. The ground floor windows are square-headed but those on the first floor, with obtusely-pointed heads and containing four lights, are of vaguely 'Perpendicular' character. Originally they contained stained glass but this has been removed. In the centre of the east and west sides on the first floor are small oriel windows. All the four sides of the quadrangle are divided into bays by buttresses which flank the windows.

Inside this cloister, the ceiling has ribbed plaster vaulting, as in the Gothic Hall, with stone bosses. The portions between the ribs and the walls are lined in imitation of masonry. Inset on the walls are classical bas-reliefs surrounded by mouldings to imitate frames. Interspersed with these are Coadeware plaques of classical scenes or amorini playing, similarly framed. Beneath the windows are stoves enclosed beneath slabs of variegated marble supported on wrought iron grilles. Though, to modern ideas, Wyatt's classical vein would have blended better with the Stuart house, this Gothic cloister is good work of its kind and date and does not disgrace the magnificent house of which it forms part. Still further alterations were possibly envisaged at Wilton at the period, but Lord Pembroke eventually lost patience with Wyatt's intolerable dilatoriness and gave him up.

Wyatt's next Gothic enterprise and one of his most important works was Belvoir Castle, Leicestershire, for the Duke of Rutland. This was begun in 1801 and was still under construction at Wyatt's death. It is probable that the work was continued by Jeffry Wyatt, as at Ashridge. But a serious fire occurred in 1816, after which the castle was completed by the Rev. Sir J. Thoroton. The result is that the respective shares of these architects are difficult to disentangle.

There is however little doubt that Wyatt built the south-east front which has a simple two-storeyed castellated elevation with square towers of three storeys at the ends. These towers contain the corner sitting-room and the boudoir of the fifth Duchess of Rutland. The former has a frieze of acanthus leaves and fleurs de lys. The boudoir has Etruscan decoration—a late use of this style. The walls are painted with three rectangular and ten round chiaroscuro panels of classical figures. The cove of the ceiling is also painted with gryphons, lyres and scrolls in the same shade of brown.

It is likely that Wyatt also designed the south-west front of the castle, though the only feature which is really typical of him consists of the two spiky octagonal turrets in the centre of the façade which are of different coloured stone from the remainder. The round tower as it is today has such marked similarity to that of Windsor Castle that it is more typical of Jeffry Wyatt. But this is probably due to the alterations to the fenestration, and the tower itself is almost certainly part of Wyatt's design. The fire did not penetrate to it, and the Regent's Gallery of which it forms part has a wide frieze of scroll-work similar to that used by Wyatt in Liverpool Town Hall.

The chapel, which adjoins the Regent's Gallery, has imitation vaulting in plaster which might equally well be the work of James or Jeffry. So also have the ballroom staircase and the ballroom itself,

164

59 and 60. Drawings by J. C. Buckler
(*Reproduced by kind permission of the Royal Institute of British Architects*)

61. Stoke Poges Park

62. Frogmore House
(Reproduced by gracious permission of H.M. The Queen)

but these probably date from after the fire, as the Grand Staircase was destroyed by the latter. There are six small rooms, three of which are called the King's rooms, with Chinese wallpapers of earlier date than even Wyatt's work in the castle, though these papers were probably inserted by him. The only other room that shows traces of the early work at Belvoir is the Elizabeth Saloon. The walls are completely lined with the most magnificent eighteenth-century gilded panelling brought from a French château, but the ceiling was painted by James's son, Matthew Cotes Wyatt. It comprises four great semi-circles with a complete roundel in the bow of the room. In two of the spaces between are medallion portraits of the fifth Duke and Duchess of Rutland. The room also contains a full-length statue of the fifth Duchess by Matthew Cotes Wyatt, who also designed the mausoleum in the grounds where she is buried.

The kitchen-garden shows signs of Wyatt's hand in the great pointed stone archways flanked by buttresses with ogee tops which stand in the centre of each side of the usual red brick encircling wall and in the similar buttresses in the four corners.

To the same period as Belvoir Castle (1802-11) belongs the great castle-palace which Wyatt built for George III at Kew. This was no doubt the most imposing of his Gothic houses in purely castle style, and it is a great pity that it no longer exits. It is described in Chapter XII.

In 1804 Wyatt received a commission from Lord Selsey to rebuilt West Dean Park, near Chichester. This house was greatly enlarged in 1893 by King Edward VII's friend, W. D. James, and the interior was entirely remodelled in the most sumptuous style of that period, largely in imitation of French eighteenth-century work. But the exterior of a large part of Wyatt's house at the west end of the main front is still intact. This is built of flints set in galletting, a local material which Wyatt had used a few years previously at the insistence of the Duke of Richmond at Goodwood, whose estate adjoins that of West Dean Park. The elevation is a plain castellated one of two storeys with a squat tower of three storeys towards the west end. The windows are casement windows with stone mullions and transoms. To the east of this surviving portion was originally a gable containing a large pointed window which lighted the entrance hall and, beyond, a single-storeyed corridor leading to a squat tower of two storeys. The gable has been replaced by another tower and the space beyond it has been filled in, but the pointed sash windows of Wyatt's eastern tower survive. Inside a few classical chimney-pieces survive, and possibly the bookcases in the study may be Wyatt's work. The service wing behind dates from Wyatt's time and possibly the stables to the east.

(5.) *Ashridge*

The year 1808 saw the beginning of Wyatt's last important and greatest surviving Gothic work: Ashridge in Hertfordshire. Unlike most of Wyatt's Gothic enterprises, this house had a real medieval connection. A College for a Rector and twenty 'Bonhommes' had been founded there in 1285. At the Reformation the buildings passed into the possession of the Crown but were subsequently, in 1605, sold to Baron Ellesmere, then Lord Chancellor, who was the founder of the fortunes of the Bridgewater family. His descendant, the third and last Duke of Bridgewater, who made a vast fortune out of the development of canals during the eighteenth century, employed Capability Brown to landscape the grounds between 1760 and 1768. He also had some thought of rebuilding the house but never carried this out, as he preferred to live at Worsley Old Hall, Lancashire, whence he could more easily attend to the affairs of his beloved canals. By the time he died in 1803 the old house at Ashridge was more or less in ruins. The major portion of his immense estate passed on his death to his nephew the Marquess of Stafford, later Duke of Sutherland. But the residue, which in itself amounted to no less than £2,000,000, devolved upon his cousin, Lieutenant-General John William Egerton, who was the heir to the Earldom, but not the Dukedom, of Bridgewater.

The seventh Earl of Bridgewater was a very different character from the eccentric and miserly old Duke whom he succeeded. He possessed all Beckford's conceit and most of his wealth but none of his talents. Pride of wealth and position was his dominant characteristic. This was, in fact, to be literally the death of him. Having arranged a shooting party for the Duke of York on what proved to be a bitterly cold day, he insisted on taking part in it though over seventy years of age and would not leave the Duke's side until he collapsed. He was then found to be suffering from frost-bite and had to have several of his toes amputated. When his doctor informed him that his position was critical, he so far forgot that he had once been a General in the British Army as to offer £50,000 if the doctor would save his life, and when told that the doctor could do nothing to help him, increased this offer to £100,000. His greatest vanity however was displayed in his will which gave his fortune to his great-nephew Lord Alford, later Earl of Brownlow, provided that the latter acquired a marquessate or a dukedom within five years from the date of Lord Bridgewater's death. The House of Lords subsequently held that this condition was void as being contrary to public policy.

This however is to anticipate. When Lord Bridgewater inherited Ashridge in 1803 he claimed that, the late Duke having planned to rebuild the house, it was a pious duty incumbent upon him to carry out this project. In actual fact it afforded him a splendid opportunity to indulge in just such a lavish display of wealth as he loved. The house, when completed, must have been one of the largest private residences in England. All the buildings were demolished with the exception of the crypt, which was converted into a wine cellar, and the conventual barn, which was made into a large summer-house after Wyatt's death. It is not known how Lord Bridgewater came to employ Wyatt as his architect. The choice of the style to be used clearly arose from the existence of the old monastic buildings. Wyatt's instructions were to site the new house between an avenue of lime trees on the east, which was only cut down in 1952, and a row of elms on the west, replaced by liquidambars in 1936.

The plan of the house was entirely classical in disposition and one that Wyatt used in many of his non-gothic houses. There was no attempt to confine the offices to a basement, as at Fonthill. At Ashridge in fact they occupy two-thirds of the ground space including the stables and workshops at the west end of the house. The state rooms at the east end were grouped symmetrically round a large square central tower, as in the castle which Wyatt had built for George III at Kew. A long rectangular hall led into the grand staircase which was contained in the tower. Beyond, facing south, was an ante-room flanked by the dining-room and drawing-room, each with a canted bay window spaced with complete symmetry. The east front is made up of the library, whose windows open on to a loggia, and a lobby. To the west the offices were arranged round two internal courtyards.

The main or entrance front faces north. The house was not completed by Wyatt's death in 1813 and was finished by his nephew, Jeffry. A great many of the working drawings have been preserved and can be studied in the Library of the Royal Institute of British Architects. But the exact extent of Wyatt's work and Jeffry's additions can most easily be seen from two sets of water-colour sketches of the house made by J. C. Buckler in 1813 and 1822 respectively. These are also in the Institute's Library. As the first set was painted in the year of Wyatt's death, it shows the sum total of the work executed by him, though much of what was done later must have been taken from his designs. The sketches of 1813 show the main body of the house without the flanking sections at a re-entrant angle. (Plate 60.) This forms three blocks, each symmetrical. The state block has a squat projecting tower in the centre flanked by sections of three storeys and four windows terminating in angle turrets. To the tower Jeffry Wyatt subsequently added enrichment and a porte cochère. The second or centre block is made up of the north face of the first office courtyard. This is slightly recessed and consists of two storeys of nine windows with buttresses between the windows and a castellated parapet above. The third or west block, forming the north front of the second office quadrangle, consists only of a screen containing nine loop windows flanked by buttresses with a squat projecting tower of three storeys at each end. This was the limit of James's work. Beyond, at an angle to the main building Jeffry added stables and workshops on the west forming two irregular courtyards and on the east a wing containing Lord and Lady Bridgewater's private apartments, with an orangery beyond terminating in an octagonal turret. This wing is now the private house of the Principal of the Bonar Law Memorial College which so suitably occupies Ashridge.

The south or garden front is not as impressive as the entrance front since, on account of the projection of the chapel and the intervention of trees, the whole length of the building is not revealed. The state block is again symmetrically arranged with the tower of the staircase dominating it. In the centre is a loggia on the ground floor with an oriel window above and a two-storeyed bay of eight lights on each side. To the west was a single-storeyed wing, originally the conservatory, containing a glazed arcade of eleven four-centred arches. This has now been bricked in and an attic storey of dormer windows added to provide bedrooms. The conservatory joined the state block to the chapel which projects at right angles to it into the garden. Its south end is splayed and at the north end is an elaborate spire which balances the tower of the staircase in the general composition of the house. Unfortunately however the 'flèche' of the spire became unsafe some years ago and had to be taken down. Its truncated state is a sad reminder of the fact that the world of today contains little Bridgewater or other wealth for the restoration of such luxuries or graces.

The *pièce de résistance* of the interior was and is the staircase round which the state rooms are grouped. (Plate 59.) This rises the whole height of the tower which is the central feature of the house. The stair is on the right on entering from the outer hall. Though the balustrade has a mildly Gothic motif, the staircase is constructed entirely on classical lines. Its plan is the same single flight branching into two at the half-landing which Wyatt used in almost all his finest classical mansions where space permitted. Above the half-landing is a niche containing a statue of Edward VI. This and the other statues above were executed by Richard Westmacott. Below the first floor is a frieze of roundels containing cusped cinquefoils. On each side of the room at this level are three four-centred ribbed arches with a balustrade of cinquefoil-headed design and quatrefoils in the spandrels. These light a corridor with ribbed vaulting which runs all round the grand staircase. In the spaces flanking these openings are small canopied niches containing statues of people connected with the foundation of the College of Bonhommes at Ashridge. On the level above the arches there are three further, but this time empty, niches on each wall, and above these a gallery with an iron balustrade all round the room supported on brackets springing from slender shafts which rise from the first floor level. This gallery is purely ornamental and does not lead anywhere. Its only use can have been to view the staircase from above. The gallery is lit by a large tripartite window in each wall, of which each section contains two tiers of cinquefoil-headed lights. Each of the three sections of these windows is flanked by shafts from which springs fan-vaulting. This supports a foliated border framing the square ceiling. Within it is another similar border edging a domed panel of fan-vaulting with the dial of a weather-vane in the centre of it. The fan-vaulting of this ceiling is all in plaster but is so realistic that it has every appearance of stone.

The only other section of the interior which was Gothic is the chapel. This was completed by Jeffry Wyatt after James's death but was almost certainly from James's designs. It is entered via an ante-chapel containing the organ, which is separated from the chapel itself by a tall four-centred archway. The stalls and oak fittings were designed by Jeffry Wyatt. At the east end, the effect of the stalls is continued in stone on each side of and behind the altar. Above the stalls rise pairs of slender engaged columns from which springs plaster fan-vaulting ribbed in stone with, between, a shallow ribbed barrel ceiling. The chief glory of the chapel was originally the sixteenth-century stained glass which filled the tall pointed windows of two tiers of two wide cinquefoil-headed lights. This was brought from Steinfeld in Germany.

When Ashridge ceased to be a private residence it was unfortunately sold and is now in the Victoria and Albert Museum. Between the windows are empty niches with cusped ogee-shaped canopies.

The remainder of the house had no Gothic decoration other than the shape of the windows. Perhaps this was because Wyatt died before the house was finished, though we have seen that in some of his other Gothic houses part of the interior was classical. Of the state rooms only the library as is it was in his day. The book-cases of ebony inlaid with brass are recessed in niches. The wallpaper had a gilt design, now faded, and the coved ceiling has gilded ornamentation in the corners. All the other state rooms were redecorated by Lord Brownlow in the second half of the nineteenth century, the billiard-room in particular being designed by Sir Matthew Digby Wyatt in 1860. Though he was not born until 1820, seven years after James's death, Sir Matthew Digby Wyatt only belonged to the next generation, being James's first cousin once removed.

If little of the internal decoration of Ashridge was Gothic in design, some of the original furniture however was so. Amongst the drawings in the Library of the Royal Institute of British Architects are two sketches of a chair and settee in Gothic taste. These are dated 1814 and signed by Benjamin Dean Wyatt, who must evidently have co-operated with Jeffry Wyatt there after James's death. A third drawing by him shows a large gilded object looking like a vase but which is labelled on the back of the drawing as a grate and so must have been an ornamental stove such as James had designed for the Mansion House at Liverpool. It is by no stretch of imagination beautiful and would hardly have been out of place in the Great Exhibition of 1851.

Ashridge represents the maturity of Wyatt's Gothic work. It comprised a fusion of his monastic and his castellated manners into a style which would probably have been called Tudor at a later stage in the Gothic revival. Of all his non-classical works it was the least scenic in character and owed the least to its situation and picturesque surroundings, the most to its own architectural character. Though it stood in a park landscaped by Brown, it had no particularly dramatic connection with this landscape and was in some ways deliberately subordinate within it, owing to its siting between two avenues of trees at Lord Bridgewater's instructions. The house also was not the production of any particular emotion, other than pride. It was not suggested by or suggestive of either melancholy or megalomania. It was neither a 'Gothic mousetrap', as Beckford called Strawberry Hill, nor a stage-set for a satrap, as his own house might have been called. It was in fact a serious Gothic building, seriously conceived and seriously executed, though it still contained such anomalies arising from the transplanting of classical ideas into a Gothic disguise as the inclusion in the house of a Gothic orangery and a Gothic conservatory. But the general effect of the building from any angle (and even seen from the air) is majestic and impressive. It appears in no sense either gimcrack or insecure. It was probably the first work of such magnitude in the Gothic revival which can be judged on its merits as a serious work. It was free both of the fanciful jesting of the eighteenth century and of the improving mania of the nineteenth. What a delivery it would have been if the revival had persisted in this vein and had not so soon vested itself in that connection with moral values which was so fatal to architecture in the nineteenth century!

A Tudoresque house that followed Ashridge was Elvaston Hall, Derbyshire, which Wyatt designed in 1812. This comprised a plain building with a castellated parapet and porch terminating in a squat square tower with an oriel window on the first floor and octagonal buttresses at its angles. Balancing this tower on the other side was an old gabled portion of the house, but this was rebuilt by Walker after Wyatt's death.

Wyatt's last Gothic work was the Market Cross at Devizes which was erected to commemorate a colossal lie. In 1753 a woman named Ruth Pierce agreed to pay her share for a sack of corn. But upon a deficiency being discovered, when she was challenged she wished she might drop dead if she had not paid her share. Having exclaimed this three times, she proceeded to fall down dead, and the money was found in her clutched hand. Her body bore no marks of violence, and the coroner's jury returned a verdict that 'from the visitation of the Great and Almighty God she was struck dead with the lie in her mouth'. If an older memorial had been erected to afford a horrid warning of Ruth Pierce's fate it had presumably fallen into ruins in 50 years and in 1813 Wyatt was commissioned to design another. This was erected posthumously. It is a florid and much be-pinnacled cross consisting of a hexagonal ground floor section on a base of six steps, each side containing a four-centred arch flanked by buttresses and surmounted by a panel of quatrefoil tracery. Inset above is a tabernacle surrounded by flying buttresses which emerge from the plain buttresses below. The whole has more the spirit of the nineteenth-century Scott-Gothic than of the eighteenth-century Wyatt. One can see that the Martyrs' Memorial at Oxford, which it considerably resembles, is only just round the corner, though this was not erected until nearly thirty years later. The cross at Devizes, like the purpose of its erection, was something in the nature of a horrid warning of what was to come from the Gothic revival in the Victorian age.

(6.) *Summary*

Wyatt's career in its Gothic phase was an evolution or progress of a very marked character. In his classical work he had as a young man acquired an elaborate knowledge of principles and details by the study of the great examples of architecture in Italy. When he first came to design a Gothic or pseudo-gothic building he had no such knowledge of Gothic work. From the nature of his first Gothic houses, Sheffield Place and Sandleford Priory, it is evident that he was utterly unfamiliar with this medium. Such Gothic flavour as these houses have is merely a hotch-potch of Gothic details grafted on to a classical body without any semblance of reality.

A few years later, when Wyatt came to design Lee Priory, he had made a small advance. Though this was still quite unrealistic and entirely rococo in spirit, it is clear that at least its architect was familiar with Batty Langley's Gothic designs and with Strawberry Hill, which was the most serious modern Gothic building in existence at the time.

Then towards the end of the seventeen-eighties Wyatt started upon his series of restorations of great Gothic buildings, beginning with Salisbury Cathedral and St. George's Chapel, Windsor, in 1787. Lichfield, Hereford and Durham Cathedrals followed; also Milton Abbey, Dorset, and the Chapels and Halls at New College, Merton and Magdalen Colleges, Oxford. All these restorations were concentrated between 1787 and 1797. Naturally they affected Wyatt's own style profoundly. At the same time he employed draughtsmen at considerable expense to visit the most celebrated monastic, ecclesiastical and baronial structures of England for the purpose of making detailed drawings of their decoration. This eclecticism by proxy alone would account for his superiority in detail to all his contemporaries.

At the end of the century Wyatt emerged from what might be called an indirect part-time study of Gothic architecture just at the moment when the romantic movement was coming to full flower. He had the good fortune to find in William Beckford a client who, on account of his great imagination and wealth, was able to commission from him the most splendid scenic composition in architecture that has probably ever been built in England. His genius was exactly fitted to this task, and the collapse of Fonthill was only in a small measure his responsibility. His castles at Norris, Belvoir and Kew were all examples of the same romantic scenic composition, and Norris Castle, alone remaining as Wyatt designed it, shows how extremely effective and arresting they were.

Wyatt's last great Gothic work, Ashridge, marked another considerable advance, though the reasons for this were probably dictated largely by the exigencies of the site and the character of the owner. Gone are the spectacular emotional associations, the grouping and arrangement for purely scenic effect. The house is a serious work, seriously conceived with intent to be judged purely by its architectural effect. It was in fact the first entirely serious work of the Gothic revival, but without any of those fateful moral aims or attributes which doomed so many of the serious Gothic works produced by outstanding architects in the later phases of the revival.

During his own lifetime Wyatt was held to be very largely responsible for the revival of interest in Gothic architecture as a whole. On his death, *The Gentleman's Magazine* wrote: 'His genius revived in this country the long forgotten beauties of Gothic Architecture. . . . Preeminently, and indeed without a rival, did he, and for the longest period of his professional life, indulge in this his favourite order.'[1] Actually he had far less to do with the original of the revival than is here maintained. Sir Kenneth Clark says: 'Literary men with no particularly architectural bent, had started the demand for Gothic, which was largely satisfied by amateurs. When professional architects employed the style, they did so purely at the dictates of their patrons.'[2] Wyatt's achievement was to shake off the almost 'chinoiserie' effect of the Strawberry Hill influence and to bridge the gap between the Gothic of literary dilettanti and that of professional architects.

It should be primarily on the unfettered and mature work of the last phase of his life that Wyatt's architectural capacity as a gothicist should be judged. He had practically no predecessors by whose example to profit. He was forced to work out for himself all the groundwork of the style. Considering these deficiencies, his work is remarkably successful. Only had he possessed a century of discovery and education behind him, could he have fully shown in this sphere what a really great architect he was and thus have done himself justice.

[1]*Gentleman's Magazine*, Sept. 1813, Vol. 83, Pt. II, p. 297.
[2]Clark, *The Gothic Revival*.

Chapter XI

WYATT AND THE ROYAL ACADEMY

For the space of one year Wyatt was elevated to the chair of the Royal Academy, a place which had never before and has only thrice since been filled by an architect. Behind this step lay a long and rather intricate dispute within the ranks of the academicians, which has long since been forgotten and cannot be said to be of great importance in anything but the history of the Academy; but is yet of some interest to anyone studying one or more of the personnel of the Academy at the time.

The incident is not particularly well documented; but we are lucky that the information that is available happens to come from both sides in the dispute. There exists an anonymous pamphlet, written by J. S. Copley or by Sir John Soane or by both together, in justification of the conduct of the party to which they and Wyatt belonged; and on the other side, the *Farington Diary* gives several interesting details of the opposition, of which Farington himself was a leading member.

The two parties in the Academy were divided over the question of what was really the governing body of the society. The direction of affairs lay normally in the hands of the Council, composed of eight persons serving in rotation for the duration of a year. One party held that the Council should determine everything. But the opposition contested that this direction of affairs must be subject to the veto of the General Assembly composed of all the academicians; or in other words that, in the last resort, the Assembly should rule. In 1800 this party tried to stop Tresham from serving on the Council when his turn came. He appealed to the King and gained his point.

When this policy of definite interference was thus checked, the Assembly turned to the idea of appointing committees to deal with certain matters. Now Richards, the Secretary, and Yenn, the Treasurer, were agitating for an increase of salary, and this was the actual beginning of the subsequent schism. The Assembly appointed a Committee to report upon the advisability of granting this increase.

But meanwhile the Council had changed, and when the Committee reported to them the Council refused to receive the report and entered a protest upon the journals.

The party in favour of the superiority of the Council had for some time wanted to make a stand and took this opportunity, when they had a majority in the Council, to resist the encroachments of the Assembly and its Committees. This majority consisted of Bourgeois, Copley, Soane, Wyatt, and Yenn. On 24th May 1803 they resolved that 'the Council is in no respect whatever subject to the General Assembly and that the members of the Council are not responsible either collectively or individually for their proceedings in the Council'.[1] They also voted that this motion be submitted to the King for his opinion.

This seems an extraordinary position to take up, as its application would have rendered the Council utterly irresponsible and is quite contrary to the usual custom of societies, whereby the committee or smaller body acts because the members as a whole are inoperative but which is, and must necessarily be, subject to a general vote, even if it overrules a previous decision of the committee.

The President summoned a special meeting of the Assembly which proceeded to suspend the five members of the Council who had voted for the offending motion. As they had thereby suspended the whole Council—three being not a quorum—the Assembly then transacted all the business of the Academy. Both sides thus proceeded with such violence that they had each acted *ultra vires* in turn: the Council in claiming to be irresponsible and the Assembly in carrying out the functions of the Council, whereas it was their business to ensure by their criticism and overruling votes that their policy was executed, and not to perform the business themselves.

Both sides then appealed to the King. His Majesty took legal advice and expressed his disapproval of the suspension of the five members, directed that the record of this be expunged from the journals and affirmed that the Assembly had no power to transact business and to vote money, as they had done, without the Council's consent. The Council party considered this verdict a victory for themselves, but it contained no support of their original motion.

The Assembly expunged the record from the journals as directed but went further and included in the deletion the original motion. The Council protested against this extra step at its first meeting and voted that it was not in accordance with the King's order. When this

[1] *Journals of the Council of the Royal Academy.*

175

was read to the Assembly, they seized the book and immediately expunged this vote also, adding that their own action was performed at the direct command of the King. When this was reported to the King, he replied that his message had been misunderstood and directed the original motion to be reinserted, and the order for its deletion to be itself erased. This was in December 1803.

It was this dispute which led up to the resignation of Benjamin West, who had been President of the Academy since the death of Sir Joshua Reynolds in 1792. The part he played in it was naturally and correctly rather of a shadowy nature, for, as chairman, he should have been impartial. But it is probable that his sympathies lay with the party of the Assembly. At one period of the dispute West fell ill, and the Council party seems to have taken advantage of his absence, which cannot have endeared them to him.

During the interval of the European peace in 1802 he, in company with Farington and Hoppner, had visited Paris. This incident and his avowed admiration of Bonaparte gave rise amongst his enemies to the accusation of being a 'democrat', as extreme radicals were then called. The charge was probably quite untrue and made his position very awkward, as he suspected that this tale had been reported to the King by Wyatt. Again this suspicion may have been without foundation. But Farington noted in 1799 that he had been told by Tresham that Wyatt had informed the King that there was a cabal within the Academy,[1] presumably not Wyatt's own party. When Academy business took West to the royal presence, the King treated him in a friendly manner and even deprecated the action of the Council in taking advantage of his illness. But West was tormented by suspicions, and even at the best of times his relations with the King were never intimate.

Of the whole body of academicians, Wyatt was undoubtedly on the most intimate terms with George III. For this reason his friends in the Council party proposed that he should contest the election for the Presidency. They gave out that, if he filled the chair for a year, at the end of that period something might have been settled concerning the government of the Academy. In fact the suggestion may even have proceeded from the King himself. The opponents, however, held that the main object of the idea was to control all affairs during George III's life and Wyatt's tenure of office.

In any case, in December 1804 Wyatt stood for election. He received

[1] *Farington Diary*, Dec. 27, 1799.

seven votes; West twenty; three were blank. The next year of office proved still more uncomfortable for West. He was elderly and not in good health. He felt all the time that the King was hostile to him and that Wyatt and his party were going behind his back and keeping the King's ear, which was probably true. So at the end of the year West resigned, and Wyatt was elected to his place.

He seems to have been a real log king and to have done nothing. His only achievement was the recovery from the Dilettanti Committee to the Academy of the appointment of a not very important committee of Artists for St Paul's Cathedral and Westminster Abbey. As a chairman he can certainly not have been a great success, as the habit of sleeping in his place at inopportune moments, to which he had always been prone, had naturally grown on him with age. He had even slept at Beckford's table at the great entertainment given to Nelson at Fonthill. So it is hardly to be wondered at that on the few occasions during his year of office when he took the chair at Academy lectures, he fell into a sound sleep, to the great amusement of the students.

After the annual dinner in June 1806 William Porden told Farington that Wyatt had been very dull in the chair. 'He said Wyatt is a man of abilities, but in private society his conversation consists chiefly of jokes and light matter.'[1] These should have been very appropriate at the dinner, but they do not appear to have been appreciated; or else, Porden had no sense of humour.

It is a pity that we have no mention of the function from some contemporary who was favourable to Wyatt at the time. The bill for the dinner amounted to as much as £300. Farington says: 'Many of the charges were shamefully extravagant and unreasonable. Such has been the management under the new government of the Academy!'[2] He himself had stayed away from the dinner, though under West's Presidency he always had much to do with the arrangement of festivities and allotted the places at the table. This would account for the last portion of the entry. But, as Auditor, it was his function, no doubt, to superintend the limitation of expenditure. If Wyatt had anything to do with the finances, however, it is hardly to be expected that they would be in anything but a chaotic condition. Farington might have added this, had he known then, as he did later, of Wyatt's personal financial embarrassments and eccentricities.

In May 1806 James Boaden told Farington that the party which had

[1] *Farington Diary*, 9 June 1806.
[2] *Ibid.*

made Wyatt President was now dissatisfied with him because he did not take enough notice of them.[1] By the end of the year he himself was content to withdraw from, and West to return to, the chair. Both sides accepted this arrangement and perhaps even welcomed West back again. Even the Royal Family seems to have have been satisfied. Association with Wyatt was far more agreeable when there was no business to be done; if there was, it was apt to be a little trying.

Wyatt's deed of appointment as President was never actually signed by the King. Consequently, on occasions, he is not included in the list of those who have held that office. But as he undoubtedly discharged all its functions for the space of a year and was recognised as chairman even by those who opposed his election, he must certainly be counted amongst those who have attained to the first place in the Academy.

[1]*Farington Diary*, 5 May, 1806.

CHAPTER XII

THE RELATIONS OF WYATT AND THE ROYAL FAMILY

THE post of Surveyor-General to the Office of Works, which Wyatt held for seventeen years, brought him into official connection with the King. But their association had originated more privately. When alterations were carried out to the official residences of the Crown and paid for out of the civil list, the architect was necessarily the Surveyor-General. But if it was a question of the houses privately owned by the Royal Family or of work privately undertaken, the choice of an architect was unlimited. After the building of the Pantheon the King had noticed Wyatt with favour, and this proved more than a mere perfunctory presentation; for in 1787 he called in his services to superintend the restoration of St George's chapel, Windsor, the expenses being largely met out of the privy purse.

The chapel had lately been in a very bad state and needed a good deal of attention. Wyatt did not work alone and seems to have had little responsibility for what was done. The whole building was repaved, the woodwork of the stalls renewed, and a vault constructed beneath the tomb-house. With the rest of the work Wyatt had little connection. A new organ, organ-screen and altar-piece were inserted, the two latter being from the design of a local architect named Emlyn.

One atrocity was committed. The whole of the east window, glass, tracery, mullions, and all, were removed in order to make way for one of Benjamin West's design, showing 'The Resurrection'. This was replaced seventy years later by one in memory of the Prince Consort. The flanking windows terminating the aisles were also removed. The west window was doomed but never destroyed. In 1797 Farington stated that 'Wyatt and Lysons much regretted taking away beautiful Gothic work at the west end of Windsor Chapel—to make room for a painted glass picture by West, who has persuaded the King to do it'.[1] The tenses of this entry are a little vague. The first half, being in the

[1]*Farington Diary*, 6 Nov. 1797.

past, would make one think that 'west end' was a slip of Farington's part for 'east end', and yet the latter half of the entry almost conveys that the change had not yet been executed. The date when this was written is seven years after the work on St George's chapel is usually reckoned to have been finished.

But as late as 1804 Farington reported that West 'was now in great apprehension that his undertaking for the chapel of Windsor would never be accomplished, which he considered to be owing to Wyatt, who would not proceed with the alterations'.[1] This almost certainly refers to the west window. West had been paid £1,500 for his former composition and was naturally anxious to secure the repetition of such a commission.

These two quotations clearly absolve Wyatt from responsibility for the removal of the windows in St George's chapel, though in the latter case his action does not seem to have proceeded from quite such pure motives. The coupling together of the names of Wyatt and Lysons is worthy of note, as it would be difficult to picture the Wyatt of tradition and one of the most respected antiquaries of his day giving utterance to the same sentiment; which is a sign that it is time to revise the tradition.

The next commission which Wyatt received from the Royal Family was at Frogmore, Windsor. This was a small estate that had been purchased in 1790 by the King for £8,000. It was then given to the Queen in exchange for Queen's House, London, afterwards Buckingham Palace, which she had renounced to the Crown to form the principal royal residence in London. Frogmore became the Queen's private domain, which was to her much that Trianon had been to Marie Antoinette prior to 1789.

Her first action was to create a garden there. This was laid out by a clergyman named Alderson, to whom the King had given a living in Yorkshire. The Queen described him in a letter to her son, Prince Augustus, later Duke of Sussex, as 'a man of great natural taste, but not of the World'.[2] According to Farington, the ornamental water was planned by a Major Price, presumably William Price who was Queen Charlotte's Vice-Chamberlain and the brother of Uvedale Price. The greenhouse was the work of W. T. Aiton. In this lay-out Wyatt designed several minor buildings: a dove-house and a rustic hermit's cottage, both since demolished, and a Gothic ruin which

[1] *Farington Diary*, 31 May 1804.
[2] 11th February 1791. Royal Archives at Windsor.

survives. (Plate 52.) This contained a room in which the Queen could breakfast, a sort of loggia attached and two little service-rooms behind. The main room has pointed windows, buttresses and a castellated parapet over it. Attached are just sufficient pieces of masonry to give the building an air of having survived from some monastic foundation. Particularly today, when largely covered with wistaria, this deception is very effective. Inside, the ceiling has a design of squares in Tudor style and tiny fan-vaulting round the edge all picked out in various colours.

Work was not begun on the house until 1792. On 13th January the Queen wrote to Prince Augustus: 'Wyatt the Architect has made me the prittiest [sic] plan imaginable for a Gothic cottage, it consists of four rooms upon a Floor besides the Towers of which there are 4, which will make eight closets alotted [sic] for Books, Plants, China and one for the Flower pieces painted by Miss Mosert [sic]. There will be a colonnade the whole length of the house which will make a sweet retirement in the summer all dressed out with Flowers.'[1] The next year she wrote: 'Mr Wyatt is just returned from Oxford with many pretty tantalizing proposals about my little paradise, of which many must be rejected, but not all',[2] probably on the ground of expense. For this reason and in order to make the pleasure of adaptation last as long as possible the Queen emphasized that she was resolved to spin out the work very gradually.

Some of the tantalizing proposals that must have been rejected were the towers (except in the stables) and indeed the whole Gothic character of the house. As realized by Wyatt it is a medium-sized country house of plain classical elevations. There was an existing building on the site, to which Wyatt added a second storey, flanking pavilions and a glazed colonnade or conservatory connecting them along the whole length of the west front. The east or entrance front is plain to the point of sternness. Its only feature is a porte cochère. The garden front of the centre block is somewhat similar but is masked by the ground floor additions which relieve its austerity. Each pavilion consists of a bowed centre portion of higher elevation than the remainder and rectangular flanking wings with a balustraded parapet. The latter is continued across the slightly recessed conservatory, whose seven round-headed French windows give the west elevation something of the light and sunny aspect of an orangery. (Plate 62.)

[1]Royal Archives at Windsor.
[2]Letter of the 8 July 1793 to the Earl of Ailesbury in the 15th Report of the Hist. MSS. Commn., Appendix Part 7.

However attractive this is, the stables surpass it and are an enchanting little building. They are faced with gleaming white stucco. In the centre is a carriage archway with flat lintel, surmounted by a semi-circular tympanum containing a single window squeezed in to the extreme head. On each side of this is a small square tower, of which the upper portion, in the place of a window, has a clock face and sundial respectively. Above each is a tiny cupola topped by a ball cap. Beyond the towers are two-storeyed wings of three windows each. The whole building has exactly the right air for an English Trianon or royal plaything. (Plate 64.)

Much of the interior decoration of the house has been renewed in the nineteenth century. But the eastern pavilion contains three rooms which retain most of their original features. The first of these (numbered 29) is decorated with large flower paintings on a black ground by Mary Moser. The white marble mantelpiece is supported on small rams'-head corbels, beneath which is a fringe of imitation drapery in marble. This is not as elegant as most of Wyatt's chimney-pieces, though infinitely more pleasant than the much heavier imitation drapery fireplace which he designed for Castle Coole at about the same period.

The adjoining room is the finest surviving at Frogmore. This occupies the bowed centre of the south-east wing, and the north end of the room is similarly curved to form an apse containing two semi-circular recesses with a doorway between and half-dome over. The walls are decorated with a charming grisaille paper[1] having a pattern of bunches of flowers set in gilt panels. Round the top is a frieze of scroll-work interspersed with a motif of two sejant lions facing a vase. The cove of the ceiling is painted with an elaborate pattern of geometrical shapes. The chimney-piece is of white marble with a rather ghoulish frieze of grotesque masks. The outstanding feature of the room is however the doorcases. These are set in an architrave surround consisting of a band of laurel leaves picked out in gold and surmounted by a cornice of acanthus design. The door in the east wall leads into a room that was possibly once the ball-room. The communication between the two rooms has one of those curious architectural pretences to which eighteenth-century architects were prone. On the west side it is a single doorway matching the other two doorways in that room. But on the ball-room side the doorway is apparently double, though the right half is actually a fixed dummy door not even leading

[1] This is probably of later date than Wyatt's time.

into a cupboard. The design of this doorcase and its companion at the north end of the room is somewhat similar to those of the adjoining room, but above the laurel architrave is a panel with a swag between this and the cornice.

The south wing contained the library with bookcases, since removed, painted in imitation of satinwood. There were two rooms called the Red and Black Japan rooms, of which the walls were painted by Princess Elizabeth in imitation of lacquer, and a third room of real lacquered wall hangings known as the Green Closet.

The staircase is in the centre of the house and is of the single-divide pattern which Wyatt so often used, flanked by Corinthian columns at the base. But the space in which it stands is of rather narrow proportions, as if the architect was constricted by the arrangement of rooms in the pre-existing house. The wrought iron balusters are of a most delightful scroll pattern, of which Wyatt used several variants, for instance at Castle Coole, Fermanagh.

Wyatt's second son, Matthew Cotes, carried out some work for the Queen at Frogmore but probably not as early as 1792, since he was only fifteen in that year. No trace of it however survives in the house at Frogmore today. But he might possibly have been responsible for the painting of the ceiling in the ruin. He began his career as a painter, and it was only later in life that he became a sculptor. One of his best-known works in the latter capacity was the equestrian statue of George III which now stands in Cockspur Street. But before turning to this second phase of work he had received extensive painting commissions from George III. About 1801 he began painting ceilings at Windsor Castle and seems to have been engaged in this work more or less uninterruptedly from 1805-1812, for which he was paid over £3,000. He also painted a series of pictures of Marlborough's battles for the Marlborough Tower at Windsor. The King seems to have been well content with the work, but Sir Francis Bourgeois told Farington that he thought it a shocking example of nepotism on James Wyatt's part that Wyatt had induced the King to pass over many more competent artists in employing his son.

In 1793, probably before the house at Frogmore was finished, Wyatt designed the decorations for a fête held in the grounds, as he did also in 1809 for the festivities held there when George III entered the fiftieth year of his reign. Farington tells us that Wyatt was paid by the Queen for these first decorations, but that the King was so well pleased with the result that he presented him with a gold watch as a mark of his approbation.[1] The Queen gave him a silver tea and coffee service and the Princesses Elizabeth and Augusta a silver inkstand with their cyphers and coronet upon it.

Yet in 1806 Farington put down in his journal that West had told him that 'Wyatt owed his situation with the King and the place of Surveyor-General of the Works to the Queen and Princess Elizabeth, which was to make him a compensation for the trouble and loss of time which he had suffered in the attendance upon the Queen and Princesses building Frogmore, etc. etc., for which it is believed he never received any pecuniary recompense. Indeed Wyatt told a person with whom West is acquainted that the expenses and great loss of time in attending upon the Royal Family had been the ruin of him.'[2]

It is at first difficult to bring these two stories into conformity with each other. The former seems to be far the more reliable. It was written nearer the date of the work concerned, at a period when Wyatt and Farington were on good terms, and apparently based on direct authority, though the nature of this is not stated. The latter comes by a more roundabout route. Yet it does not altogether contradict the other statement. No doubt Wyatt was paid a percentage of the total expenditure for his work. But when summoned to attend the King and Queen he did not charge both for the time which he spent at the palace and on the road, as he was accustomed to do to ordinary clients. Hence the difference in financial advantage.

This brings us to his appointment as Surveyor-General in 1796. For one reason or another, this sprang directly out of his employment at Frogmore. The Queen, whom Wyatt himself considered to be a warm friend to him, may have been influential in securing this position for him; and the Princesses, with whom also he was a great favourite, may have added a word of commendation. But there is no reason to believe that the King was not equally responsible for the choice, both on account of past satisfaction and general appreciation of his professional merits.

Two years before the death of Sir William Chambers the King promised Wyatt the reversion of the office, should he be the survivor. There was nothing unusual in this practice, which was a common one in the eighteenth century; but the emphasis seems to lie here upon the fact that no request for such a favour had been made on the part of the recipient, which was much more remarkable for the period. The King

[1] *Farington Diary*, 23 Nov. 1793.
[2] *Ibid*, 11 Dec. 1806.

told Pitt at once that he had disposed of the reversion to the office, to save applications. Several of these, nevertheless, were made to him direct but were refused on the grounds that the place had been given to the first architect of the kingdom. The Prince of Wales also espoused Wyatt's interest, and sought for him from his father the same favour, only to find that the decision to grant it had already been made. When the King promised Wyatt the reversion he said that he considered him 'the first architect of the Kingdom and the most proper for it'.[1] When the post was actually conferred the King repeated this and added that he had given it to Wyatt because Wyatt had not asked for it.

The salary was supposed to be £500 a year, plus £10 for stationery, as Sir William Chambers had received. But Wyatt's widow, in petitioning for a pension after his death, wrote to Lord Liverpool that the actual amount paid had been £200 a year less than this; a sum which Wyatt had been told would be made up to him, but which never had been received. His attendances at the office were so irregular that one of the clerks told John Bacon that the woman cleaner kept a girls' school in the Surveyor-General's room and turned all the pupils adrift whenever she learned that he was likely to put in an appearance.

As Surveyor-General, Wyatt was naturally responsible for the repairs to all the official residences of the Crown. The Tower, Hampton Court, St James's and Kensington Palaces received much attention, in particular the last which the Board of Works was occupied in making habitable for the Duke of Kent. Former royal houses, too, such as the palaces at Winchester, Newmarket, Greenwich and Richmond fell within the supervision of the Surveyor-General; and in addition, the prisons of the Marshalsea, the King's Bench and the Fleet, at the two former of which extensive repairs were undertaken in the first years of the nineteenth century. But in all these cases, the work done was mainly structural restoration; and it was in the houses actually occupied by the Royal Family at the time that Wyatt was entrusted with more important and more personal work.

There is a curious entry in *Farington's Diary* for the 22nd December 1798 to the effect that Wyatt proposed to build a royal palace in Hyde Park (as had William Kent before him) on the high ground near Kensington Gardens. He even suggested that St James's Palace should be sold to offset the expense.

From 1796 onwards he was almost continually employed by George III. Work began immediately at Windsor, as the King had put off

[1]*Farington Diary*, 14 Feb. 1794.

several changes there during Sir William Chambers's life. But of what was carried out at this period little remains as it was nearly all swamped in the subsequent reconstruction by Sir Jeffry Wyatville.

Wyatt rebuilt the great staircase inserted by Hugh May for Charles II in the Upper Ward and a connecting vestibule. He erected two octagonal turrets on the north front of the castle, caused the interior of the Blenheim Tower and some ceilings in other rooms to be redecorated, substituted at the west end of the inner face of the north wing Gothic windows with tracery and mullions in Portland stone for the circular ones of May's insertion, and built a two-storeyed cloister, as at Wilton, round the small interior courtyard then known as Horn Court, on the site of which Wyatville subsequently constructed the Waterloo Chamber. Wyatt also designed Sandpit Gate in the park.

When George III first went to live at Windsor he was prepared to have the actual castle buildings adapted for his reception but was told that they would not prove comfortable. Consequently in 1776 Chambers enlarged for him the detached building opposite the south terrace called the Queen's Lodge, which had been occupied by Queen Anne.[1] Here the Court had lived when at Windsor since 1778. Wyatt however reported to the King that the castle could be made comfortable, and it was no doubt due to this encouragement that in 1800 the King ordered Wyatt to prepare for his own habitation the ground floor of the north wing under the state apartments. The King moved into residence there in 1804, and it was there that the poor blind old man passed the years of his mental affliction.

Wyatt built a staircase and a range of buildings for the accommodation of the pages at Queen's House, London, and made several internal alterations, again lost in a mass of later work by Nash. He also carried out many repairs at Kew Old House. But his most important enterprise was the new palace at Kew which is usually referred to as 'His Majesty's new Lodge, Richmond Gardens'. The old house had been inherited from the Princess Dowager and was completely unsuited to the requirements of so large a family. The Princes had, indeed, been forced to lodge in separate houses nearby, which was a most inconvenient arrangement.

Work was begun on the new building in 1802. Wyatt was well advanced in his Gothic progress by that year, and though we do not absolutely know that it was he and not George III who suggested the adoption of Gothic here, yet it seems much more likely. In 1804 the

[1]This was afterwards demolished by George IV.

63. Plas Newydd. The Stables
(*Country Life Photograph*)

64. Frogmore House. The Stables
(*Reproduced by gracious permission of H.M. The Queen*)

65 and 66. The New Palace, Kew
(*Reproduced by gracious permission of H.M. The Queen*)

King told West that 'he should have thought it impossible thirty years ago that he should ever encourage Gothic'. 'Wyatt', he said, 'is now in the habit of it.—At Fonthill he had done a great work.'[1] Yet James Elmes maintained that not only did Wyatt come to study Gothic by the desire of the Sovereign, but that also the latter was himself responsible for the design of the new palace at Kew.[2] It seems to be generally accepted that, as a young man, George III had shown some talent for architectural draftsmanship under Sir William Chambers's tuition, but the idea that he had to his credit any larger enterprise than perhaps some garden buildings in the grounds of the old house at Kew is highly fantastic and must be dismissed along with Elmes's other inaccuracies. Whatever the new palace was, both as to style and design, Wyatt must certainly bear the praise or blame for it.

In 1804 the King thought that he would live to inhabit the new palace in two or three years. His expectations of life were realized, but not of the progress of the building. Two years later Farington records that the building was at a standstill, after costing £100,000.[3] The King was fast losing his sight and when he could no longer see the progress of the work he lost interest in it. The Queen never favoured its construction. Work appears to have dragged on until 1811, when the building was nearly covered in. By this time it had cost £500,000, and £500 a year for repairs. The King's permanent illness put an end to all work. The palace remained in this unfinished condition until 1827-8, when it was demolished by order of George IV—one of the few destructive acts of that very constructive king.

Fortunately not every record of the size and character of the building has perished. There is a ground plan of the palace in an album of Wyatt drawings recently acquired by the Victoria and Albert Museum. This shows it to have been the shape of a wide aeroplane with a short tail. The wings comprised stables and coach-houses on one side and possibly a theatre and riding-school on the other. The centre portion was hollow and enclosed a square courtyard with curved corners. The main buildings round this courtyard comprised two L-shaped portions separated in the centre by a carriage archway which was the principal entrance. The other ends of the L-blocks were joined by quadrants of the curved corners of the courtyard to an otherwise free-standing square block with a porte-cochère over the state doorway. This square

[1] *Farington Diary*, 8 Jan. 1804.
[2] *Civil Engineer and Architect's Journal*, 1847, Vol. 10, p. 301.
[3] *Farington Diary*, 26 March 1806.

187

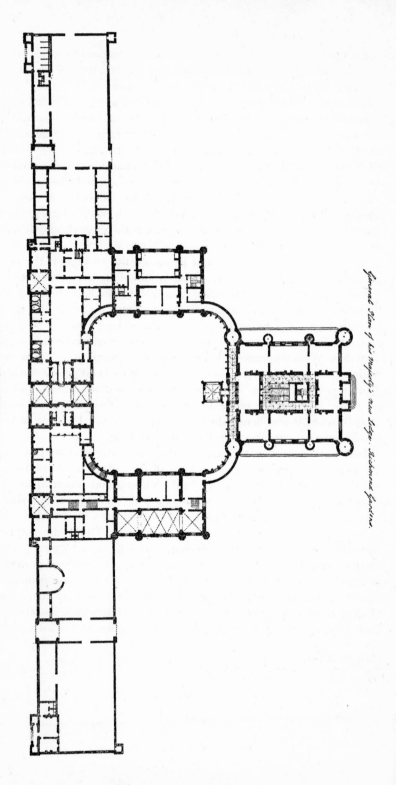

General Plan of his Majesty's New Lodge, Richmond Gardens.

Plan of the New Palace at Kew

block was the most impressive part of the building, presumably containing the state rooms. At its angles were four circular towers and between these on the flanks two smaller circular turrets. In the centre was the main staircase with a square tower over it that dominated the whole building.

Two sketches of the palace have also been preserved and can be seen in Kew Old House. (Plates 65 and 66.) These are such delightful composition, with a lake in the foreground of one and figures strolling in the park beside the palace in the other, that they probably give a rather more romantic than truthful picture of the nature of the building. The entrance front is a plain enough castellated affair. But the square block behind the courtyard with its eight round towers and the tall square tower in the centre was plainly intended to show Windsor what the early nineteenth century could do in the way of castle construction.

It is generally said that the whole building was constructed of cast iron, except the floorboards, after an invention of Wyatt's patented in 1808. But one of the original windows, complete with the panelling of the embrasure, is built into one of the houses in Kew Gardens that is used as an office, and this shows that the surrounds of the windows were of wood, though the casements themselves were of iron. It is greatly to be regretted that this window is the only surviving portion of such an interesting and spectacular building. The use of cast iron in the palace ante-dated by several years Nash's use of the same material in the Royal Pavilion at Brighton, which Doctor Pevsner has cited as the first use of cast iron in England in a non-commercial building.

As George's palace at Kew is said to have cost £500,000, it is strange that this expenditure has excited very little adverse comment either amongst contemporaries or since. This sum was the same total as was spent by George IV on the Pavilion at Brighton, including the purchase of the land, the construction of both Holland's and Nash's versions, the remarkable Chinese decoration of the interior, and the fittings and furniture now in Buckingham Palace. Owing to the rhyming jingle of 'the Pavilion' and 'million', the cost of the Pavilion has usually been much exaggerated, but George IV's expenditure on it was so much blamed at the time that one cannot but be surprised that little or nothing has been said about the outlay of a similar amount upon the construction of a palace which was never occupied, without this including any interior decoration or furniture.

Benjamin West thought that Wyatt had ruined the King with his

189

building enterprises. Most monarchs are usually held responsible for their own architectural expenditure, rather than their architects; but if in his case Wyatt played the part of tempter, it must have been due to the intimate relations which existed between him and the King. He himself told Farington that he was treated with great respect at Windsor and always dined at the equerries' table. This respect Wyatt in theory reciprocated. At the time of the scandal about the Duke of York and Mrs Clark he wrote: 'The respect due to such characters' [the Dukes of York and Kent] 'should never be infringed, and nothing should ever take place to lessen their consequence in the Public mind.'[1] But Wyatt did not always manage to put this respect into practice in his dealings with the much more respectable George III. He carried his slovenly and unbusinesslike manners to the palace and even there could not manage to be punctual. The King was a notoriously early riser and once ordered him to be in attendance at 7 a.m. He arrived half an hour late. The King asked how many hours he usually allowed in bed. 'About eight, an' it please your Majesty', was the reply. 'It is a maxim with me', said the King, 'to allow six hours for a man, seven for a woman, and eight for a fool. Think of this, Wyatt, think of this.' Wyatt was fond of repeating this anecdote.

This was apparently not the only occasion when he kept the King waiting, and the Queen is said to have observed once that he had better be careful or he might make the King wait for him once too often. Perhaps George III's gift of a watch to Wyatt was as much in the nature of a tactful hint for future behaviour as an appreciation of services rendered.

It would seem that these erratic ways, which the Royal Family cannot have construed in any manner but as amounting to disrespect, rather diminished their enthusiasm for Wyatt and possibly prevented him receiving a knighthood. In 1805 the King had a temporary fit of insanity, and while this lasted, the Queen and Princesses had to deal with his architectural concerns and incidentally with the architect. It may therefore be due to this that West was able to think in December 1806 that they would welcome his return to the chair of the Academy on account of dissatisfaction with Wyatt's year of office. As the King's infirmities increased, Wyatt was less and less connected with the palace. After 1811, when the insanity became permanent, for the two remaining years of his own life he faded permanently into the background.

The Prince Regent never substantially employed Wyatt. The fact

[1]Letter of the 14th December 1809 to his son, Matthew Cotes Wyatt.

that, unsolicited, he recommended him to the King to succeed Chambers at the Office of Works shows that he thought well of him as an architect. He remained well disposed towards him until the end of Wyatt's life. When Drury Lane Theatre was burned down in 1809 Wyatt's sons, Benjamin Dean and Philip, both submitted designs for its reconstruction. Wyatt supported the latter very strongly, probably because he was somewhat of a ne'er-do-well, and this design no doubt represented a material hope of at last making his fortune. A letter from Wyatt to a third son, Matthew, dated 24th October, 1811, says: 'I saw the P——e yesterday who said he has said and done all he could without absolutely quarrelling with that obstinate pig W——d' [Whitbread] 'but that he had spoken his mind very freely and decidedly to him about his choice of Plans, that he preferred P——p's all to nothing and that in his opinion there was no comparison as to merit. He said *"I am very sorry for poor P——p but however"* and there he stopd [*sic*]—he was amazingly gracious indeed—I think I shall see him again tomorrow.' The Prince was not however successful in his intervention, as the commission was given to Benjamin Dean Wyatt. His father quarrelled with Benjamin as the result and ceased all connection with him, probably until Wyatt's death two years later.

Though the Prince Regent was friendly to Wyatt, it was not until the year after the letter quoted above was written that he showed any intention of employing Wyatt to execute anything but the merest structural repairs. In 1812 he instructed him to fit up the room adjoining the library at Carlton House as an additional library and to furnish the strong-room with plate-glass cases to contain the Prince's plate. In August of the following year Wyatt went down to Brighton to survey Marlborough House, which adjoined the Pavilion on the north and which the Prince had just purchased from the Duke of Marlborough. He accordingly prepared an estimate for its adaptation amounting to £200,000. He must evidently have considered the commission as fairly definite and that it would involve his being much in Brighton from then onwards, for his intimate friend, Dr. Thorpe, told Farington in 1818 that at the time of Wyatt's death 'an agreement had been made for them to take jointly a house in Brighton for the accommodation of their families'.[1] Unfortunately Wyatt's death the very month his survey of Marlborough House was made put an end to the only chance of large-scale employment by the Prince Regent which had ever come his way.

[1]*Farington Diary*, 17 May 1818.

When Philip Wyatt announced his father's death to the Regent, 'the news very much affected the Prince Regent, even to shedding tears, accompanied by his saying that he had just found a man to his mind, and was thus unhappily deprived of him'.[1] But this habit of weeping copiously in a rather maudlin way was a trick that the Prince Regent was able to produce on all occasions and arose much more largely from self-pity than from any genuine motive of sorrow or sympathy at Wyatt's death. This case proved no exception. His esteem for Wyatt did not induce him to bestow any of the posts that Wyatt held upon the latter's sons, as they supplicated; or even to take notice of his widow's petitions for a pension.

So altogether, all one can say is that the Prince Regent admired his work in a general sort of way but, in spite of a remark in *The Monthly Magazine* that he 'frequently consulted him',[2] never held any serious practical connection with him. For some reason or other, he evidently preferred Henry Holland and John Nash. If it had not been so, perhaps we might have had a Gothic palace at Brighton? However much one would have liked to see another Gothic palace from Wyatt's hand, one cannot regret that the way remained open for Nash's delicate and unique oriental fantasy, without which Brighton would scarcely be Brighton.

[1] *Farington Diary*, 18 Sept. 1813.
[2] *Monthly Magazine*, Oct. 1813, Vol. 36, p.266.

CHAPTER XIII

DEATH

DURING the last decade of Wyatt's life Farington records three separate reports of his health having been adversely affected. On the 1st December 1804 he noted that Samuel Lysons said that he had heard 'Wyatt was paralytic and had his mouth to one side'. Three years later West spoke of Wyatt's state of health and said 'it was not probable he would ever be restored to what he was before his last illness. He said his mind seemed to be gone. The cause of his illness was as follows:'.[1] But the rest of the page in the Diary is tantalisingly blank. The cause alleged was sure to have been one of those pieces of gossipy scandal of which Farington was so fond. In February 1811 Dance told Farington that there were 'visible marks of age and care in his' [Wyatt's] 'countenance.'[2] This is not surprising, as he was then sixty-four.

It is likely that the first two of these rumours were at least greatly exaggerated if not definitely untrue, as right up to Wyatt's death his professional activities and peregrinations continued unabated. In August 1813 The Monthly Magazine stated that Wyatt 'promised, as far as regarded his constitution, his general good health, his habitual activity, temperance, and good spirits, to live to extreme old age'.[3] Fate willed otherwise.

On 4th September he was accompanying his friend and employer, Christopher Codrington of Dodington Park, Gloucestershire, on his return to London from this country house. They travelled in Codrington's coach-and-four. About two miles east of Marlborough, while travelling at a great speed, the carriage met a returning post-chaise travelling in the opposite direction and a man on horseback riding by the side of the chaise. This rider was forced to take his way between the two vehicles; and his horse, being young, became restive and unmanageable. It ran against Codrington's carriage and was thrown

[1] Farington Diary, 20 Nov. 1807.
[2] Ibid., 3 Feb. 1811.
[3] Monthly Magazine, Oct. 1813, Vol. 36, p.265.

over. The wheel of the carriage passed over the rump of the struggling horse, and the vehicle overturned.

'Mr Codrington, falling under, received no injury.'[1] Wyatt at the time had removed his hat and was reading a newspaper. His head struck the roof of the carriage or the handle of the door with great violence, producing concussion of the brain according to one account, or fracturing the skull according to another. Death was either instantaneous or followed after a very short period of insensibility. Farington recorded, on the authority of Dance, that Wyatt had wished to die a sudden death.[2]

The letter which Christopher Codrington wrote to James's son, Matthew, two days later, has survived:—

Park Lane.

September 6th 1813

My Dear Sir,

Indeed I have not the Means of expressing my feelings on your account; But it is the Will of Heaven, and we must submit with fortitude. How I escaped God only knows, but it is perhaps still more miraculous that the Man and horse whom we ran over shd. not have suffered more. Indeed I know well the loss you have sustained, and am sensible of the state of anguish you are in; Would to God, that the slightest particle of Comfort was within my reach! I feared I was doing wrong in leaving Marlbro' before you came, but I know Reports had gone down and up the Road I had also suffered, and Mrs C. was in a state easily to be affected; Nor could my longer stay have been to any other purpose than to have added to the misery of my own mind by witnessing the state of yours. I will add no more; It was the Will of Heaven. I have not the means of comforting you, but you have the most heartfelt good wishes of My dear Sir

Yours most unfeignedly

C. CODRINGTON.'

The body was conveyed to the Castle Inn, Marlborough, where an inquest was held. A verdict of accidental death was returned. The body was then transferred to Wyatt's house in Foley Place, where it lay until the funeral which took place on 28th September.

Sir John Soane proposed that the funeral should be academical; but West ruled that Wyatt's position in the Academy was not such as to

[1]*European Magazine*, Oct. 1813, Vol. 64, p.275.
[2]*Farington Diary*, 3 July 1815.

justify any particular action by them as a body. He was buried in the south transept of Westminster Abbey, rather on account of the position that he held as Surveyor to the church than because of his eminence in his profession; and his grave, which is marked by a stone slab in the floor, fittingly adjoins that of his predecessor, Sir William Chambers, and of his early rival, Robert Adam. The inscription is as follows:—

'Sacred to the memory of James Wyatt, Esq.; who, having devoted many years of his youth to the study of the pure models of Antiquity abroad, was, at the early age of Twenty-two, transcendently distinguished in his Profession as an Architect, in this country: and having sustained the dignity of that Profession for Forty-five years, during the principal part of which he held the Offices of Architect of this Church and Surveyor General of His Majesty's Works, departed this life on the 4th day of September 1813. In private life he was remarkable for his meek, unassuming, and dis-interested dispositions. His professional Ability was the combined result of superior genius, science, and energy.'

Chapter XIV

CHARACTER

SEVERAL portraits of James Wyatt exist, mostly painted towards the end of his life. His son, Matthew Cotes Wyatt, painted him sideface with his hair dressed in the old-fashioned queue of the eighteenth century, though this had probably gone quite out of date at the time when the picture was painted. This portrait was engraved by C. Turner. The Royal Institute of British Architects possesses a portrait of James by Opie with a rather dark background. Another by Sir William Beechey hangs in the Council Room of the Royal Academy. (Frontispiece.) Owing to its position with its back to the light, and to the fact that it badly needs cleaning, it is not seen to advantage. But it is the best of Wyatt's portraits. It was painted about 1800 when he was fifty-four. It shows him to have had a pair of thick bushy eyebrows, a large and slightly arched nose and a determined mouth—much more determined in fact than his easy-going character would suggest. But humour shines from his eyes. Ozias Humphrey also painted him, and this head was engraved by Henry Singleton. (Plate 47.) It was reproduced in Humphrey's *Correspondence*. Wyatt also appears in the picture by Singleton of the Royal Academicians in General Assembly under the Presidency of Benjamin West, which is dated 1795. He is standing at the back of the picture towards the right beside the plinth of a piece of sculpture. In the same year George Dance made a portrait drawing of him which is amongst the series of drawings of the first academicians still in the possession of the Royal Academy. It is dated the 31st March. He was then forty-eight but appears younger, and the profile is not at all like his other portraits. In the National Portrait Gallery there is a bust of Wyatt by C. J. F. Rossi which was cast in 1797.

There is an overwhelming consensus of opinion that Wyatt had three very outstanding faults: an entire lack of business capability, complete incapacity for constant or intensive application, largely resulting from the first, and utter improvidence.

The first two cannot be considered separately. There are various witnesses of these failings. James Wyatt's nephew and pupil, Jeffry, stated that when his uncle received a commission from a new employer for whom he had not worked before, he eagerly attended to all the instructions necessary for the commencement of the work but soon became indifferent to it and casual in his attention.

His designs were struck out in his carriage or at dinner amongst company, wherever he happened to be when they occurred to him. Farington records that, on an excursion to Frogmore, after tea Wyatt sketched a design for a new accommodation for the Royal Academy, the Royal Society, and the Society of Antiquaries on the site of the King's Mews, in order that Somerset House, in which they were then located, could be given over to public offices. These sketches were then left to be worked up by his clerks.

Occasionally he did labour at the big works himself for a certain length of time. William Owen found him employed for three weeks on end in his office at Ashridge. During these periods of application he deserted society and worked incessantly; but at certain particular buildings only. Meanwhile the rest of his work accumulated, and his other buildings stood idle in a manner which was purely the result of bad management and unequal division of his work.

Farington gives a good picture of one of his periods of inactivity. 'Beckford is much dissatisfied with Wyatt, who perpetually disappoints him. He said if Wyatt can get near a large fire and have a bottle by him, he cares for nothing else. He lately left him at the Abbey on the pretence of being obliged to go immediately to town. He (Wyatt) stopped at Fonthill House belonging to Mr Beckford, three miles from the Abbey, there found Foxhall the Carver, and stayed with him there secretly a day and a half enjoying himself, which Beckford a week after discovered.'[1] Meanwhile he was probably charging Beckford five guineas a day for attendance! On the other hand, his periods of concentration were just as complete, and then he left both the company and the bottle to shut himself in his office.

On the whole, it was easier for Wyatt's employers to obtain plans from him than supervision of their execution. The designs cost little effort; but to have them carried out was more laborious. If he did concentrate, it was on the larger houses: Fonthill, Dodington, Wilton, Ragley, and Ashridge. But even here he evidently did not give continual satisfaction, as Lord Pembroke gave him up when his patience was exhausted. The best example of his maddening negligence comes

[1]*Farington Diary*, 29 March 1804.

from two letters of William Windham, which are worth quoting in their entirety.

In 1793 he wrote: 'I shall no longer insist upon a right I have no longer a means of enforcing, nor complain of injuries which it is not in my power to redress. It is near two years since you undertook a business for me neither requiring nor admitting delay, and which you have not done yet. I have written you no less than five letters, desiring to know whether you meant to do this or not, and you have returned no answer.

'You may think perhaps that this is a mark of genius, and the privilege of a man eminent in his profession, but you must give me leave to say that it must be a profession higher than that of an architect, and eminence greater than that of Mr Wyatt, that can make one see in this proceeding anything but great impertinence and a degree of neglect which may well be called dishonest. It is dishonest to make engagements which you are either not able or not willing to fulfil: it is in the highest degree uncivil to receive letter after letter containing a question which the writer is entitled to ask: and to send no answer.

'Pray, Sir, who are you, upon whom engagements are to be of no force; and who are to set aside all the forms of civility as established between man and man? Had the most private Gentleman of the Country written to the first minister of the Country, he would have received an answer in a quarter the time. And what is this privilege denied to persons in that station which you suppose to be possessed by you? A privilege not allowed to a man's betters may be expected to be one of which he has no reason to boast. But of this, I leave you to judge. There is one privilege that you shall not possess, that of acting with rudeness and contumely without being told of your conduct. If you are fond of placing yourself in a situation, in which you must hear these charges without the power of refuting them, I wish you joy of your choice, and with that reflexion shall take my leave of you.

'PS. Am I to expect that the metal frames which you ordered at Sheffield, will come at last when they are no longer wanted: or am I to understand only that what you told me is untrue; and that no such order was ever given?'[1]

Yet eleven years later Windham does not appear to have obtained what he sought. 'I do not like even yet to quit the style of friendly communication, though I must confess that my patience is nearly exhausted; a person has some right to feel impatient, who at the end

[1]Windham Papers, 23 Nov. 1793.

of seven or eight years, (I believe I might say ten), is going into the country with the certainty of finding the principal rooms of his house near uninhabitable, because he has not been able to obtain from you what would not be the work of a couple of hours: the dissatisfaction may reasonably be stronger because my late applications have been, not that you would at all events do what was required, but that you would either complete the design, or tell me at once that you would not do so: this application I must now renew, suggesting to your consideration that the plea of this being your way, and that you treat everyone else so, is really not sufficient to justify a mode of proceeding so remote from all that is expected and all that is observed by the rest of the world. If I receive a letter from you saying that you will without delay complete the design, I will repeat to you in detail what I before stated of the manner in which I would wish to have it done; If you say you cannot do it, I shall then apply to someone else, but a letter I must beg to receive.'[1]

Nothing could be more outspoken than these letters; but they do not appear to have had the smallest effect upon Wyatt. Shute Barrington, Bishop of Salisbury and later of Durham, was another client whom Wyatt treated in this cavalier fashion. William Beckford's half-sister, Elizabeth Hervey, wrote to Beckford from the Palace at Salisbury on the 3rd October 1790: 'I found the Bishop fretting to the greatest degree at Wyatt's provoking delays. He even sent a person to him lately to fetch him here, and as a further inducement, he desired he would bring with him his wife and family. But he was not to be had, and the Bishop is afraid of stirring from Salisbury to see the Fleet, lest he should miss him. In short this said Wyatt seems to be an universal plague.'[2] He was playing the same game with Beckford at the time that Mrs Hervey wrote, as no doubt she knew. The remarkable thing was that anyone of the distinction of William Windham or the Bishop of Salisbury was willing to put up with this casual behaviour. One can only conclude that their anxiety to secure Wyatt's services was very considerable. Of course their patience was not always equal to the demands made upon it: Lord Pembroke gave Wyatt up, and Jeffry Wyatt said that his uncle had lost many clients through his dilatory habits. But on the whole they seem to have been very submissive.

Beckford alone appears to have brought Wyatt to heel in similar circumstances. After the collapse of the first tower at Fonthill he ended

[1]Windham Papers, 12 Jan. 1804.
[2]Letter in the Hamilton Papers.

a long letter of remonstrance addressed to Wyatt in this fashion: 'Determined to sink no longer from disappointment to disappointment I give you this plain and decided warning. If you take it as it is meant I shall see you soon at Fonthill. If not—the whole shall be stopped, every work man shall be discharged, the reasons which have compelled me to adopt so violent a measure stated at large in the (Morning Chronicle)[1] and every other Chron. Morn. or Eve. which appears in London.'[2]

This charge of dynamite seems to have worked, but no milder measure. If it is wondered how any of Wyatt's clients were willing to put up with such treatment at all, the reply was, according to John Bacon, that when Wyatt did appear, 'he had such a peculiar talent in making everyone feel that he was so entirely absorbed in the wishes of his employer that his want of respect in not coming was soon forgotten.'[3] It is a pity that more of his clients did not show some of Beckford's autocracy in the matter.

If Wyatt did let slip some potential engagements, the fact neither was, nor is, at all to be lamented; for the press of his affairs was almost as much to blame as his innate slackness for his inattention. After his death, Lord Liverpool, writing to the Duke of Richmond, remarked upon this: 'Tho' he was in my judgment a man of most considerable talents as an architect, he was certainly one of the worst public servants I recollect in any office, not, I am persuaded, from dishonesty or want of zeal, but from unsteadiness and from his always choosing to engage in a great deal more business than he was capable of.' A man of method might just have managed to keep pace with the demands of his enormous practice. But an erratic cycle of intensive application, preoccupation with particular works and complete inactivity could not but produce a grand muddle.

Those same authorities which cite these unbusinesslike characteristics are very anxious to stress Wyatt's 'mild and gentlemanly manners.'[4] It has been said that these were as responsible as his genius for his distinction. But it would probably be more true to say that they were all that made his outstanding professional faults tolerable. Wyatt was admitted by the majority of his patrons to a considerable degree of intimacy—perhaps because they found private relations an agreeable substitute for the strain of professional intercourse.

[1]Crossed out in the Manuscript.
[2]Undated draft letter in the Hamilton Papers.
[3]Unpublished Diary of John Bacon Junior.
[4]*European Magazine*, Oct. 1813, Vol. 64, p.275.

But one cannot help feeling that the particular insistence of the obituary notices upon his 'irresistible' manners is a rather patronizing approval extended to an individual who had risen from insignificance to fame and association with the great.

Also the quality comprehended in the word 'manners' is here rather that of amiability than that of politeness. It would be difficult to credit a man who failed in all his appointments, even with the King, and never answered letters, with even as much politeness as Dr Johnson considered himself to possess. But it is not difficult to believe in the agreeableness of one whom Jeffry Wyatt again called 'one of the best-tempered men living'.[1] He had the real artistic temperament; was erratic, unreliable, casual in his work and general conduct, and withal charming. It can only have been this genial disposition which accounted for his acceptance as more or less of an equal by many who were really his superiors.

One unpleasant characteristic that Wyatt seems to have possessed was a lack of respect for fellow artists. Lord Pembroke thought he had a mind which was 'narrow towards his profession, having heard him speak in company disadvantageously of professional men'.[2] Perhaps a snobbish liking for aristocratic society had something to do with the matter. Hoppner, in opposing Wyatt's candidature for the Presidency of the Royal Academy, said that 'a man who speaks as he' [Wyatt] 'does against artists not only those in his department, but in every other, is a very unfit man to be placed at the head of such a Society'.[3] William Porden, who had been his pupil, went so far as to say that Wyatt 'had no feeling for anybody'.[4]

In spite of the size of his practice and the amount of his commissions, Wyatt never accumulated a fortune. His friend Dr Thorpe thought this was due to his professional irregularity, his neglect of his appointments, and his general bad management of affairs. But it was really due to his improvidence; he must have earned a fortune but never saved any of it.

Directly after the building of the Pantheon, he had received from certain noblemen a retaining fee of £1,200 a year; and all through his life, his commissions were very substantial. One of his surviving letters for instance refers to the fact that he was owed at least £4,000 for work done at Bulstrode, Buckinghamshire. Yet he spent all that he

[1]*Farington Diary*, 2 Nov. 1812.
[2]*Ibid.*, 7 May 1804.
[3]*Ibid.*, 27 Feb. 1806.
[4]*Ibid.*, 26 Dec. 1804.

received and was frequently in financial difficulties. In 1782 we find him applying to E. Davey of Yoxford, Suffolk, for the loan of £80, which was the amount of a bill due to him and not yet paid, an amount which he needed for other engagements. In 1807 when his wife wrote to him at Fonthill asking for £20, he was not able to pay it and had to request his son, Matthew, in London to advance it for the time being. A few months later he was unable to return to London from Belvoir Castle as bailiffs were in occupation of his house in Foley Place. On this occasion he forwarded a draft for £1,800 to Matthew for the discharge of the debt and asked him to advance the balance if the liability exceeded this amount. On other occasions he borrowed £4,000 from his bankers, £500 from a Mrs Elizabeth Kendal, and applied to Beckford for the loan of an unspecified amount on his bond. Farington also records that he had been bailed out of a sponging house by Beckford.[1]

Probably he found money too easily acquired to rate it at its proper value and was naturally thoughtless and unheeding. William Porden told Farington that Wyatt lost £2,000 or £3,000 a year 'from mere neglect in respect of order in his accounts'.[2] Consequently, when he died he left to his family little more than his reputation. Indeed his affairs were in a terrible condition. He owed £900 to his draughtsman, Joseph Dixon, and £2,000 to Bertolini, the plasterer; his house in Foley Place was mortgaged to the utmost; and his estate amounted to less than £10,000. The latter was renounced by his widow to their eldest son, Benjamin Dean Wyatt. Consequently she was left entirely without means of subsistence until granted a pension of £100 a year by Lord Liverpool in December 1814.[3] She died in 1817.

Rachel Wyatt is a shadowy figure, of whom little is known. A few of Wyatt's letters to her have survived. They invariably begin 'My dear love' but are mostly about commonplace subjects and contain nothing of interest with regard to either his work or his character. There is nothing to lead one to suppose that the marriage was not a success; and Rachel Wyatt, in her petitions after her husband's death, stated that she had been accustomed to peculiar affection and indulgence.

Yet there is one very curious entry, somewhat in this connection, in *Farington's Diary*. On 17th May 1818 he was told by Dr Thorpe, who claimed to have been an intimate friend of Wyatt's, that the latter's

[1] *Farington Diary*, 7 Sept. 1813.
[2] *Ibid.*, 26 Dec. 1804.
[3] Her will was made on the 13th April 1816 when she was living at St. Michael's Place, Brompton, Middlesex.

'love of women led him away from other pursuits, and at the time of his death, one of his female servants was pregnant, and within three weeks of her confinement'.[1] Farington took a curious delight, quite inappropriate to a respectable old widower of sixty-five, in retailing in his private journal the moral lapses and peculiarities of his large circle of acquaintances. Perhaps he might be pleased to think that this entry quoted above is the only accusation laid against the morals of a man to whom he was not particularly favourable.

Nothing is known of Wyatt's daughter Jane except that she died in 1789, no doubt when still a child. Farington describes her mother as having been so much affected by her death that five years later she had still not entered the dining-room since Jane's death and had only recently gone into the drawing-room. Wyatt's relations with his four sons were unusually affectionate for that formal age. Through the patronage of Queen Charlotte, Wyatt was able to place two of them in the service of the East India Company as Writers. These were the eldest son, Benjamin Dean, who was always called Ben in the family, and the third son, Charles Burton. Ben sailed for Calcutta in February 1798 and Charles about a year later. But they did not like life in India and found that the prospect of making a fortune quickly, which apparently was their main objective in following such a career, was not nearly as substantial as they had been led to hope. Charles returned home in October 1801 and Ben probably the next year. There is in existence a doctor's certificate, dated January 1803 and signed by James Earle of Hanover Square, stating that a return to India would be harmful to Ben's health. But as the voluminous memorandum of seventy numbered paragraphs, which he sent home from India to his parents to try and induce them to consent to his return, hardly mentions the question of health at all, one cannot help feeling that this doctor's certificate was somewhat of an afterthought. His cousin, Jeffry Wyatt, in fact told Farington in 1806 that Ben's ill health was only 'a Home-fever—a desire to go home'.[2]

While in India Ben had been attached to the personal staff of the Governor General, Lord Mornington, later Marquess of Wellesley. The latter evidently gave him an introduction to his brother, then Sir Arthur Wellesley, who was Chief Secretary in Ireland for a few months during 1806. Ben accompanied him there as his Private Secretary. This was the beginning of his substantial connection with the future

[1] *Farington Diary*, 17 May 1818.
[2] *Ibid.*, 16 Oct. 1806.

Duke of Wellington later in life when he had entered upon an architectural career.

His initiation of such a career was in 1809, when he submitted a design in the public competition for the rebuilding of Drury Lane Theatre, which had been burned down that year. This in fact led to the only family quarrel of which there is any record. His father was incensed with Ben for entering for this competition, as his youngest son. Philip, had also done so, and James was very anxious for the latter to succeed. Philip had had no previous employment and was somewhat of a problem to his parents. There are numerous references to this in the family correspondence which survives, but the most outspoken is a letter to Philip from his father dated Christmas Day 1806, which is worth quoting in full: 'It is totally impossible for me to express my feelings to you, on the subject of your conduct; or what is still worse I am afraid that nothing I say can say or urge against it will have any weight with you. You have deceived me so often and pay so little regard to what is said to you that I have very little hopes of ever seeing you otherwise than in distress. I will however for this once endeavour to furnish the sum necessary to pay your debts tho' I can very ill afford it, and as to the second part of your request for £120-11-6 I will endeavour to let you have that as well upon your showing me what is to be done with it. Your debt to Stevens' [possibly a servant] 'is abominable and hurts me more than all the rest. Let me know when you want this money to be advanced as it will put me to a very serious inconvenience to spare it.

Yrs Dr. Philip
Most affectly.
James Wyatt.'

Two years later James was so much pledged for Philip's debts that he would not let Philip into the house. His anger with Ben over the Drury Lane competition no doubt resulted from the fact that he considered that this was the one chance of giving Philip a solid hope for the future. Ben however persisted and through the influence of Samuel Whitbread was successful. As a result his father ceased all connection with him at least until 1812 and possibly until his death in the next year.

The two brothers do not however appear to have been estranged, as after James's death they worked largely in co-operation. Ben in fact became a very successful architect.

Charles after his return from India later tried a second job in the

Empire. He became Surveyor-General of Crown Lands in Canada but is said to have returned home after a quarrel with the Governor of the province in which he was working. Thenceforward he devoted himself to his father, though in what capacity is uncertain. After James's death he seems to have become a private tutor and to have had some dealings in the wine trade.

The steadiest member of the family was the second son, Matthew Cotes. He first worked in his father's office and seems to have looked after the business side. His chance came when he was commissioned by Queen Charlotte to carry out some paintings at Frogmore and later by the King to paint ceilings at Windsor Castle. Later he became a sculptor and had a successful career as such. On the 29th December 1801 he married Maria McClellan, widow of Edward McClellan, a sea captain in the East India trade. In 1803 Farington recorded that one of Wyatt's sons—and presumably this was Matthew—married without telling his father of his intentions 'the natural daughter of someone, a very pretty woman with a fortune of one or £2,000'.[1] Matthew and his wife had a large family whose descendants are living today, though none still bear the name of Wyatt.

[1]*Farington Diary*, 21 Dec. 1803.

CHAPTER XV

REPUTATION

WRITING in 1872 C. L. Eastlake said: 'No English architect has perhaps been so much overrated by his friends, or so unfairly abused by his enemies as James Wyatt.'[1] This is really the secret of Wyatt's reputation both during and since his lifetime.

He was at the age of twenty-six raised by popular approbation of a single work to be the chief fashionable architect of the day. As he had not achieved fame by a gradual professional progress in which his merits were consistently displayed in his buildings, the character of his conquest of society was, if more brilliant, much less real than the normal process. It was the caprice of a moment and not obvious sterling qualities which made his name, though the qualities were present. The persons who employed him did so, for the most part, without questioning his merits and just because of his fashionable reputation. But there was also a group of people who were more honestly and sincerely convinced of his worth and who were apt to express their admiration as much in the form of flattery as of praise.

When Wyatt turned his attention to Gothic, a change took place in contemporary appreciation of him. His admirers soon accepted this new phase as easily as the old and, after his first composition, ranked him as high in the Gothic as in the classical sphere of construction.

But they did not carry the whole country with them. If Wyatt had confined his Gothic energies to house building and ruin building, they might have done so. But it was his treatment of English cathedrals which offended the susceptibilities of some of his contemporaries.

There were two sections of opponents with separate objections, aesthetic and archaeological. The one thought Wyatt's activities in bad taste, the other that they were sacrilegious. The latter were the more important. The antiquaries of the period happened to be a more than usually prolific and vehement body of writers. They managed to broadcast their unfavourable opinion of Wyatt quite as effectively, if not

[1] *History of the Gothic Revival.*

more so, than his uncriticizing disciples. It was an evenly balanced dispute.

Then Wyatt died. In the latter years of his life his classical work had been, naturally, rather a modified version of his earlier style, for the demand for what had been the rage in 1772 was not so great in 1800 to 1813. The Greek revival and Regency simplicity were becoming the vogue. Many of his most fervent admirers had died before him. Consequently his reputation as a classical architect was already declining before his death. After 1813 this decline was accentuated, and all his classical work was soon swallowed up in the general appellation of 'the Adam style'.

But the legend of ill-repute still lingered. The antiquaries continued implacable. In fact their vituperation increased and was expressed in a much less justifiable manner than by contemporaries. Carter and his band had known exactly what Wyatt had executed. They took a wild delight in retailing all the details of his work. But successive generations were not similarly well-informed. They knew that he had been condemned for destruction. They seized hold of his bad name and proceeded to use it as a target for all the evil things that critics had to say about eighteenth-century gothicists. They did not inquire into the nature and extent of what he did. Pugin and his followers invented the phrase 'Wyatt the Destroyer' without inquiring how many of the accusations levelled against Wyatt were misattributions or contained exaggerations. His original Gothic construction was as much anathema to them because it was not 'pure' enough to please them. Meanwhile his classical work was quite forgotten.

This process of intensive depreciation on a large scale continued right into the present generation and almost increased in vehemence. This is well demonstrated by the admission of a verger of Salisbury cathedral that every discreditable alteration in that cathedral is attributed to Wyatt. As the early days of the Gothic revival grew more dim, Wyatt stood out more and more as the one well-known figure who had to bear the blame for all the misdeeds of the early Gothic practitioners. Everyone had heard of his existence and of his iniquities in a general way and of few others who lived at about the same time and who did the same things. So the refrain 'Wyatt the Destroyer' became louder and louder. In fact from his death until quite recent years no one ventured to mention his name without indulging in wholesale condemnation. Indeed it is true to say that from 1814 until 1926, with the exception of Mr Potter of Lichfield, not one protesting voice was raised against this flood of often vitriolic abuse.

In 1926 Mr H. Avray Tipping put in a plea for Wyatt's work at Ashridge and in 1928 appeared Sir Kenneth Clark's book *The Gothic Revival*, in which he suggested that Wyatt had been unfairly treated. Sir Kenneth Clark pointed out that even those who most abused his activities were often unaware of the exact extent of these and suggested that there might be a further inquiry into Wyatt's alleged guilt and the circumstances of his condemnation.

As the result of such an inquiry one sees that the volume of accusations levelled against Wyatt is quite out of proportion to the amount of his crimes. He has suffered condemnation for other people's misdeeds, for the exaggeration of his own, and because he has been remembered, and they forgotten.

It is impossible to deny that he was destructive; or that he was not an archaeologist; or that he did not treat Gothic architecture as we should treat it today. But with all that, he had a genuine admiration for medieval buildings. He may have expressed this in a peculiar way; but then, at the period, it was still an unusual sentiment not common to many and was expressed very differently from its equivalent today.

The list of churches with which Wyatt tampered is not large: four cathedrals, Westminster Abbey, St George's Chapel, Windsor, Milton Abbey, Dorset, and three college chapels at Oxford; an imposing, but hardly an exorbitant list as compared for instance with the 39 cathedrals and 476 churches submitted to the attention of Sir Gilbert Scott. But the important point is that, even had the list been longer, these and all the other cathedrals were in a very bad state at the end of the eighteenth century and were bound to receive some attention. The chapter acquiesced in all Wyatt's suggestions and was as destructive as he. So Wyatt was not an isolated vandal in a generation of antiquaries, but one of many who held views similar to his own on the subject of medieval architecture. Also, it is only fair to note that to whichever of his contemporaries had been entrusted the restoration of the cathedrals which Wyatt repaired, even had they belonged to the party of the real antiquaries, we should now be no better pleased with the result.

Meanwhile in all this controversy and vituperation Wyatt's original compositions were overlooked. But in the work of any architect his restorations, whether good or bad, cannot be so important as the new buildings designed by him. Wyatt was no exception to this fact.

Every generation causes a swing of the pendulum in matters of taste. This has perhaps been more marked in the sphere of neo-Gothic architecture than amongst other buildings. The association by the Victorians of moral considerations with aesthetic judgments, in addition to their condemnation of Wyatt's restorations, ruled his new Gothic buildings out of favour with the next generation even more decidedly than is the case with the usual reaction of taste from one age to another. But viewing the Gothic revival from the vantage point of our own day, we can see the greatness of Wyatt's Gothic work and its importance to the revival as a whole. In works such as Ashridge he was the first serious architect of the movement and one of the last to be uninfluenced by irrelevant moral conceptions that were so disastrous to nineteenth-century architecture. His romantic buildings were not romantic to the generation of his grandchildren who remembered their grandparents and their peculiarly distressing ideas. But to later descendants, who had not known these ancestors and who contemplated their ideas with more detachment and less irritation, Wyatt's romantic compositions can be appreciated as they were meant to be viewed, without arbitrary restraint. This is even facilitated by the fact that the greatest of them, Fonthill, no longer exists, thus allowing the imagination to picture it in perhaps greater splendour and mysticism than even that most romantic of all houses may have presented.

But despite the excellence of some of Wyatt's Gothic work, it does not constitute his chief claim to distinction. It was his classical interior decoration that made him famous to his contemporaries. After his death this work was largely forgotten in the acute controversy as to his Gothic enterprises or was engulfed in the general term, 'the Adam style'. Again the wheel of taste has come full circle. The delicacy and elegance of this late eighteenth-century work is now seen and appreciated in its full beauty. Wyatt was no less skilful and hardly less prolific in its practice than the Adam brothers. If there are some who are disposed to say that one of these architects excelled the other in this sphere, I am not amongst them. To me they reign jointly in a realm of unsurpassed beauty. Despite the unpredictable changes of future taste, it seems unlikely that the judgment will be reversed that Wyatt's classical work was superior to his Gothic construction. His career leaves no doubt that he was considered to be, and was, one of the finest architects of the eighteenth and early nineteenth centuries. Since we can now look at his classical as well as his Gothic work in its proper perspective, it seems no exaggeration to claim that on the strength of this at least James Wyatt can be accounted one of the great English architects.

APPENDIX

LIST OF WORKS BY JAMES WYATT

1770-2   The Pantheon, Oxford Street, London; (interior burned in 1792 and 1811; finally demolished in 1937).

1771   Hagley, Staffordshire, for Asheton Curzon Esq., a ceiling.

1771   Fawley Court, Oxfordshire; interior alterations.

1771-81; 1789-93; 1801-12 Cobham Hall, Kent, for the 3rd & 4th Earls of Darnley; alterations and additions; 1783 the Mausoleum in the Park.

1772   Heaton Hall, Lancashire, for Sir Thomas Egerton, later first Earl Grey de Wilton; also the Temple in the park.

1773 (circa) Crichel House, Dorset, for Humphrey Sturt, Esq.; interior alterations.

1773-83 Christ Church, Oxford; 1773-8 the north and east sides of Canterbury Quadrangle rebuilt and the Gate erected; 1778-83 the south side of the Quadrangle built; 1805 a new staircase and lobby built to the Hall; 1809 the Lodgings of the Regius Professor of Hebrew rebuilt.

1774   Charlton Park, Wiltshire, for the Earl of Suffolk and Berkshire; alterations.

1774   Aubrey House, Notting Hill, London, for Lady Mary Coke; alterations.

1774 (circa) Shardeloes, Buckinghamshire, for William Drake Esq.; alterations to the Library; 1785-6 & 1789 garden buildings, (since demolished).

1774 (circa) Erdigg Park, Denbighshire, for Simon Yorke, Esq.; internal alterations.

1774 (circa) Nos. 11-15 Portman Square, London.

1775   Copped Hall, Essex, for John Conyers, Esq.; improvements of white brick, and redecoration of the Library (burned out about 1917).

1775-6   Milton Abbey, Dorset, for Lord Milton, later Earl of Dorchester, interior decoration; 1789-91 the Abbey Church restored.

1776   St. Mary's Church, Cheltenham, Gloucestershire, a wall tablet in memory of Katherine, wife of P. A. A'court, Esq.

1776 (circa) Sheffield Place, Sussex, for John Baker Holroyd, later Lord Sheffield.

1776-7   Belton House, Lincolnshire, for James, Lord Brownlow, alterations including the Library and Boudoir.

1776–8   Burton Constable, Yorkshire, for William Constable, Esq.; the north west Drawing-room and the Lodges.

1776–84   Heveningham Hall, Suffolk, for Sir Gerard Vanneck; the interior; also the Orangery, Heveningham Rectory and the farm known as Huntingfield Hall.

1776–94   The Radcliffe Observatory, Oxford, for the Radcliffe Trustees; continued the building after Henry Keene's death in 1776.

1778   Blagdon, Northumberland, for Sir Mathew Ridley; internal alterations; 1787 the Lodges of the Park; 1789-91 the Stables.

1778   Bryanston, Dorset, for H. W. B. Portman Esq.; (rebuilt by Norman Shaw in 1890, except the kitchen wing and the Lodge).

1778–9   A house on the south side of Grosvenor Square, London, for Mr Delvine.

1778–80   Hothfield Place, Kent, for the Earl of Thanet; (the wings added in the nineteenth century; the whole demolished in 1954).

1779   No. 9 Conduit Street, London, for Mr Viner.

1779–80   Brasenose College, Oxford; redecoration of the Library.

1779–83   Badger Hall, Shropshire, for Isaac Hawkins Brown, Esq.; also a Pigeon-house in the grounds; (demolished in 1952).

1780   The Music School, Holywell, Oxford; rearrangement of the interior.

1780   Roundway House, Wiltshire.

1780 (circa) Ragley Hall, Warwickshire, for the first Marquess of Hertford; alterations.

1780–6   Sandleford Priory, Berkshire, for Mrs Elizabeth Montagu; alterations and additions.

1781–2 (circa) Fornham Hall, Suffolk, for Sir Charles Kent; (demolished in 1951).

1782   Richmond House, Whitehall, London, for the third Duke of Richmond; the addition of two rooms and a staircase; also a temporary Theatre in 1787; and another in the adjoining house in 1788; (destroyed by fire in 1791).

1782–4   Pishiobury Park, Hertfordshire, for Jeremiah Milles, Esq.; reconstruction of an older house after a fire.

1782–90   Lee Priory, Kent, for Thomas Barrett, Esq. (altered and enlarged by Sir Gilbert Scott about 1865; demolished in 1954).

1783 (before) No. 69 Queen Anne Street (later No. 1 Foley Place), London, for himself; (demolished about 1925).

1783   The Assembly Rooms, Chichester, Sussex.

1783   The Kentish Town Episcopal Chapel, Lower Craven Place, London; (rebuilt in 1842).

1783   Worcester College, Oxford; the interior of the Hall and Chapel.

1783   New Park, Devizes, Wiltshire, for James Sutton, Esq.

1783–95 and 1811 Plas Newydd, Anglesey, for the 9th Lord Paget, later first Earl of Uxbridge; alterations and enlargements.

1784 Sudbourne Hall, Suffolk, for the first Marquess of Hertford; (since enlarged and greatly altered).

1784 Westminster Abbey and the Pantheon, London; arrangements for the Handel Festival.

1785 Gunton Hall, Norfolk, for Edward Harbord, Lord Suffield; enlargements; (since partly burned down).

1785 (circa) Leinster House, Dublin; the decoration of the Picture Gallery over the Supper Room.

1785 (circa) Sunningdale Park, Berkshire.

1785 (circa) Cremorne House, Chelsea, for Viscount Cremorne; alterations; (since demolished).

1785–8 The County Prison, Petworth, Sussex; (altered by Monypenny in 1816 and demolished in 1835).

1785–8 Wynnstay, Denbighshire, for Sir Watkins Williams Wynn; (rebuilt in the late nineteenth century); also a Doric Temple and a fluted Column in the grounds.

1786 Milton Abbas Church, Dorset.

1786–91 Stansted Park, Sussex, for Richard Barwell, Esq.; rebuilt the house of 1686, attributed to William Talman; (rebuilt by Sir Reginald Blomfield after a fire in 1900, except the Stables, the service wing, and the Lodges).

1787–90 St George's Chapel, Windsor, for the King; alterations.

1787–93 Salisbury Cathedral; alterations.

1787–94 Brocklesby Park, Lincolnshire, for Charles Pelham, Lord Yarborough; the Mausoleum in the grounds.

1787–1806 Goodwood House, Sussex, for the third Duke of Richmond; enlargements; also the Kennels in the Park, and the dower house, Molecombe.

1788 (before) Powderham Castle, Devonshire, for William Courtenay, second Viscount Courtenay; additions to the north wing.

1788 Westminster Abbey, London; arrangements for the installation of the Knights of the Bath.

1788 Chiswick House, Middlesex, for the fifth Duke of Devonshire; addition of wings and the alteration of the interior; (the wings demolished in 1952).

1788–91 Oriel College, Oxford; the Library and the Common Rooms beneath; also alterations in the Provost's Lodgings.

1788–94 St. Peter's Church, Manchester; (the tower by Francis Goodwin; the whole redecorated by E. Salomans in 1860 and since demolished).

1788–95 Lichfield Cathedral; alterations; also a monument to David Garrick, Esq. (died 1779).

1788–97 Hereford Cathedral; alterations.

1783–1813 The Exchange or Mansion House, Liverpool; additions and redecoration of the interior after a fire in 1795.

1789–94 New College, Oxford; alterations to the Hall, Chapel and

Library; (the Hall and Chapel again reconstructed by Sir Gilbert Scott in 1865 and 1877–81 respectively); also a monument in the Chapel to John Oglander, Esq. (died 1794).

1789–1813 East Grinstead Church, Sussex.

1790   Strawberry Hill, Middlesex, for Horace Walpole, later fourth Earl of Orford; the Offices, from the design of James Essex.

1790 (*circa*) Gresford, Denbighshire, for John Parry, Esq.

1790–4   Merton College, Oxford; the Hall rebuilt; (again reconstructed by Sir Gilbert Scott in 1872–4).

1790–5   Hartham Hall, Pickwick, Wiltshire, for Lady James.

1790–8   Castle Coole, Fermanagh, for S. L. Corry, Earl of Belmore; (the Offices built by R. Morrison in 1828).

1791–4   Lichfield House, No. 15 St James's Square, London, for Thomas Anson, Esq.; alterations to the Drawing-room.

1791   Lincoln's Inn, London; the Chapel repaired, a new roof and east window inserted.

1791–1804 (between) Felbrigg Hall, Norfolk, for William Windham, Esq.; minor alterations.

1792   Frogmore House, Berkshire, for the Queen; also the Stables, the Gothic Ruin, a hermit's cottage and a dovecote in the grounds; and decorations designed for a fête in the Park.

1792   Balliol College, Oxford; the Old Hall rebuilt, and the interior of the Old Library redecorated.

1792–5   Magdalen College, Oxford; alterations to the Hall and Chapel.

1792–5   Sundridge Park, Bromley, Kent, for E. G. Lind, Esq.; (continued by John Nash and/or Samuel Wyatt after 1796).

1793   Montagu House, No. 22 Portman Square, London, for Mrs Elizabeth Montagu; the addition of two Nurseries; (the house demolished by enemy action in 1940).

1793–7   Henham Hall, Suffolk, for Lord Rous, later Earl of Stradbrooke; (altered by Sir Charles Barry; demolished in 1953).

1795   Purley Park, Berkshire.

1795–6   Durham Cathedral; alterations.

1795 (*circa*) Bishop Auckland Palace; for Bishop Shute Barrington; the addition of the Gothic screen and the inner gateway to the south front.

1796   Bowden House, Wiltshire, for B. Dickenson, Esq.

1796   Corsham House, Wiltshire, for P. C. Methuen, Esq.; alterations.

1796   Longford Castle, Wiltshire; designs and a model for additional towers.

1796 (*circa*) Hinton St George, Somerset, for Lord Poullett; alterations and additions in succession to Sir John Soane.

1796–1800 Windsor Castle, Berkshire, for the King; alterations; (rebuilt by Sir Jeffry Wyatville in 1824-8).

1796–1805 The Royal Military Academy, Woolwich Common, Middlesex.

1796–7; 1802-8 The Royal Artillery Barracks, Woolwich, Middlesex; a new Riding School; (also ascribed to Jeffry Wyatt).

1796–1813 Fonthill Abbey, Wiltshire, for William Beckford Esq.

1797 Peper Harrow, Surrey, for Lord Midleton; a conservatory (since demolished, probably in 1913).

1797 (before) Trentham Hall, Staffordshire, for the Marquess of Stafford; alterations and enlargements; (rebuilt by Sir Charles Barry).

1797–1802 Stoke Poges Park, Buckinghamshire, for John Penn, Esq., following work by Robert Nasmith; 1799 the Memorial to Thomas Gray near the churchyard; 1800 the Column in the Park in the memory of Edward Coke; 1802 rebuilt the Vicarage.

1798 (before) Canwell Hall, Staffordshire, for Sir Robert Lawley; new wings added and the interior altered; ground filled up in the park.

1798 Swinton Park, Yorkshire, for W. Danby Esq.; the north wing (the drawing-room by John Foss of Richmond); (the east wing added by Robert Lugan about 1820).

1798 The Hen and Chickens Hotel, Birmingham.

1798 (circa) Wycombe Abbey, Buckinghamshire, for Lord Carrington.

1798–1808 Dodington Park, Gloucestershire, for Christopher Codrington, Esq.

1799 Cassiobury Park, Hertfordshire; alterations and additions, including the Gothic Stables; (since demolished).

1799 Norris Castle, the Isle of Wight, for Lord Henry Seymour.

1800 Pennsylvania Castle, Dorset, for John Penn, Esq.

1800 (?) Cranbourne Lodge, Windsor Park, Berkshire, for the Duke of Gloucester; additions to the rear; (the main portion of the house demolished in 1830).

1800–13 The Parliament Buildings, Westminster, London; a general restoration; the House of Lords transferred to the Old Court of Requests; new accommodation provided in the House of Commons.

1801 (before) Nacton House, Suffolk, for Philip Bowes Broke, Esq.

1801 Queen's House, London, for the King; a range of buildings erected for the accommodation of the Pages and internal alterations; (rebuilt by John Nash in 1825–30).

1801 The Town Hall, Ripon, Yorkshire.

1801–11 Wilton House, Wiltshire, for the Earl of Pembroke; alterations.

1801–13 Belvoir Castle, Leicestershire, for the Duke of Rutland; alterations; (continued by the Rev. Sir T. Thoroton).

1802 St. Kea Church, Cornwall; (demolished in 1895).

1802–11 The Old Palace at Kew, Surrey, for the King; repairs.

1802–11 The New Palace at Kew, Surrey, for the King; (demolished in 1827-8).

1803   Westminster Abbey, London; revaulting of the central tower, after a fire in July 1803.
1803   No. 22 St James's Place, London, for Samuel Rogers, Esq. (cornice and chimney-pieces by John Flaxman); (damaged by enemy action in 1940, and since demolished).
1803   Hafod Church, Caernarvonshire; (burned down in 1931).
1803   Weeford Church, Staffordshire.
1803–4 The King's Bench Prison, London; restorations and alterations.
1803–5 The Marshalsea Prison, London; restorations and alterations.
1804 (before) Roehampton Grove, Surrey, for Sir Joshua Vanneck, Lord Huntingfield; (enlarged about 1890).
1804   West Dean Park, near Chichester, Sussex, for Lord Selsey; (enlarged in 1893).
1805–6 St Paul's Cathedral, Westminster Abbey, and Westminster Hall, London; arrangements for the funerals of Lord Nelson and William Pitt, and for the trial of Lord Melville.
1806   The Naval Arsenal, Great Yarmouth, Norfolk, with the stone roof; (broken up in 1829).
1806   The Armoury, Shrewsbury, Shropshire.
1807 (before) Bulstrode Park, Buckinghamshire, for the third Duke of Portland; (altered and enlarged by P. F. Robinson and rebuilt by Benjamin Ferrey in 1862).
1807–12 The Royal Military College, Sandhurst, Berkshire.
1807–13 Henry VII's Chapel, Westminster Abbey, London; restorations.
1808   Dorset House, Whitehall, London; adaptation into Government offices.
1808–13 Hanworth Church, Middlesex; (rebuilt in 1865).
1808–13 Ashridge, Hertfordshire, for the Earl of Bridgewater; (completed by Jeffry Wyatt, 1813-18).
1809   Decorations for Festivities at Frogmore, for the Queen; assisted by J. W. Hirst of the Board of Works.
1809   Croome Court, Worcestershire; terra-cotta Casket in the grounds to the memory of Lancelot Brown; perhaps also the Temple seat on the island, but this may be by Robert Adam.
1809   The Banqueting House, Whitehall, London; alterations to the staircase at the north end and conversion of the interior into a military chapel.
1810   A house at Streatham, Surrey, for the Dowager Countess of Coventry; (since demolished).
1811–12 Devonshire House, London, for the sixth Duke of Devonshire, the staircase; (demolished in 1924).
1812   Elvaston Hall, Derbyshire, for C. Stanhope, Earl of Warrington; (completed by Walker).
1812   Carlton House, London, for the Prince Regent; fittings in the additional Library and in the strong-room.

1813   Swinton Park, Yorkshire, for William Danby, Esq.; the south
          wing; built posthumously by John Foss from Wyatt's design.
1813–14   Chicksands Priory, Bedfordshire, for Sir J. Osborn; altera-
          tions.
1814   The Market Cross, Devizes, Wiltshire, for the Corporation of
          Devizes; built posthumously from Wyatt's design.

UNDATED WORKS

Alton Tower, Staffordshire, for the Earl of Shrewsbury; (rebuilt by
     A. W. Pugin in 1836-44, except the Lodges; the whole demolished in
     1952).
Apuldurcombe, the Isle of Wight; interior alterations; (now in ruins).
Ardbraccan House, Meath, for the Bishop of Meath.
Badminton Park, Gloucestershire, for the Duke of Beaufort; alterations.
Belmont House, Clehonger, Herefordshire, for John Matthews, Esq.
Delamere House, Cheshire, for the father of George Wilbraham, Esq.
Escot House, near Honiton, Devonshire, for Sir John Kennaway (after
     1794).
Fonthill House, Wiltshire, for William Beckford, Esq.; the chimney-
     piece in the Ante-room, the ceiling in the Egyptian Hall, and a
     fishing seat by the Lake; (demolished in 1807).
Hanworth Farm, Middlesex, for himself.
Hanworth Park, Middlesex; the Stables, for the Duke of St Albans.
Holkham Hall, Norfolk, for the Earl of Leicester; entrance gates and
     unexecuted design for a lakeside pavilion.
Hurstbourne Park, Hampshire, for the Earl of Portsmouth; erected by
     Meadows from Wyatt's design; (burned down about 1870).
Little Aston Hall, Staffordshire, for William Tennant, Esq.
Llandygai, Caernarvonshire, for G. H. D. Pennant, Esq.; a new front.
Newark Park, Gloucestershire, for Lewis Clutterbuck, Esq.
New Hall, Nunton, Wiltshire.
Somerset House, London; arrangement of rooms.
Sophia Lodge, Clewer, Berkshire, for William Dawson, Esq.
Sudbury Hall, Staffordshire, for Lord Vernon.
Sunninghill Park, Berkshire, for G. H. Crutchley, Esq.; alterations;
     (since demolished).
Thirkleby Park, Yorkshire, for Sir T. Frankland, Bt.
Thornden Hall, Essex, for Lord Petre, of white brick; added or com-
     pleted the Hall; (burned down in 1878).
Worstead Hall, Norfolk, for Sir Berney Brograve.
Monument in Shrivenham Church, Berkshire, to William Wildman,
     Viscount Barrington (died 1793).
Monument in Wilton Church, Wiltshire, to Henry, tenth Earl of
     Pembroke (died 1794).
Monument in Hale Church, Hampshire, to Joseph May, Esq. (died
     1796).

Broome Park, Kent (1778) for Sir Henry Oxenden; alterations; but also attributed to James Gandon.

Combe Hay Manor, Somerset; additions.

Gidea Hall, Essex, for R. Benyon Esq.; a bridge of three elliptical arches (now called Black's Bridge, Raphael Park, Romford).

Heytesbury, Wiltshire (*circa* 1780), for William P. A. A'court, Esq.

No. 18 New Cavendish Street, London; alterations to the Drawing-room.

Rudding Park, Yorkshire.

Swinfen Hall, Staffordshire, for J. Swinfen, Esq.

White's Club, Nos. 37 and 38 St James's Street, London; (altered in 1811 and 1850).

West Itchenor House, Sussex, for the third Duke of Richmond; also the Stables.

Willingdon Hall, Cheshire.

Winnington Hall, Cheshire.

INDEX

Hanworth Farm, Middlesex, 17–18, 216.
Hanworth Park, Middlesex, 216.
Harcourt, First Earl, 133.
Harcourt, Second Earl of, 116, 133.
Hartham Hall, Wiltshire, 213.
Harvey, Elizabeth, 199.
Hatcher, Henry, 108.
Hawksmoor, Nicholas, 91.
Haymarket Opera House, London, 6, 12.
Heard, Sir Isaac, 148.
Heaton Hall, Manchester, 27–31, 39, 41, 42, 63, 69, 71, 210 (Plates 8, 10, 13).
Hen and Chickens Hotel, Birmingham, 214.
Henham Hall, Suffolk, 68–69, 213.
Hereford Cathedral, 109–111, 143, 172, 212.
Hertford, First Marquess of, 58, 160, 211, 212.
Hertford, Second Marquess of, 116.
Heveningham Hall, Suffolk, 30, 31, 32, 33–42, 75, 96, 211 (Plates 14, 16, 17, 18, 45, 46).
Heveningham Rectory, Suffolk, 42, 211.
Heytesbury, Wiltshire, 217.
Hinton St George, Somerset, 213.
Hiorne, Francis, 139.
Hirst, J. W., 215.
Hodges, William (Plate 2).
Holkham Hall, Norfolk, 216.
Holland, Henry, 63, 98, 116, 120, 189, 192.
Holroyd, Maria, 129.
Hope, Thomas, 89–90, 124–125.
Hornsby, Thomas, 82, 93.
Hothfield Place, Kent, 43, 69, 211.
Howard, Sir George, 70.
Howard, John, 52.
Hoppner, John, 176, 201.
Humphrey, Ozias, 196 (Plate 47).

Hunt, T. F., 6–7, 18, 93.
Huntingfield, First Lord, 33–34, 42, 76, 215.
Huntingfield Hall, Suffolk, 42, 211.
Hurstbourne Park, Hampshire, 216.
Hyde Park, London, 185.
Itchenor House, Sussex, 56, 217.
James, W. D., 165.
James, Lady, 213.
Jolliffe, Thomas, 59.
Johnson, Dr Samuel, 10, 201.
Johnston, Francis, 139–140.
Jones, Inigo, 16, 73, 162, 163.
Keene, Henry, 20, 82, 211.
Kendal, Elizabeth, 202.
Kennaway, Sir John, 216.
Kensington Palace, London, 185.
Kent, Sir Charles, 50, 211.
Kent, Edward Duke of, 185, 190.
Kent, William, 49, 185.
Kentish Town Episcopal Chapel, London, 211.
Kew Old House, Surrey, 186, 187, 189, 214.
Kew New Palace, Surrey, 165, 167, 173, 186–189, 214 (Plates 65, 66).
King's Bench Prison, London, 185, 215.
King's College, Cambridge, 90–91.
King's Mews, London, 197.
Langley, Batty, 172.
Lansdown Crescent, Bath, 151.
Latrobe, Benjamin, 128–129.
Lawley, Sir Robert, 214.
Leadbitter, Stiff, 97.
Lee Priory, Kent, 43, 132–138, 139, 143, 157, 172, 211 (Plates 51, 53, 54).
Leicester, Lord, 116, 117, 216.
Leigh, Fifth Lord, 84.
Leinster House, Dublin, 64, 212.
Le Nôtre, André, 53.
Leverton, Thomas, 36.
Liancourt, duc de, 34.

223